FOOTLIGHTS AND SPOTLIGHTS

OTIS SKINNER
in The Honor of the Family

Portrait by George Luks

Footlights *and* Spotlights

RECOLLECTIONS OF MY LIFE ON THE STAGE

By OTIS SKINNER

GREENWOOD PRESS, PUBLISHERS
WESTPORT, CONNECTICUT

The Library of Congress has catalogued this publication as follows:

Library of Congress Cataloging in Publication Data

Skinner, Otis, 1858-1942.
    Footlights and spotlights.

    1. Actors, American--Correspondence, reminiscences,
etc. I. Title.
PN2287.S5A3 1972   792'.028'0922   76-164474
ISBN 0-8371-6216-5

Originally published in 1924
by the Bobbs-Merrill Company, Inc., Indianapolis

Reprinted with the permission
of the Bobbs-Merrill Company, Inc.

First Greenwood Reprinting 1972

Library of Congress Catalogue Card Number 76-164474

ISBN 0-8371-6216-5

Printed in the United States of America

To

M. D. S.

But thy eternal summer shall not fade.

—Sonnet xviii

CONTENTS

CONTENTS—*Continued*

CONTENTS—*Continued*

LIST OF ILLUSTRATIONS

LIST OF ILLUSTRATIONS

FOOTLIGHTS AND SPOTLIGHTS

Footlights and Spotlights

CHAPTER I

FROM A GALLERY SEAT

As he was writing, Barnum chuckled to himself and then, with a twinkle in his eye, handed me this astonishing document impersonally and generously addressed "To Whom It May Concern," and asked me if it would do. I assured him that it would and that I was most grateful.

The bearer, O. A. Skinner, Esq., is known to me. His parents whom I have known in Hartford, Conn., for several years are eminently respectable. Mr. Skinner has an ambition, a talent and a *yearning* for the stage. I have no doubt that he will prove an important acquisition to any theatrical corps which he may join.

P. T. Barnum.

After I had definitely decided to go on the stage I began answering advertisements in THE CLIP-PER, the theatrical paper, which entreated the services of "gifted young persons who were good dressers on and off the stage." I wrote to metropolitan managers setting forth my desirable qual-

1

ities and my experience, but the only replies came from traveling impresarios offering chances in Eufala, Alabama, or Streator, Illinois, and always there was the proviso that I should furnish a complete wardrobe and pay my railroad fare to join the company. Finally came a gleam of hope—a chance for an opening, as far away only as Philadelphia. My eye fell upon an announcement that William Davidge, Jr., was organizing a company for the Philadelphia Museum, and a correspondence followed which ended in an offer from Davidge to do utility business at a salary of seven dollars a week. This good news came to me in the summer of 1877—a summer that dragged by with intolerable slowness, for my season was not to open until the autumn.

When September arrived I began to grow anxious. After the first two letters I had heard no more from Davidge, and he did not forward the promised contract. I wrote but received no reply. In a panic at the thought of my golden opportunity slipping from me, I determined to go to Philadelphia, and packing my belongings into two small trunks, I bade farewell to my parents. My mother viewed my going with misgiving. My father was wholly philosophical. Just as I was about to leave an inspiration came to me. I might be going on a fool's errand, but I knew of one whose name would be of the greatest value. I asked my father to give me a letter of introduction to P. T. Barnum.

My father, the Reverend Charles A. Skinner, a

The Rev. Charles A. Skinner and Cornelia Bartholomew Skinner
The Author's Parents

minister of the Universalist Church, and Barnum had long been friends. The great showman was an ardent and liberal upholder of Universalism. It was just the sort of religion that agreed with his philosophy and his business. In his WHY I AM A UNIVERSALIST, published shortly before his death, he wrote: "The Universalist Church is the only one that believes in success."

Barnum attended regularly the New England annual convention of the Universalists where my father found him an amusing companion. One year they were proceeding arm in arm up to the Convention Hall when Barnum spied a huge ink-stain on the step of the wooden stairway. Pointing down to it he said with great solemnity: "Some nigger had the nose-bleed!" This story I heard many times in the family circle.

On my way to Philadelphia I arrived in Bridgeport about noon and walked to "Waldemere," the Barnum home. "Waldemere" was of the architecture of the 'sixties—pretentious, somewhat mongrel, pleasantly shaded by trees and overlooking the waters of the sound. When I entered the grounds I noticed a white flag with the initials, P. T. B., flapping on a flag-pole. This I learned was the announcement that the proprietor was at home.

The great man was at lunch, but would see me presently and in good time I was ushered into the library which was filled with many curiosities, savage and Oriental. African spears and shields, Malay knives, Moorish guns, Japanese carvings and

3

grotesque masks. Some story-telling oil paintings hung on the wall. That day I was too deeply absorbed in my quest to be interested in any of these things which ordinarily would have delighted me. My business was with their owner. He came in, big, corpulent and smiling, with an air of having lunched heartily. He quite filled the doorway as he entered. Loose lipped, red nosed, bald headed, he was geniality itself. Success and power were stamped all over him.

"What a make-up for Falstaff," I thought.

Settling his immense bulk in his desk chair he inquired after my father's health. "My son," he said, "your father is one of the finest men I know."

I felt my nervousness slipping away in spite of my awe of "The Great Showman."

He listened to me indulgently, even with interest, and I had no difficulty in telling him that I was starting on a stage career, and that I wanted his written endorsement. He had no objections, none whatever. He whirled his swivel chair to his desk and wrote the "To Whom It May Concern" letter.

I then asked if he knew William Davidge, Jr., of Philadelphia and could he give me a note to him? No trouble at all. He knew Davidge—of course he knew him, he knew all these theatre chaps. If I had asked him for an introduction to the Czar of Russia I believe he would have given it to me.

I reached Philadelphia late in the evening of the same day that I had seen Barnum and went to an humble hotel, The Merchants', in Fourth Street. I was awake by daylight—indeed I think I had scarcely slept at all—and, unable to remain abed, I strolled out to the Delaware water-front and walked about until breakfast time. The Museum was at the corner of Ninth and Arch Streets, and as soon as a decent observance of time served I presented myself there.

The manager's office was exactly like a scene in a play. People rushed in and out for hurried consultation, telegrams were sent and countless letters signed. I came to know later that very little of this activity was genuine, but that day it impressed me mightily. I thought Davidge the busiest man I had ever seen.

At last he turned to me. He was a small tenor-voiced man with a ready smile and a bird-like turn to his head; frankness and geniality fairly oozed from him. He seemed to extend tenderness to the whole world, in a manner not wholly convincing, but he charmed me. He had forgotten me. An oversight—quite an oversight, really! He knew that there was something he had omitted to do—that was it. And he was sorry—truly sorry, but he feared everything was full now, and I should have written sooner to remind him. I had kept the Barnum letter in reserve; I presented it now.

He sent a shifty little look at me from his grayish eyes, and said: "Perhaps there might be something turning up to-morrow. Drop in at, say, nine o'clock."

I was there at nine—and so was my contract.

5

FOOTLIGHTS AND SPOTLIGHTS

As I walked back to my hotel the whole business seemed strange and unnatural, strange to find myself in this city, almost a foreign one to me, and stranger still that I, with my heritage and upbringing, should be embarking on the career of an actor. I felt then as I have ever since felt when I have looked at the many-branched family tree of the Skinners that the sap of infinite righteousness must have flowed from its roots. Splendid and conscientious citizens are the hard-faced men and women whose names are written on the limbs. In a lithograph of this chart which I possess, the trunk rises bravely from the ground with "Timothy Skinner born at Mansfield, Massachusetts, February 10th, 1761" lettered up and down its bark; the name of Ruth Warner, in smaller print, appearing as consort. These were my great grandparents. Timothy, descendant of Thomas Skinner, who in 1650, at the age of thirty-three, settled in America, lived a God-fearing and patriotic life. I find in the records of New Hampshire and Massachusetts that he is credited with several enlistments in the Army of the Revolution during his youth. I also discover a blot on Timothy's (and my) scutcheon in the HISTORY OF SALEM WITCHCRAFT. It is there recorded that the Reverend George Burrows was charged with witchcraft and hanged. The unfortunate Burrows was Timothy's great grandfather.

But this graft of the gallows on the family tree does not seem to have impaired its growth. From the parent stem of Timothy spread nine limbs, variously labeled with such names as Warren, Alanson,

Waldemere,
Bridgeport, Ct.

Oct 19 1877

The bearer, O A Skinner
is known to me. His parents
whom I have known in
Hartford Conn for several
years are highly respectable.
Mr Skinner has a talent,
an ambition and a yearning
for the stage. I have no
doubt that he will prove
an important acquisition
to any theatrical corps which
he may join.

P. T. Barnum

To Whom it may Concern

THE BARNUM LETTER

Cynthia, Hiram, and from these, lesser shoots in profusion.

And so it fell that Timothy begat Warren, and Warren begat Charles A. Skinner, and Charles begat Charles, Otis and William who grew to man's estate. The great uncles who blossomed on the tree became doctors, merchants, jurists and clergymen.

My grandfather, also a clergyman, a man of overwhelming presence and—when I knew him—of great age, viewed his annually-assembled grandchildren at the family homestead in Proctorsville, Vermont, with an impersonal eye. We might as well have been his chickens or his cows. We used to greet him decorously, as if he were a mayor or a president. His air of aloofness had perhaps come from long years of sermon-preaching in high pulpits where he was separated from his flock.

He had married twice. From each union had come a considerable crop of offspring. It was my father's stepmother whom I knew—and hated—a sour soul who never had a kindly word for any of us. To her lord and master she never spoke except in a snappy growl.

Wife collecting seems to have been traditional in early New England. One finds "wife of the above" duplicated repeatedly on the same headstone over many graves there. Was it the interminable toil of the household, or the constant bearing of children that plucked them forth before their time, I wonder? Or the bleak climate; the long cold winters, housed in frame dwellings heated only in

7

spots by wood-burning stoves? Or was it the bad cooking? Perhaps it was all these put together. . These summer round-ups of the Skinner clansmen were largely attended. There was my Aunt Harriet, tall, broad-shouldered and spectacled, whose personality was dominant and assertive. She was the wife of a lawyer in Washington, and she had done work in the military hospitals during the Civil War, after giving to her country the lives of two of her sons. They brought with them a group of pretty girl cousins, the youngest of whom wore her hair flowing away from a horse-shoe roach-comb, like Alice in Wonderland, and in her web of brown tresses my youthful affections became sadly entangled.

My Uncle Bill, an engineer who had run the first train through Dismal Swamp in Virginia, brought his hard-favored wife and my Cousin Bert from their home in Indiana. Bert, bigger and rougher than I, generally came off the victor in our frequent squabbles which sometimes took on a note of seriousness.

Then there was my gentle and sweet-faced Aunt Nancy and her husband, a newspaper editor over in New Hampshire, who came with their children. And my Aunt Martha, whom I adored for her great beauty, her freckles and her auburn hair. And my Uncle Eugene, whom I thought something of a sport: he was certainly rather out of the family picture for he had once been connected with a troupe of negro minstrels—a monstrous affiliation!

8

But he made full atonement by a life devoted to pulling the teeth of the village folk in his little dentist's shop at Proctorsville.

My mother's ancestors were farmers and landowners. Their family name of Bartholomew suggests a French origin, and I find this country's first representative in Colonial times, one William of Ipswich, Rhode Island.

The din of war rumbled in my childish ears. My father was made chaplain of a Massachusetts regiment. It all seemed quite terrible but rather vague to me. One of my early diversions was to pour over a collection of hundreds of Civil War envelopes in my father's study. They were used for ordinary correspondence and had patriotic devices, state coats-of-arms, or comic cartoons directed against the "Secesh" printed on their faces. Some of them were of rebel origin and bore sentiments equally bitter against the North.

For the summer outings in Vermont, nor in fact, at any time, was I allowed spending money. My father's meager salary as a preacher sufficed to make us decently comfortable at home and no more. Sometimes he would bestow a few cents on me for candy, pickled limes or licorice sticks, but these occasions were rare. Most of the small money in the early 'sixties was not in the form of coin, but paper —like the fifty centime paper pieces that France issued after the late war—"shinplasters" they were called and came in denominations of five, ten, twenty-five and fifty cents. In my greatest af-

9

fluence I never rose above the ten-cent shinplaster. My usual allowance was one of the thick, palish one-cent pieces then in circulation, or a tiny three-cent silver piece.

It used to be something of a mystery to me how my own vocation as an actor could have found root in soil so unsympathetic, or that of my brother Charles, a writer and poet of nature, or that of my younger brother William, an artist. It appears that at the time Charles was born my father was a young clergyman in a small New York state town, producing his sermons at the expense of much mental labor, and carefully going over them later with my mother. Before I came into the world, my parents had moved to Cambridge where neighboring Boston afforded the young couple delights undreamed of in the little up-state town of Victor. The fairy-land of the theatre had opened to my mother's imaginative mind when the cue was given for my entrance. Eight years later my mother had taken up painting during time spared from manifold parish duties, and she pursued the art with an appreciation and an efficiency that had the mark of genius, when my painter brother William was born. I know that biologists will tell me that prenatal influence is a theory long exploded, but I like to think of my mother battering down New England tradition and in her varying moods, coloring the dispositions of her sons. Indeed when I recall her wide dark eyes, her rippling black hair, her voice "ever soft, gentle, and low—an excellent thing in woman," I am sure there was little of the Puritan in her. I know now, as I could not know in days of adolescence, that she ever yearned for the companionship of her sons; but we were kept at distance by the strict rule of the household—obedience to discipline. Our parents were our superior officers. Had not they been privates, as we were, and obeyed their commanders?

And my father? No more tender-hearted man ever lived, but he did not know how to express his feelings and still maintain the authority handed down through generations of Puritan Skinners. He found this means later when his boys were earning their livelihood and could come home on a new basis of love and understanding. The old commander was off duty then—retired.

He once caused a youthful stage situation of mine to fall quite flat. I was eighteen. The call of the theatre had just come to me, and my blood was boiling for a chance to begin. One Sunday my father preached a sermon on the duties of parents toward their children. I had been scarcely conscious of his words when, suddenly, I heard him advocating the allowance of a choice to the boy in his selection of his life's work. It was a bolt from clear skies. Did my father really believe what he said? If so, my secretiveness in ransacking the Public Library of Hartford, where we were then living, for knowledge of plays, players, the theatre and the art of acting had all been for nothing. It had been wholly unnecessary for me to steal into uninhabited woods to recite *Shylock's* lines, or to shout *Rich-*

11

ard's villainy at unappreciative cows in lonely pastures. However, I could not believe that my father would admit play-acting as a possible occupation, I determined to hold up his openly expressed theories to his very face. Putting myself in the center of the stage, and with lofty speeches casting back his own words at him, I dramatized the scene, and when a small chance in the shape of a very doubtful theatrical engagement opened to me, I felt the time for the deed had arrived. My father must be told. He was in his study at work on his Sunday sermon. Outside his door I did not feel nearly so valiant about the business. But I went in. He was absorbed in his work, and I had time to pull myself together. Finally, "What is it?" With deepest chest tones I delivered my prepared speech, and braced myself for the shock of his wrath. It came. He looked at me for a moment over his spectacles, a curious gleam came in his eye, and he said: "Very well, Otis, if you've made up your mind, I suppose that is what you are going to do. Perhaps you'll speak to your mother about it. Don't bother me now. I'm busy." That was all. It was my first lesson in anticlimax.

I did speak to my mother, and received my second surprise. I had expected sympathy and understanding from her, but she upset all my anticipations by a manner as nearly derisive as I can remember in her, and told me that I could never succeed on the stage because I couldn't even talk straight.

THE BOSTON MUSEUM

My theatre-going probably began when I was about five. Charlie and I were frequently allowed, on a Saturday afternoon, to accompany our parents across the Charles River from Cambridge to the Boston Museum. This dignified place of amusement was exempt from Puritan prejudice; its very name gave it a propriety denied to other theatres. A visit there was most instructive. In orderly alcoves, shelves of minerals, cases of stuffed birds, fossil remains, and curiosities from various parts of the world formed a collection that was presided over by busts and portraits of gentlemen whose respectability no one could doubt. A large painting called THE ROMAN DAUGHTER hung over the entrance into the hall of curiosities, representing a beautiful matron who visited her starving father in prison and nurtured him by suckling his parched old lips at her breast. I was duly impressed by an ingenious piece of faking known as BARNUM'S JAPANESE MERMAID, a mummy, the size of a small cat, with female head, hair and breast, arms and claws of an animal and the tail of a fish. I used to wonder why the Japanese were so clever in catching mermaids.

But the place of dread in this enchanted palace was the gallery of wax-works on the upper floor. Here I drank horrors by the bucketful. There were the Siamese Twins in ill-fitting black suits, the ligature of realistic wax binding their bodies in perpetual companionship. And Daniel Lamber', the celebrated fat man, seated in a huge chair, a dimin-

13

utive wax boy struggling to hand him a mug of
beer the size of a coal scuttle which he was receiving
with great joy.

A particular terror was wrought upon me by a
moral lesson called THREE SCENES IN A DRUNKARD'S
LIFE and another entitled THE PIRATES' CABIN. The
dominant feature of these silent and awful dramas
was blood—lots of it. The *Drunkard* and his family had begun their pestilential caree_ pleasantly
and prosperously. Father, Mother, Son and Daughter were seated about the festal board, the expression of their faces fixed in a beatific trance, and
the gorgeousness of their raiment only matched by
that of the wall-paper and the tablecloth. They
were drinking champagne, the cotton wool foam of
which was greatly in need of dusting. This was
the first step in their downward path. The second
house, meaner—much meaner; furniture and tablecloth shabby and the drink *RUM*—labeled in bold
letters on the family bottle. The fashionable garments of the first scene were things of the past.
Son and Daughter were degenerate and obviously
bilious; Mother's rum had not agreed with her; and
Father was truly no fit company for any one. In
the last group the family had moved up to the garret and again changed their clothes to their disad-
vantage, except Daughter who had found profitable
employment in the streets and had blossomed into
colors like the butterfly. The others were sad
sights. Father, shrunken and haggard, a sore in
the corner of his mouth, had just dealt Mother a

14

blow with the gin bottle, and the poor soul lay prone
in her dingy calico dress, rivers of blood ebbing
from a hole in her waxen head. Son had become
a moron, and Father was being arrested by a policeman at the very moment of murder.

Horror mounted on horror in THE PIRATES'
CABIN, where the immorality of piracy was set forth
in lasting lesson to the youth of Boston who had
formed the habit of sailing up the salt creeks of the
Charles on heavily armed rafts in search of treasure galleons. Never was such scene of carnage as
that cabin presented. Corpses oozing blood, and
pirates, armed to the teeth, gloating over them. A
particularly awful ruffian was standing in the fore-
ground with ax uplifted to tap a fresh blood supply
in the head of a gentleman with white whiskers. A
beautiful maiden raised arms of supplication over
him, and the pirate captain descended the compan-
ionway with an arresting gesture.

These were the gory objects that pursued my
waking and sleeping hours. Especially did they
busy themselves at night and hide under my bed
and in the dark corners that pirates and drunkards
know about. Sometimes, after dusk, I was sent to
Kennedy's Bakery in the main street of Cambridge, on the servant's bread-baking evenings, for
a cent's worth of yeast, and then there was an inevitable chase of these hobgoblins in my wake.
Sometimes they would get ahead of me and hide
behind trees and in black doorways, and little it
mattered that I jangled the penny vigorously in my

tin pail! That scared them not at all; my path was sore beset by demons. Nor in my dreams did they cease from troubling, but came flocking in new forms, committing dire deeds.

The recollection of this horror chamber lies far deeper than the plays I saw. These were given in what, for politic reasons, was first termed, "The Lecture Hall" of the Museum, and which gradually assumed the proportions of a stage and auditorium. Ministers of the gospel could freely patronize such a place of entertainment; their attendance was even sought on a complimentary basis. That, perhaps, is why my family became frequent patrons of the Museum at a time in my life when the play was a mixture of things too vast for my infantile mind. To my brother Charlie, drama meant art with definite ideas of management. He organized a company of boys and girls, wrote and produced plays, war plays inspired by the conflict of the North and South then being brought to a close. Soldiers and sailors, both Federal and Confederate, slaves, planters and overseers formed the characters in Charlie's tragedies which were given in our cellar kitchen where the young manager, also his own scene painter, had sketched a landscape in charcoal and chalk on the boarded walls. Properties were few and poor, but our imaginations were rich. To transform a packing-case into Libby Prison, a board tilted on a saw-horse into Seminary Ridge at Gettysburg, barrels into cotton presses, and wash tubs into gun-boats was an easy matter.

MY FIRST PART

Usually ostracized from active part in these performances on the score of my extreme youth, and forced in spite of entreaties to be one of the audience admitted for a stated number of pins, I clamored to be enrolled in the company, until, disgusted at my importunities, they cast me for a shipwrecked sailor. This was a silent part, requiring merely that the actor should sit still in a wash tub while two stage hands waved a large gray shawl of mountainous seas in front of the craft. The title of the drama was ALLIGATOR SWAMP.

One hair-raising act of Charlie's was rehearsed upon me when I wasn't expecting it. With gore-smeared face he emerged suddenly from behind a door and committed hari-kari with a wooden sword. The howl I set up brought the dead to life with amazing speed, and I was bribed to silence by being allowed to daub myself with beet-juice blood.

My brother was my hero. Never had he appeared so fine as that time, during the war, when he gathered two of his playmates under his banner, marched across Cambridge Bridge to the Boston recruiting offices, and offered to the cause of flag and country the services of three earnest volunteers. The youngsters, not one of them over ten, had visions of defending redouts and leading charges against the enemy, but were willing to begin as drummer-boys. The recruiting officers received the lads with gravity, examined their eyes, noses, teeth, made them strip to the skin and thumped them; then told them they could not be

perfectly sure of their qualified character until they
had passed them on with a note to another station
where the urchins were submitted to a second haz-
ing. At night three weary little boys dragged themselves homeward, and Charlie said his country had
refused his services. Humiliation became abysmal
when father said the soldiers were making fun of
them. I was furious and said I was going to join
the Rebels.

Not long after this the news came of Lee's sur-
render. I remember how my father, a member of
the Cambridge public school board, came one morning into our class-room where our juvenile fingers
had been daily employed in picking lint from cotton rags for the hospitals (think of the insanitation
of it!) and said, "Boys and girls, the war is ended.
You may all have a holiday." Then in a few days
the assassination of Lincoln at Washington and the
buildings of Boston and Cambridge hung in black.

Of the pieces I saw, one stands out from all the
rest, RUTHVEN, or THE CASTLE OF TORMINAR. In it
was a group of characters such as are seldom met
with to-day. Vampires, ghouls and such uncanny
cattle mingled with noble lords, soldiers, persecuted
maidens and comedy servants. The hero was a
vampire whose existence was sustained by the blood
of an innocent maiden once a year, and who was
apparently unkillable. The nine lives of the cat
were as nothing to the frequent deaths and resur-
rections of *Ruthven*. It was his custom, upon being
killed, to request that his body be placed on a cer-

tain crag where the beams of the moon would strike him at the hour of twelve. And *somebody* always did it! No one ever stayed to see what the audience saw at the midnight hour. The prostrate figure, at first enveloped in the darkness of night, became illuminated by the calcium's rays, a quiver ran through its limbs, its hands moved, its head raised and finally it stood upright on the cliff, and stretching itself, disclosed a huge pair of bat-like wings attached to its body! To all appearances it was as sound a specimen of vampire as it ever was, ready for more villainy and prepared to meet death in any form. Charlie and I never attempted to enact RUTHVEN in our cellar kitchen theatricals. It was too awful. There was something even sacred about it.

Those Museum days came to an end when I was nine or ten. My father moved his family to Hartford, Connecticut, whither he had been called by the Universalist Church, and a curtain dropped upon the playhouse, not to rise for several years.

It is a quaint figure that I see—the ten-year-old lad who found himself in a big roomy house, far too big for the little family that could occupy but half of it. This small person is somewhat imaginative and shy, and there are nights in his bedroom when he lies awake and listens to the moaning of banshees that contrive to get through gusty keyholes and cracks, and to the snapping of old wooden beams on frosty nights, which phenomena he can not quite attribute to natural causes. He has a

19

strong suspicion that ancient and uneasy ghosts are revisiting the scene of crimes committed in this old colonial mansion when its state was more gracious. The shutters of his bedroom are not stable. On windy nights they sometimes become wrenched from their fastenings and pound against the window, sending terror through the echoing rooms. And there is one especial night when he is awakened from a nightmare of murder, to which he has been a partner and is being tried for his life, to find a storm has arisen that fairly rocks the old house, and in the corridor beyond his bedroom door a Walpurgis orgy is in full swing—demons, ghosts, warlocks and all.

His habit of novel reading helped along his terror. Dime novels—Beadle's, DeWitt's and Munroe's. Beadle's novels with their bright orange covers had an odor all their own. They smelt differently from other publications. Tales of assassins, Indians and specter skippers; narratives so gruesome that he dared not continue reading, nor yet did he dare to blow down the chimney of the unlawful midnight lamp, because then it's all dark and things can get you before you can dive under the bedclothes. He had a cache of these forbidden paper-covered volumes at the foot of an apple tree in the yard which he secretly visited from time to time, and took one from the store to be read up among the branches in a seat he had built there. At other times, at a prearranged signal, a fistful of tales of horror which he had already read, would be exchanged *quid pro quo* with the boy who lived on the other side of the fence.

It was under this same apple tree that he took his first remorsefully-ended lesson in smoking, that time when his pride fell and he gazed into the jeering countenances of a ring of young ruffians who couldn't smoke either, only it didn't happen to be their turn just then. But youth is persistent, and though its discouragements are acute and grievous, they are soon over. Lighted by the' glow of Mrs. Miller's Best Smoking Tobacco in a T. D. clay pipe, this youth's path to manhood was trod with increasing success and fewer disasters.

Desultory spasms of histrionism took place in our high barn loft which Charlie had frescoed with an Alpine scene; but when a load of hay was suddenly pitched into our temple of art, drama died.

Came years at the Brown Grammar School and the Hartford High School. Among the pupils of the latter was William Gillette, a senior during my beginning year, even then enacting humorous pieces of his own composition at class recitals in something of the dry manner that became his characteristic in THE PRIVATE SECRETARY. I did not graduate. My parents resigned themselves to this disappointment cheered by the enthusiasm with which I took up the work of clerk for an insurance company where for the first time in my life I felt I was accomplishing something of my own choice. Yet in this I achieved no distinction; the end of the year found me quit of insurance policies and en-

21

gaged as assistant shipping clerk in a wholesale
commission house. This change I shall always regard as one of the most beneficial that ever came
to me. I had for years been physically weak, subject to blinding headaches that lasted for hours,
sometimes for days. The confining duty of an insurance office was telling on me; this new work was
of entirely different character. The shipping of
cases of goods entailed real physical exercise in all
kinds of weather. Often, when the laboring force
was short-handed I was obliged to assist at hoisting
heavy boxes into high lofts, trucking them into
storage, or to walk a mile of railroad track, seeking
lost cars in freight yards. Sometimes I had to rise
in blackest winter mornings before the dawn, go
into the stinging cold and work for hours in an un-
warmed warehouse addressing goods-cases in marking ink, my finger-tips well nigh frozen. Though I
grumbled at these hardships I felt exhilarated—
alive. I laid in a lasting supply of health which
stood me in stead when later periods of stage work
drew heavily on my vitality.

On a certain Saturday I was given leave to visit
my brother in New York. Charlie had left home
and secured a position as the cub reporter on the
BROOKLYN TIMES, where his talents as a writer
were bearing their first fruits. His assignments
were all in the way of news-gathering, police reports, accounts of street accidents and hospital
cases, but even in this hack work he evolved an individuality of style, his destined vehicle for the ex-

pression of the most human, most poetic of thoughts and fancies.

Charlie had invited me to come over for an introduction to the big town. He had ever been sagely watchful, leading my mind into the paths of good taste. It was he who explained some of the mysteries of nature and of the skies to me; it was he who pointed out the best in books, and interpreted for me the meanings in music and in painting; it was he who treated me to my first opera—FAUST, with Pauline Lucca as *Marguerite,* by buying me a seat in the gallery of Roberts' Opera House in Hartford.

In the afternoon of this particular Saturday he met me at Grand Central Station and gave up to me the day's liberty he had succeeded in borrowing from his newspaper. We wandered down Fifth Avenue gazing with awe at the homes of millionaires below Forty-Second Street. That thoroughfare was as a country highroad to the turmoil-racked street of to-day. Long rows of "brown stone fronts" through whose windows one caught gas-lit glimpses of heavy, costly furnishings. No big buildings; no handsome shop windows, trade was very far from the dwellers of this avenue; a few slow cabs rolled along the cobbles and a line of little white omnibuses, horse-drawn, ran between Fulton Ferry and Forty-Second Street. We reached Union Square whose hundred gas lamps seemed like the illumination of Aladdin's Cave. At the Lyceum Theatre, subsequently renamed the Fourteenth

Street Theatre, we purchased two tickets for the gallery. This playhouse had sometime before passed from the management of Charles Fechter and was now prospering in the run of a dramatization of Hugo's HUNCHBACK OF NOTRE DAME, with T. C. King as the star playing *Quasimodo.*

In my most excited dreams I had never beheld such splendors as that play unfolded. King's *Quasimodo* reached heights beyond my imaginings, and Charles Wheatley's *Claude Frollo* moved me to pity and terror. Jeffreys Lewis, a vision of beauty, made her New York début in this play as *Esmeralda,* John Jack was the *Clopin* and Sol Smith the *Gringoire.*

I sat in my gallery seat in a daze. I was not in New York: I was not in the theatre: I was in Paris, five hundred years ago, the companion of priests and gypsies, poets and fools, soldiers and cutpurses. The play ended. The gallery crowd moved slowly down the stairway and out into the cool night air. We walked down the Bowery to Grand Street. We crossed the Williamsburg ferry and then home to my brother's humble boarding-house in Brooklyn, and to bed. But there was no sleep for me. I lived through the play a dozen times during the night. Over and over did I see *Esmeralda* whirling in her dance before the motley crowd in the Cathedral Square—her black eyes ablaze, and her beautiful figure pulsing with joy; again did *Claude Frollo,* overcome and pale with passion, balefully glare at her from the church steps; again did the

24

poet *Gringoire* face the doom of hanging in the thieves' den and protest his innocence and fear; again did the gypsy girl repulse the unholy advances of the monk and tear herself from his arms; and yet again did *Quasimodo* creep after the black-cowled figure up the steps to the high gallery above the roofs of Paris, and there, among the stars, hurl him shrieking to his death on the stones of the street below.

I stayed in New York during the following Sunday. What I did I do not know, and I never shall. It is all a blank. At night I took the train back to Hartford.

I had found my life's work.

CHAPTER II

WITH this introduction to the playhouse, I set about to devour all the plays and all the works on the stage I could procure. My father's library had a complete set of Hudson's SHAKESPEARE, and a volume of Byron containing his dramatic writings. I usually carried one of these in my pocket, to be picked up anywhere in the halt of a leisure quarter of an hour during storehouse work, with hands soiled by marking ink. In the Wadsworth Library I was able to obtain Beaumont and Fletcher, Jonson, Congreve, Sheridan and Bulwer Lytton. The librarian, with whom I had become friendly, assisted my search and unearthed some treasures of Elizabethan drama, climbing ladders to remote shelves, and digging them out of the accretions of dusty years. It would rejoice my soul to see him come forward, slapping the sides of a dingy volume, and blowing a fine dust cloud from its top. In the columns of the NEW YORK CLIPPER I found an advertisement of the Lacy and French editions of plays; some of these I sent for, comedies of Tom Taylor, Robertson and H. J. Byron, and some tearing old melodramas of the Adelphi school. My reading was fuel to consuming fires. There was no sort

26

of character from Addison's *Cato* to *Old Eccles* in
CASTE that I did not fancy myself as playing with
unheard-of success.

My world became strange and lurid. Worthy in-
dividuals who walked along the streets became characters in my gallery of impersonations. Their gait,
voices, hair, noses, movements were noted and set
down in a little book that I came across not long
ago. It contained the descriptions of some forty or
fifty of Hartford's well-known men. I presume I
had intended to reproduce their various qualities
in future plays, but the tricks, mannerisms and even
their owners have long since been forgotten. It is
singular that my favorite characters should have
been old men. *Shylock* was my first love. I had
read that when Kean, at Drury Lane, made his
début in *Shylock*, the audience applauded his, "I
will be assured I may." As my youthful idea of
his reading was that of great vocal stress, my ren-
dition was like the roar of a mad bull. Now I am
sure that Kean spoke the line quietly and with much
humor. Henry Irving had made a success in Eu-
GENE ARAM, and reports of it had appeared in
American papers. I immediately devoted myself to
a study of the character in a bad version that I
found. It was not Irving's, but it served.

There were lax days at the storehouse when I
could steal off to remote lofts, and behind closed
iron doors hiss and writhe myself into physical
fatigue. The rag of a play-book is extant, and I
discover by copious penciled notes that I read cer-

tain lines in a "cold level tone;" that at times I
spoke so hoarsely that my *Aram* must have been
afflicted with chronic bronchitis; that I "trembled
violently" before speaking and clutched my side in
agony. Altogether it was a fine study in remorse
and hydrophobia.

Acting, however, is an incomplete thing if the
actor has to be his own and only audience. I sought
out latent talent in my father's congregation, and
to the shock of certain worthy ladies, produced a
costume play in the basement vestry of the church
—John Tobin's old comedy, THE HONEYMOON, without scenic setting, and garbed in what raiment
the town costumer could afford in periods ranging
from Elizabeth to Queen Anne. I chose the part of
Rolando, the woman hater, for my début. The other
parts I cast to the young Siddonses and Gar-
ricks who had won favor in former elocution con-
tests, and their efforts gained the approval of the
audience. But *my* acting met with a mixed verdict;
in fact it stirred up a pretty row. Some were enthusiastic in praise of it, others, I think the major-
ity, rejected it utterly as being altogether too dramatic for so churchly an environment, and gray
heads nodded ominously at the downward path the
pastor's son had taken.

Among the new acquaintances I made was that
of a young musician who played several instruments well, and who had even appeared in min-
strel and variety shows. His professionalism quite
over-awed me. He was always *ennuyé*, and ap-

peared saturated with the aroma of footlights and burnt cork. He proposed that we should give a show together. There was a hall in East Hartford that could be had for fifteen dollars and we could raise the price. The programme was arranged under the caption of:

A GRAND LITERARY, MUSICAL AND DRA-
MATIC ENTERTAINMENT:
By the
EMINENT MUSICAL ARTIST
Professor Cheney
and the
FAVORITE ELOCUTIONIST and IMPERSON-
ATOR
Mr. Otis Skinner

We were to make alternate appearances in choice selections, the whole to wind up with:

THE SCREAMING FARCE
No. 1 *AROUND THE CORNER*

Flipper ....Mr. Skinner
Nobbler ....Prof. Cheney

Thus read the bill which concluded with the information that tickets would be but twenty-five cents; children fifteen. We were our own advance agents; there was no bill posters' union to prevent our going forth with hammer and tacks to affix programmes on fence, tree and telegraph pole, or to present them politely in a house-to-house visit.

We traveled the mile or so of road that evening on foot with our hand luggage containing books, musical instruments and a few properties. We didn't find our hall of Thespis surrounded by waiting throngs. The janitor was sitting on the steps enjoying his evening pipe, and a couple of idle urchins were playing with a dog. But we gave our performance. We gave it to an audience whose aggregate admissions totaled three dollars and seventy-five cents. We spread the treasures of our art before them. I gave them tragedy of deepest hue, and comedy of button-bursting variety, while the professor poured forth dulcet music, but the effect did not seem to be electric. Our bucolic spectators made no sound either of moan or laughter, though there was occasional squabbling during quiet moments by the janitor's sons who were admitted free. In the second part of the varied and brilliant programme we gamboled through the "screaming farce." The janitor, who acted as our treasurer, had agreed to come back to the stage and lower the curtain at the end; but at this important crisis when *Flipper* and *Nobbler* had settled their differences and had thrown themselves into an embrace of reconciliation, we waited in vain for the curtain on the tableau. The janitor had tilted his chair against the wall at the back of the hall and was sleeping sweetly. Rather shamefacedly we walked off the stage, and rang down.

It was like the old mummer who always had to have melodramatic music for prolonged death

Otis Skinner

AT THE AGE OF TWENTY

Young Men's Club Hall,
NEWINGTON JUNCTION,

Wednesday Evening, Sept. 12.

MESSRS.

Skinner and Cheney

Will, by GENERAL DESIRE, give the second
of their

SELECT ENTERTAINMENTS,

CONSISTING OF

READINGS,

Character Sketches,

AND

HARMONICA SOLOS !

The evening's entertainment concluding with
the LAUGHABLE FARCE,

No. I, Around the Corner

Mr. O. A. SKINNER will appear in an entirely
new programme, of READINGS and SKETCHES,
including selections from the leading Comic
Writers and Poets.

Mr. W. L. CHENEY, the well-known and popular performer on the MOUTH-HARMONICA, has
arranged some of the finest of his Solos, which
have been received with great favor in numerous New England cities.

☞ "The gentlemen have given satisfaction
wherever they have appeared." — *Hartford
Times.*

PROGRAMME.

PART I.

1. The Death of Little Dombey......*Dickens*
2. The Yarn of the "Nancy Bell". *W. S. Gilbert*
3. Harmonica Solo—"Sweet Spirit Hear
   My Prayer".....................*Wallace*
4. The Experience of the McWilliamses
   with the Membranus Croup. *Mark Twain*
5. The Witch of Wenham...........*Whittier*

PART II.

6. Harmonica Solo—March—Selected.
7. An Advertisement Answered........*Anon*
8. Laughin' in Meetin'............*Mrs. Stowe*
9. The Reading Class..............*Skinner*
10. No. 1, AROUND THE CORNER.
    Flipper.. ....Mr. Cheney.
    Nobbler.............Mr. Skinner.

Admission. . . . . . 25 Cents.
Children, ... 15 Cents.

TICKETS FOR SALE AT FISH'S STORE.

Commence at 7.45 o'clock.

Fowler, Miller & Co., 2 State Street, Hartford.

scenes. On one occasion when the orchestra went on strike, this genius, being himself a musician, died with head and shoulders in the wings and, reaching his hands over his head, played *his own death music on the violin.*

Our patrons tumbled noisily out of the hall, and disappeared down dark lanes. We gathered our belongings and walked back across the Connecticut in the peace of the autumn night, perfectly satisfied.

There was an old English actor established in Hartford as a costumer. He had supplied costumes for THE HONEYMOON and this gave me open sesame to his graces. Papa Payn was picturesque. He had wonderful white hair which he would allow to grow until it fell about his shoulders, and then every year or so he would cut it off and sell it. Never-to-be-forgotten days those in the little mildew-smelling shop in Asylum Street where I sat listening to stories of Phelps of Sadler's Wells and other London players with whom he had acted. There were no good actors in America, Papa Payn would say; in truth all the fine ones in the world were either dead or retired. That was the reason for his present occupation. His was the manner of the pompous tragedian, and from imitations he gave of his ancient comrades he must have been one of the bad old actors of the good old days.

Week-end trips to New York occurred as often as Saturday leave and sufficient savings would permit. Among the plays I saw were THE TWO OR-

PHANS with its celebrated cast, Clara Morris in THE SPHINX, SARDANAPALUS at Booth's Theatre with Frank Bangs and Agnes Booth, and Charlotte Cushman as *Queen Katharine* in HENRY VIII, the one fine example of old-school American acting I ever saw.

One holiday I look back upon with unalloyed delight. It was a walking tour through the Berkshires with Dwight W. Tryon. His fame as a landscape painter had not then spread beyond Hartford. A primrose by a river's brim had always been a yellow primrose to me, but in his enthusiasm I saw with new eyes. Often we would halt by hill or stream and while he sketched the spot that intrigued him, I propped my elbows in the grass and studied my play-book.

Among my new advantages was that of the position of Hartford correspondent for the NEW YORK DRAMATIC NEWS, and I had a perfect gorge of plays and stars. Lotta, Maggie Mitchell, Lawrence Barrett, E. L. Davenport, Edwin Adams, George Rignold, Madame Janauschek gave notable impersonations. Fechter played *Hamlet* and *The Count of Monte Cristo*, Barry Sullivan, *Richelieu* and *Richard III*, Ristori appeared as *Elizabeth*, Salvini as *Samson, Othello* and *the Gladiator*, and I had the joy of seeing Booth's incomparable *Hamlet*, and HUMPTY DUMPTY with the drollest of pantomimists, George L. Fox.

Later, I became editor of the HARTFORD CLARION, a weekly newspaper made up of "patent insides," an advertisement or two, and the stolen contents of the dailies. Its circulation was among farmers. The plant and good will had been thrown in as bonus on a printing deal to one of my friends.

This friend, Eugene Jepson, later an actor—his name appears in one of the casts of PETER PAN with Maude Adams—met me on the street and asked what I was doing.

"Nothing," I said. I had left the commission house.

"Then come around and edit THE CLARION for me. I'm too busy with my printing orders to attend to it myself."

Installed in the sanctum with scissors and paste pot I gave the rural subscribers the best of local news. I also evolved for each issue a column of original humorous paragraphs, wrought in the depths of agony; wrote spirited editorials on topics of the day and carried my own copy to the composing room. It was not always easy to maintain editorial dignity when the grimy journeyman printer, receiving my effusions, would ask derisively, "Did you write this?"

It is worthy of note that to our printing office came Frederic Courtland Penfield, to work as compositor. Penfield had his training from the ground up. When my first traveling engagement took me to Hartford, he had become a writer on the EVENING POST; next I met him in London where he was filling the position of vice consul, and our last meeting was in my dressing-room shortly before his

33

death. This was after the severing of diplomatic relations between the United States and Austria and his return from his post as Ambassador to the Court of Vienna. He had written to me:

My dear Skinner:

I am bringing a boxful of friends to see the play to-morrow—Saturday—afternoon.

Might I come behind for a moment to reassure you of my high esteem and admiration, and this after many, many years?

Sincerely,
Frederic C. Penfield.

We had a happy reunion recalling old times.

During the short time that I was editor, "Professor" Cheney and I repeated our combined entertainment several times in towns adjacent to Hartford. Sometimes we made our expenses; often we walked home. Thus I learned at an early age one of the trials of the acting profession—getting home.

But now these youthful episodes were at an end—at the other side of my burned bridges. The world of the theatre lay before me enticing and lovely. I knew nothing of stumbling-blocks and heart-aches ahead. If I had I should not have cared. Though my beginning was humble, it was real. I was a professional actor.

CHAPTER III

On the night of October 30, 1877, I made my professional début at the Philadelphia Museum in the part of *Jim*, an old negro, in a play of the North and South called WOODLEIGH, by Phillip Stoner. I recollect little about *Jim* beyond the fact that I costumed him from a collection I had made of red vests, trousers of extraordinary plaid, collars of the vintage of 1840, loud ties and odd hats, and that I wore a darky wig made of gray horse hair. My performance was no doubt wholly negligible; I was too confused to remember. There had been hours of anxiety as to how I should render my lines, and precisely what movements, gestures, tremble of voice, or variety of facial expression I should use; nights of restlessness when fear of failure banished sleep, or waked me suddenly from dreams of having forgotten my lines completely. And I did forget them. Several days before the performance I would find my memory playing me every sort of trick. The few lines I had were poor and unimportant, but they were an affair of life and death. There was small matter for apprehension, as it proved. The audience gave me but meager attention, and the members of the company ignored

35

me. The stage manager, a palish, tired sort of man who appeared to regard actors as the bane of existence, had flung me a word or two of instruction which I had hungrily seized. I was made to feel that a utility man in a dramatic company was not admitted to the companionship of Olympians long-serviced to a public that had hailed them kings, and I found fellowship among the lowlier members from whom I learned wise and useful things. It was a picturesque little group of men and women with which I had cast my lot. Most of them had known the vile blows and buffets of this world, and took their fortunes lightly—true bohemians.

Our manager had married into the Harold family of actors, and his prolific wife had regularly presented him with an increasing herd of small Davidges who looked out upon a sea of troubles in the doubtful financial returns of the Philadelphia Museum—a minor theatre, reduced to slight market value through maladministrations of bad managers. Under the banner of the Davidges and the Harolds, family hostages were given to fortune in the positions of leading woman, juvenile woman, walking lady, orchestra leader, call boy, business manager, and that of the impresario-in-chief who, although a comic actor, frequently seized upon the parts of the leading man or the old man if they were particularly fat. Cynics spoke of the Museum as "The Snake Shop, located at the corner of Harold and Davidge Streets."

The serpentine allusion referred to a collection

like that of the Boston Museum, of pickled reptiles
and stuffed animals. There was also a wax-works
gallery, much gone to seed, the *chef-d'œuvre* of
which was a stiff representation of THE LAST
SUPPER, wherein the Apostles were regaling themselves on a frugal feast of onions. At the date of
my writing the building has been turned into a
house of negro minstrelsy—the only one of its kind
in existence, I believe. A few years ago it was a
hall for the exhibition of freaks, and where the sacred wax tableau had stood, I beheld a fat woman's
six day, go-as-you-please race.

Our leading man was Mark Bates, husband of
Marie Bates, so many years with David Warfield,
who had filled numbers of prominent positions, and
filled them well. He was a handsome fellow and a
good forceful actor, but years of dissipation had
caused him to grow lax and undependable. He was
the first actor to tell me I had any ability.

Lawrence Barrett's brother, Louis, did the
heavies; a little consumptive fellow named Rothwell
purveyed rather doleful comedy; and Saville, an
old English clown, much crippled with rheumatism,
was useful in pantomimes.

By far the most notable member of the company
was William A. Chapman, who, in his day, had been
a favorite comedian in New York and Philadelphia,
and who was now very old and crusty, resembling
more than anything else a worn edition of The Duke
of Wellington. I appeared to have got somewhat
on his nerves, for I overheard an irritable reference

37

to me as a "damned amateur" after one of our
scenes together. As the season passed on, I found
myself becoming less annoying to the old comedian.
His bark was worse than his bite. Seeing that I
was a very earnest youngster he began to tolerate
me. Finally he thawed and talked to me of his
own early days in the theatre. His first engagement in England had been in a traveling troupe
shepherded by a man named Davenport who was
the father of Mrs. Jean Davenport Lander, at one
time a popular star on the American stage. Davenport was a very pompous person and the descrip-
tion that Dickens gives of *Vincent Crummles'* bow
—"something between the courtsey of a Roman em-
peror and the nod of a pot companion"—fitted Davenport exactly. When Chapman had acted for a
short term with Davenport and his itinerants, a
young man joined their forces to play unimportant
parts; a gawky, delicate-looking fellow but quite
alert, with an eager eye. No one especially marked
his advent, recruits were constantly falling in hope-
fully, and falling out again for lack of pay. This
young man kept his own council and was reserved to
the point of shyness. Somebody said he was a
newspaper man or a writer of some sort, but nobody knew, and his stay in Davenport's grand ag-
gregation of talent was short.

Several years later Chapman had advanced
from his provincial novitiate and had become a
player at one of the London theatres. One night
the rumor went about that Mr. Dickens was in the

audience. Between acts Chapman hastened to the peep hole in the curtain. The celebrated author was pointed out to him, and the actor recognized the brief associate of his days in Davenport's company.

"And could Dickens act?" I asked.

"Oh, yes, he was pretty fair as an actor. Nobody could do much with the parts he had to play, and I guess Dickens didn't think it worth while to try hard with his. He always looked out of place in the queer costumes Davenport gave him to wear."

I asked Chapman if other people in Davenport's troupe were recognizable in the personnel of the *Vincent Crummles'* company who acted with *Nickleby* and *Smike* in the Dickens' story.

"Every one of them except that there was only one young male *Crummles* instead of two. I'll swear our leading woman was *Miss Snevellicci,* and if our heavy man wasn't Dickens' *Mr. Lenville,* he was the very spit of him. Davenport's fat wife certainly had a 'charnel house voice' like *Mrs. Crummles.*"

"How about the 'infant phenomenon'?"

"Absolutely."

"But Mrs. Lander," I said, "denied point-blank that she was the model for this character."

"Of course it was exaggerated," said Chapman, "but she was *Crummles'* daughter. Dickens dressed her up—that's all. The company often walked from town to town while the properties were carried in a rickety cart, drawn by a weary pony— *Crummles'* pony, whose mother had 'been on the stage and whose father was a dancer.'

"As for Dickens, well, he might have been *Nicholas Nickleby.*"

Dickens, avid for character and detail, was possibly at work on *Nickleby* at the time and needing veritable models for his already conceived characters, turned stroller and lived the life until his purpose was served. All this is probable.

Our season started bravely and busily with two performances a day. The evening bill was also presented at Wednesday and Saturday matinées, while at the other four afternoon performances, which were called "off matinées," a short drama and farce were given. Of the former I recall the names of BEN BOLT, MICHAEL EARL or THE MANIAC LOVER, THE IDIOT WITNESS, FANCHON, BLACKEYED SUSAN, THE SEVEN CLERKS, etc., lurid specimens of mid-Victorian playwriting; while the farces were of the Madison Morton variety,—BOX AND COX, SLASHER AND CRASHER, MY TURN NEXT, and a score of others. The regular evening bill was usually a melodrama in the repertory of a visiting star—the kind one finds now in the cheaper city theatres.

It will be seen that we had no time for idleness at the Museum. Morning, afternoon and night were occupied by rehearsal and performance. Parts were scantily studied, inadequately rehearsed and slovenly performed. Heaven knows how many dead-and-gone playwrights turned in their graves during that season! If we said anything approximating the meaning of our lines, we were doing well by our standard. I learned the useful arts of faking and winging. To "wing" a part meant to have the manuscript of it tucked in your sleeve or your pocket, or thrust into the framework of the wing near your exit to be seized and scanned between scenes. Should you see an individual gazing intently into his hat while playing an intense, dramatic scene you knew he had his part concealed there. Writing sketchy cues on your cuff was an old trick. One character I never studied at all— *The Admiral,* in BLACKEYED SUSAN. The admiral was seated at a table conducting a court martial in a ship scene, with a large book in front of him. I put the part in the open book, and read the whole of it. Many a Saturday night I have gone to my lodgings with three parts to study for Monday matinée and night, and walked the floor till daybreak, my forehead wound in a wet towel to avoid falling asleep, cramming the words into my brain somehow—anyhow. But what a school it was! I learned my art crudely, roughly, but by leaps and bounds, driven by necessity to an intuitive grasp of character and the way to express it. To sing; to dance; to fence with foil and broadsword; to kneel; to fall in combat; to work up the crescendo movement of a scene; to sit or to rise; to play fair in a give-and-take episode with a fellow-player; to learn how to make up, and above all, to do nothing. Repose was as foreign to me as to a French dancing master. No one ever had more unruly legs. The wearied stage manager, Reynolds, in a voice verging on tears, used frequently to exclaim at rehearsal, when I was cast for a calm and slow-going old gentleman, "For God's sake, Skinner, keep your legs STILL!" There was no kind of part I did not play—advancement had been rapid—even sex was no bar, for I was sometimes clapped into skirts for nigger wenches and coarse old hags. I scowled as villains, stormed as heavy fathers, dashed about in light comedy, squirmed in character parts, grimaced in the comics, and tottered as the Pantaloon in pantomime. *Miss Smithers* in Wanted One Thousand Milliners in the afternoon would be followed by the aristocratic *Count de Linieres* in The Two Orphans, or hundred-year-old *Solomon Probity* in The Chimney Corner at night.

My companions were adepts at improvisations of costume and make-up. I was taught how to make lace neck falls and Charles II collars out of white wrapping paper, to transform a frock coat into a military uniform by pasting disks of gilt paper on the buttons, and pinning strips of yellow braid on the shoulders for epaulets. On one occasion, when cast as a rich banker in Aurora Floyd, and hurriedly dressing for the part, I discovered I had no white shirt, nothing but the flannel thing I had worn in the street, and inquiry through various dressing-rooms, revealed a dress-shirt famine. The curtain had rung up before I chanced upon a discarded paper cuff thrown into a corner which I hastily seized, straightened flat, cutting a curved yoke at one end. This I fastened to my collar button, and when it was ornamented with a fake diamond and my coat buttoned across, my linen was faultless. At another time, having to build up a whiskered face for an Irish cutthroat in KATHLEEN MAVOURNEEN, I found no crêpe hair in my dressing-room, and no one had any.

"Here, I'll fix you," said an incorrigible fakir named Brooks who was never at a loss on occasions like this. Diving into his pocket, he fished out a package of fine-cut tobacco and removed two liberal wads which, pasted to my jowls, formed convincing-looking mutton-chop whiskers. The only trouble was that they slowly disintegrated during the evening, and I was left, after a scene of assault upon the heroine, with nothing on either jaw but a dark brown smear.

In some forgotten storage trunk I still have my first pair of fleshing tights, which have been preserved in memory of the sensation they caused on the opening night of ALADDIN. When the season began I owned but one pair of tights, dark blue worsted, and they had served me for every costume play we did until this especial production, when it became necessary to provide fleshings for the Chinaman I was cast for. These are strictly home-made—a triumph of ingenuity and economy. They are a pair of ladies' long cotton stockings, dyed with annatto and sewed with black coarse thread to the seat of a pair of underdrawers. Covered by the outer casing of Chinese trunks, their constructive crudities were hidden, and my legs looked truly Mongolian. Six of us had to perform a Chinese

43

dance with jumpy steps and pointing forefingers before the *Khan* and his daughter, and as we gyrated in a circle past the royal throne there was a broad smile on the face of the *Princess.* When the revolving wheel brought me again before her, she shot a whispered aside and pointed vigorously. I was not to be caught; the victim of many practical jokes had grown wise. Shaking my head knowingly, I danced on. As I reached the front of the stage, a titter went through the audience, and when I looked about the players were all convulsed, and the *Princess* was nearly beside herself. One downward look, and I grew cold. My trunks had slipped from my waist and were sagging lower and lower, hanging but by a tape-end to an anchoring belt, and my personally-constructed tights were displayed in ghastly realism. I fled from the stage with the shouts of the audience in my ears.

Since October I had heard regularly from home. My mother's letters were particularly anxious. I wrote glowing descriptions of the company, the productions and of my domestic quarters on Wood Street, in reply. I was too proud to reveal the real truth—that small as my pay was it was not regularly forthcoming. Business was pretty bad at Ninth and Arch. My room was a tiny garret chamber for which I was charged a dollar and a half a week by the sweet-faced old lady whose advertisement of lodgings to let I had answered. An incongruous figure in a most dubious part of town— (there were lodging-houses of no uncertain char-

acter to the right and to the left of us) this gentle-
woman knew intuitively that I was but nineteen and
had just tumbled from the parent nest; she was always kind and solicitous even when my rent was in
arrears—and it often was. My whole life ran in the
narrowest groove, bounded on every side by the demands of the theatre, and my daily walk rarely
varied from the direct route that lay between Wood
Street and the Museum. Practically my only asso-
ciates were my co-workers. If they were simple
folk who talked shop overmuch, sound wheat lay beneath their chaff. Over the nightly beer at Liszt's
—not the Abbé, but one whose liquid melody
wrought harmony in our souls—our gathering place
across the way, I listened to tales that interested
me mightily.

Out of these dark ages emerges a vision of myself and a penniless fellow-player sitting in the
moonlight on the marble steps of a Ninth Street
mansion that had seen better days. We gaze lovingly at a stream of yellow light flooding the sidewalk over the way from beneath swinging lattice
doors. Our throats are parched, for we have finished an evening of strenuous acting at the theatre
and the May night is hot and humid. The golden
radiance flows from the *bierstube* of Liszt, the port-
ly—the immaculate—whose starched shirt-front is
never without its three little diamond studs, and
whose smile is sunshine in dark places. A few belated pedestrians pass by, and their inhospitable
"good nights" fall dry and unproductive. Sudden-

45

ly the swinging doors fly open and mine host steps
forth in his shirt-sleeves. With a slow survey his
gaze sweeps the gloomy street, then rests on our
still figures. Hope springs from the marble steps
only to die as Liszt turns and waddles back again
without a word. The world has neither pity nor
profit, for in that saloon is a score on the slate
against us longer than Rip Van Winkle's on the
shutter of Nick Vedder's tavern. We dare not come
within its monstrous presence. But lo! a miracle!
A waiter, all in white, bearing two glasses, amber
and effulgent! Before our amazed eyes he crosses
and silently places in our hands something long and
cold and wet. After a few minutes that are full of
prayer, we go to make acknowledgment and find
our host has been watching behind a window curtain, shaking with silent laughter.

There came to the Museum on a time when
stage manager Reynolds was taken ill, a strange
creature names Lascelles. A more incompetent old
bluff I never met. He would sit at the rehearsal
prompt table with an expression of beatific rapture,
his thoughts miles away from the book wherein he
was supposed to be following our lines, and when
some one struck verbal snags and commenced to
flounder, the old rascal became Quilp-like in his
gloating over the unhappy one's difficulties. A
fiendish look appeared in his eye, and raising his
hands he would pantomime the playing of an imag-
inary flute, saying, "Music! deedle! deedle! dee!"
It was he who responded to an actor in the midst of

a mental morass when he whispered savagely into the prompt entrance, "For God's sake, give me the word!" by replying, "Certainly, son, what word do you want?" One night he fairly went into a doze at the prompt stand. We were doing a spectacular play—THE CATARACT OF THE GANGES, I think—and we were all floundering in our lines. A messenger came on announcing, "The Rajah of Bramapootrah sends you greetings." Brooks, who had been sadly in need of prompting, gave a look of helplessness at the slumbering Lascelles and exclaimed, "Well, thank God, somebody sends me *something!*"

At the little play-house finances were at low ebb. One afternoon the receipts were seven dollars. Salary days went by and the "ghost did not walk." Whenever I was hungry I braved the manager in his den. His compassion was tempered with indignation at my unreasonable demands.

"You don't want to forget this opportunity I am giving you."

"I am not forgetting, but I must live," I answered.

Davidge's tremulo deepened; he glanced mournfully, meaningly at the photographs of his large family on the desk before him, with a look that said, "You helpless darlings! And this monster would take the bread out of your mouths!" then turning to me with—"Don't you consider I am making some sacrifice in allowing you to play all these prominent parts?" Quite true, but who else had he to play them? I was politic but insistent.

"Look at these!" He waved a package of bills. "Gas bills! If I don't pay them they'll remove the meter. Then what'll you do?" My distresses seemed to me as great as those of gas magnates.

"Oh, well!"

Blood money! But he couldn't part with me—not at *my salary!*

Depositing a few bills in my hand with the air of a monarch signing his abdication, his face brightened, his smile returned, his squeaky pathos departed; all was well again.

"Come around in a few days. We've got a great part for you week after next."

I gritted my teeth. A line to my father would have brought financial aid, but I remembered my mother's prediction of failure. No, not yet! My penates were few—everything I owned, even my most juvenile treasures I had brought from home—but they were productive. After a trip to the pawnshop with a packet of rings and pins and things, I had a sense of becoming some kind of Bank, and my companions and I feasted royally. Ordinarily financial recoupment took place at Leary's Old Book Shop on Ninth Street. Here I could exchange mental for material food by dipping into a stock of school prizes and Christmas presents, sets of Horatio Alger, Mayne Reid and Oliver Optic. When it came to the sacrifice of some works on the stage, volumes of plays, and a set of Victor Hugo, it hurt.

TEN NIGHTS IN A BAR ROOM was put on with the dissipated Bates as the drunkard, *Joe Morgan.* It was the last of his appearances. I encountered him one rainy night—or early morning—homeless, penniless. I conducted him to a cheap lodging, and then had to stay with him several hours to prevent him from jumping up to dress and go out. The following season, he was picked up from the sidewalk and died in the station house. A fund was raised for his funeral at the Church of St. John The Evangelist on North Thirteenth Street. His only enemy was himself.

UNCLE TOM'S CABIN we gave every afternoon and night for a week, and I blacked up twelve times for *Uncle Tom*. Old Bob McWade (he who had played *Rip Van Winkle* with us the week before) said it was a good performance. I wonder if it was! I was nineteen. Scarcely an age for *Uncle Tom!*

During the holidays, Davidge followed English tradition and presented pantomimes; and there were nights of actual physical pain when I would drag myself homeward, scratched, bruised and beaten, my lot being to endure, as *Pantaloon*, falls from ladders, disappearances through traps, and always the noisy belaborings of the slap stick and bladder on my tender anatomy.

A delicious example of faking through a *contretemps* was shown one afternoon at a performance of THE SEVEN CLERKS, which, by the way, used frequently to appear in the announcements under a new title. One week it would be THE SEVEN CLERKS, the next, THE MISER OF MARSEILLES, and yet again,

THE THREE THIEVES AND THE DENOUNCER. In the first act the miser has to exhibit the contents of a cabinet containing seven bags of gold. It is imperative that their display to the audience should be actual, since in the following act one bag is found to be missing. Louis Barrett and Brooks were breezing through the scene. Barrett with due impressiveness handed a key to Brooks and bade him "unlock yon cabinet." Brooks inserted the key, fussed with it but couldn't open the door. Turning, he said, "Master, here is some mistake; this is not the key." Then followed a scene, purely extempore:

> BARRETT: "How, varlet! Not the key?"
>
> BROOKS: "No, Master."
>
> BARRETT: "Try again: thy fingers are clumsy."
>
> BROOKS. (*Making a second attempt and pulling at the door*) "'Twill not yield."
>
> BARRETT: "Ha! I do remember. I but mistook. The rightful key lies within my chamber, Bide here, young sir, till my return." (*Exit.*)
>
> (*He is seen in the wings, grabbing keys from stage manager, property man, carpenter, stage hands—everybody, and returns laden. Throws everything in a heap on center table.*) "Now! Do as I bid you!"
>
> BROOKS: (*Who has shown pantomime of mystification during Barrett's absence, takes keys one after the other, and struggles with the lock in vain, uttering frequent ejaculations*: "Not this! Nor this! Still in vain!" etc., *while Barrett sits grunt-*

ing and growling. Turns finally, and throwing the keys on table with a grand gesture, exclaims:) " 'Tis useless, Master, not one will fit the lock."

BARRETT: "Is't e'en so? I see it all! Some usurper has stolen the key. But remember, sir, in yon cabinet *are* seven bags of gold. Let them be found there in the morning." (*Exit.*)

CURTAIN

We had great mirth over this afterward. Some one asked Barrett, "Why 'usurper'?" "It was the only thing I could think of, and—isn't it a splendid word!"

Barrett had never been at a loss for words that would carry him over a lapse of memory or unstudied speeches. Cast for the *Khan of Tartary* in MAZEPPA with Kate Fisher who, as the hero of this equestrian drama delighted the Bowery playgoers of the 'seventies with her silk-clad limbs and her strapping figure, Barrett observed at rehearsal that while he was calling for the "fiery, untamed steed!" and shouting out the edict that the suffering hero (Miss Fisher) should be lashed to the sides of the unconquered one and sent galloping over the desolate plains of Tartary, the horse was stamping in the wings and the supers making a general hullabaloo. Why study that speech? Nobody would hear it. After a night or two the star detected through the noise that the *Khan* was saying a quantity of things in language unknown to human tongue. At the next performance Barrett was in

51

the midst of the dread proclamation, when suddenly the cries of supers and the noise of horses' hoofs were stilled, and the *Khan's* voice rang out with: "Ains! Blains! Fortescue! One, two, three! Humpty Dumpty sat on a wall! Blamfy! Boom! San Francisco!"

Now came the great part Davidge had promised me. The Frank Frayne family of actors and rifle shots, six in number, had played an engagement early in the season in Si Slocum—a drama of the West, in which they performed dangerous feats of marksmanship with real rifles and bullets. They returned for a repeat minus one member of the family who had played the villain. This character was seized by the neck at the end of Act Three by a ferocious bulldog. The parts were all fraught with danger; deadly action was, however, undertaken only by the stars themselves, leaving the company immune.

Davidge was distressed at the break in their ranks until he thought of me. Calling me to his office and fairly inundating me with beneficence, he unfolded his plan. I was to be one of the Frayne family and have my name announced in the same type as theirs. Either I could play the *Nigger* and have a clay pipe shot from my mouth, or I could do the *Mexican* and wrestle with the dog! The offer dazed me. It was surely a wonderful chance. But of my choice I was doubtful. The missing member, Butler, who usually did the *Mexican,* had on the previous occasion, showed me his scarred chest where the dog had accidentally seized him.

"He's a gentle dog," he told me. "Whenever he gets me instead of this pad around my neck, he always lets go. But sometimes I'm not quick enough to slip the pad into his jaws." I chose the *Nigger*.

In the act where the shooting took place, a number of fancy shots were executed—one was a sort of William Tell effect and an apple was shot by Frayne from his wife's head. My duty was to stand still, facing the footlights on a line between the two proscenium sides, Frayne's sombrero pulled over my face with the stem of a T. D. clay pipe stuck through a hole in the brim and held between my teeth. Frayne with his rifle *reversed,* and the butt against his forehead, sighted along *beneath* the barrel and shattered the bowl with a bullet that entered a foot-thick, hard-wood target on the opposite side of the stage.

All was well for a few nights. I was part and parcel of a big sensation, and my name was featured outside the theatre and on the house bills.

Then I began to think!

Frayne wasn't a drinking man: he was never ruffled or nervous: he was a sure shot, but suppose—suppose! By the end of the week I was nearly a nervous wreck, and Frayne sometimes took *three shots* instead of one to hit the shaking pipe bowl.

But I had been starred.

A few years later, a despatch from Providence appeared in the morning papers, announcing that Frayne had accidentally shot his wife through the head in his William Tell act, instantly killing her. I read the account in a cold trance.

Some wild pranks were played now and then. Wood Benson, an absurd actor, a veritable Count Johannes, appeared for a week in a "protean" piece called KATIE. One night one of our practical jokers fastened some twenty feet of thread to a nail in the side wall near the prompt entrance, to the other end he fixed a bent pin. He stood behind Benson who was ready to enter briskly on a front scene, and as he started the pin was caught neatly in the star's wig. The slack allowed the victim to advance about ten feet toward the middle of the stage when the audience was regaled by the sight of the wig flying from Benson's head, and the unfortunate man standing before them, bald as an egg.

The season drew toward its close. The personnel of the company had suffered change; those who could get engagements elsewhere had deserted. Chapman and Barrett had gone, Bates was a wreck, and little Rothwell had succumbed to tuberculosis. The Harolds and the Davidges, assisted by a handful of the remnants, held the fort against fearful odds. Financially I was worse off than when I began, but in experience rich beyond measure.

A slight recoupment of depleted fortunes came before summer finally put an end to everything theatrical in Philadelphia. The Chestnut Street Theatre was opened for a few weeks by Louis James, Van Horn, the costumer, and William E. Sheridan. A fairly good company was got together, and I had the advantage of playing prominent parts with excellent actors. *Malcolm* in MACBETH and juvenile parts in THE SEA OF ICE, OLIVER TWIST, EAST LYNNE, THE CHILD STEALER and other standard plays, and the chance to study such men as Sheridan and James. Sheridan was a man of splendid power, with one of the most intriguing voices I ever listened to. For years he was a favorite in Philadelphia. His fine acting as *Macbeth*, *Don Carlos* and *Fagin* was enormously stimulating to me. His *Louis XI* was, to my thinking, a finer impersonation than Irving's. He starred with the play in this country, received much praise but little fortune, and died in Australia where he had gained great popularity.

Hot weather soon brought the Chestnut Street enterprise to a close. The year's work was ended. My gentle landlady, when I confessed I had no means of settling her bill, protested at my leaving as security for future payment, a trunk still containing a few saleable things—among them books of value whose loss grieved me. "Take your time," she said, but I left the trunk; it was little enough. My purse was empty, but I had a home to go to and a contract duly signed by George K. Goodwin, manager, and Otis Skinner, actor, for the services of said Skinner at the Walnut Street Theatre for the following season. Goodwin had seen me play *Malcolm* at the Chestnut Street.

I had played from the previous October to the closing in June, counting "doubles," precisely ninety-two characters.

William E. Sheridan

Louis James

CHAPTER IV

THE season of 1878-79 at the Walnut Street Theatre saw the last of the stock company in that historic house. The system of theatres was changing. Hitherto the custom had prevailed of local companies in the larger places—Boston, Philadelphia, Baltimore, Cleveland, Cincinnati, Chicago—and in a few cities of the South—to whom came the visiting star with his repertory. When a number of pieces were to be produced during the engagement, the star's stage director would precede him (or her) to conduct rehearsals in advance; the star and company coming together on Monday morning for the first time to run through the lines "perfect," and the bill presented that night. The copyright law was a lax ineffective thing. One of its absurd provisions was that if a person could prove that he had witnessed a public performance of a play, and memorized it, he *had the right to produce it!* Thefts were frequent; to guard against them, manuscripts of privately owned pieces would not contain a complete text. The speeches of supporting characters would be given in full, as well as the stage business, but the star's part would be indicated only by a cue of three words. These were

57

known as "skeleton manuscripts." Sometimes
there would be but one play for the engagement; at
others a long list, changing nightly, would strike
havoc among the entire personnel from the director
and leading man to the mechanics.

Rehearsals were called at ten o'clock, and if, after ten minutes' grace to allow for a difference in
clocks, some one came late, he was subject to fine.
Old John Jack, a popular favorite in this country
and in Australia, told me shortly before he died at
the Edwin Forrest Home in Philadelphia, how
punctilious Forrest had been in this matter. "He
was never late for rehearsal and had no patience
with anybody that was. Should there be a wait for
a tardy member, Forrest would sit silent and majestic, watch in hand marking the overdue minutes,
and when the culprit appeared, breathless and apologetic upon the hushed stage, the tragedian after
an impressive pause, would snap his watch shut,
and rise with his best King Lear manner: 'Sir!
You are late. You have taken from these ladies
and gentlemen that which Almighty God himself
could not restore to them—their time!'"

Caste distinctions were observed; if the leading
man or woman noticed the utility people at all, it
was with condescension, but the comfortable green
room was common ground where all met. The call
boy notified only the star at his dressing-room; all
others from the green room. An institution of the
virtuous days of yesteryear was the call boy. He is
now defunct. His pale descendant of to-day, the

assistant stage manager, is a weak imitation. The call boy did more than shout, "Beginners! All down for the act!" He was the young person who kept the play going. Five minutes before the entrance of a character, or group of characters, on the scene, he would pop into the green room with his manuscript call-plot, issue the summons and pop out again. And woe betide any who loitered or neglected the call. He was fined outrageously. The green room, like the call boy, has become extinct.

Cases of intoxication were subject to fine or discharge.

There were no modern drops in the stock scenery; the box set so common to-day was unknown. The interiors and exteriors in the scene-dock bore such descriptive titles as; Oak Chamber, Gothic Palace, Red Drawing-room, Rustic Kitchen, Prison, Roman Street, Rocky Pass, Cut Wood, etc. In the property room were paraphernalia from throne chairs and royal couches to masks, helmets, blunderbusses, red fire and Yorick's skull. Scene painter and property man were kept busy constructing special scenery and articles for new plays. Electrical lighting had not been invented; when the gas man had lighted the "borders" at seven-thirty p. m. with torch and long pole, and his "foots" in front of the curtain, and turned them "down to the blue," all illumination was ready, except for the calcium lights of blended gas from the red and black cylinders.

Of such kind was the organization at the Walnut

Street Theatre, now rebuilt, but the oldest in America, whose date 1807 stands on its façade to-day.

The company for this season was efficient and hard-working. Mr. and Mrs. Charles Walcot were in the leading parts. Mrs. E. L. Davenport, old woman; Lizzie Creese, juvenile woman; Harry Meredith, heavies; Atkins Lawrence, juveniles; James Dean, old men; George Howard and Sam Hemple, comedians. John B. Mason ("Jack" Mason), who later achieved distinction and is remembered for his fine performance in THE WITCHING HOUR, and I were engaged for general business. This meant anything and everything. Once in Webster's tragedy, THE DUCHESS OF MALFI, we assembled under the stage and were "the groans of the dying."

The manager, George K. Goodwin, knowing very little about the artistic side of the theatre, left the direction to Charles Walcot who ruled behind the scenes, and selected all the "fat parts" for his own playing, sometimes to the disgust of the heavy man or the leading juvenile. Goodwin had made his money by running a "dollar store" (these were days before Mr. Woolworth) and by perfecting a magic comb for dying hair. He was extremely vain about his personal appearance, much given to fawn-colored coats, loud vests, padded shoulders, telescope hats and jewelry.

The patriarchal title of "Pop" was bestowed on John Reed, the gas man, father of Roland Reed and grandfather of Florence Reed. He had seen the rise

60

and fall of generations of actors, had illuminated productions without number, and had bequeathed to the theatre his own skull to be used in the graveyard scene of HAMLET after his death.

I was engaged at a salary of fifteen dollars a week, and I was happy in the fact that "treasury days" were regular and prompt. Stepping down somewhat from my long parts at the shabby Museum, in this established company I must be content with lesser ones. I took lodging in a respectable quarter near the theatre. Almost my first act was to look up my old landlady on Wood Street; but there was a to-let sign on the brick front; no one could tell whither she had gone. The loss of the little zinc-covered trunk and its treasured contents has been a lasting regret.

My first appearance in the new company was a small part in OLIVER TWIST, in which Rose Eytinge, in the full bloom of her oriental beauty, starred as *Nancy Sykes*.

Then came one star after another and in the support of these great and popular people, whose abilities differed as much as their methods, I was given many parts as utility man. It was a splendid opportunity, to be associated with and to watch these artists. The present-day verdict on some of them might be different, but they were all great in their time. To many these will be but names with little association. The deeds of all actors are written in water.

Early in the season Fanny Janauschek swept

across the stage in a repertory of plays both awesome and exacting. Gloom sat in her train for four weeks. Though a short, rather stockily built woman, "Madame" could rise seemingly to physical heights that were overpowering. Her eyes were of hazel-gray, large and weary-lidded, but when they suddenly opened, it was the unmasking of a battery. They quite terrified me the first time I played with her. I had not encountered the tragedienne until I met her on the scene—her rehearsals having been conducted by her stage manager. As *Seyton* in MACBETH I entered to announce the coming of *King Duncan* and was instructed to wait my speech until *Lady Macbeth* demanded my news. Madame's massive back was toward me, her gaze fixed on *Macbeth's* letter, and she showed no recognition of my presence. I blurted out, "The King comes here to-night." Thereat she whirled like an enraged tiger, her eyes two fiery search-lights, and with a deep vibrato thundered out: "How now, sirrah, vot noos?" With wilting legs I reiterated my speech and retired clammy. Her eyes had given me a distinct electric shock.

Another luckless wight, Maylin, had to precede her exit from the court in HENRY VIII. Blazing with offended royalty she bade him "Go before!" and he started. He made the least miscalculation in his line of direction, but backed away before the queen step by step with a debonair grace that in his heart of hearts he did not feel. A commotion arose among the occupants of the left-hand stage box, and

62

Madame Janauschek.

a large frightened lady got up in haste to escape holding the actor in her lap. There was an unrehearsed back fall, a flourish of gray worsted tights, and a smashed chair. The awful part of it for Maylin was that he had to recover himself, gather up the crown and cushion he was bearing, and after getting back to the stage, resume his backward minuet step until he got round the fatal curve and into the exit. Meanwhile Janauschek stood frothing with fury.

There was a husband attached to Madame Janauschek whose companionship she bore with patience; his name was Pillot. When some one told her the news of the deaths of several noted people, Madame sighed and said: "Yes, everybody dies but Pillot."

A woman of Janauschek's temperament could not help but act well: Madame did more; she was both majestic and irresistible. Her *Catherine of Russia, Lady Macbeth, Brünhilda* and *Medea* were figures stepped out of classic tragedy; her *Katharine of Aragon* profoundly pathetic; her *Mary Stuart* feline, tender and queenly. Her most sensational performance was the dual rôle of *Lady Dedlock,* and the French maid, *Hortense,* in CHESNEY WOLD, taken from Dickens' BLEAK HOUSE. She was never truly happy in a part unless she had a drapery to handle—her very clothes acted. She could be almost as eloquent with scarves and hangings as in her voice and gesture. No other woman I ever saw on the stage made so much of the definite business of handling her garments—and they were ample, yards and yards! She would stop in the middle of a sentence to rearrange the fall of a cloak, and as Janauschek did it, the action was convincingly natural.

The lady's temper was none of the sweetest. There was a night in MEDEA when one woe trod upon another's heels in faulty scenery and properties. She clutched a chair, it wabbled. She leaned against a braced pillar, it gave way. She walked up a flight of steps, they nearly collapsed under her weight. To steady herself she seized the hand-rail, it came off in her hand!

Hell let loose when the curtain fell. Pretty soon there was a circle on the stage consisting of Walcot, his assistant, the carpenter, the property man, the gas man, the stage hands, even the call boy; in the center stood Janauschek, revolving in turns to different ones like the pointer on the dial of a weighing machine, telling them what she thought of them. Her personal stage manager, Smith, who lived a life of perpetual panic, had hidden in the darkest corner he could find. One of the company who had been out of the cast, came back from the front of the house where he had been spellbound by Madame's acting. Overhearing his enthusiastic comments, Smith crawled from his hiding-place and pushed him violently into the group on the stage, saying, "Tell it to Madame." The infuriated star turned on the newcomer with a look of amazement, and the confused actor stuttered out his lame compliments. Janauschek's anger vanished in a flash. In the softest voice and most coquettish manner she purred: "Oh, thank you, Meester Dean!" The lately berated culprits were forgotten: they tiptoed out of sight.

In grateful relief to the gloom of Madame Janauschek's visit was that of Lotta who in LA CIGALE crowded the old Walnut nightly. The figure of a child, eyes that held a world of laughter, set in a dimpled roguish face, crowned by a fluff of curling bronze hair, a voice that sang and feet that danced, fingers that tripped nimbly over banjo strings, spirits that never flagged; that was Lotta— Charlotte Crabtree in private life—and if her plays were slight things, nobody cared. Probably those who regarded the effervescent little actress as the embodiment of joy and thoughtlessness would have been amazed to know that she was perfectly cool-headed and businesslike, with an eye to box-office returns and a knowledge of stage generalship.

And what a contrast there is between the last scenes in the eventful history of these two women! One famous in two continents, favored by royalty, her very jewels used for exhibition in shop windows of the towns where she played as evidence of the admiration bestowed upon her, an acknowledged queen of tragedy, dying at last, forgotten, old, ugly, nearly blind and saved only by the charity of her fellow-players from burial in the Potter's Field. The other a witch of fascination, a dazzling sunbeam, dancing, singing, cooing, kicking her way into the hearts of thousands, and retiring at last from public life, the mistress of a fortune.

Ada Cavendish, who had made some stir in her native England, played with us. In the warmth of her early thirties, comely and magnetic, diction that was clear and distinct, her *Jane Shore* and *Rosalind* charmed and delighted her audiences. Her voice was intriguing; it made me think of distant church bells.

Stars arrived and departed with each week: Chanfrau, the Kiralfys, Mary Anderson and Mc-Cullough prospered in their engagements. Frank Chanfrau had passed through the popularity of Joe, Mose and Sam, and was devoting his later years wholly to Kit, The Arkansas Traveler. Referring to the Walnut programme I find that *Kit*, in the prologue, was "aged 25, a right smart sort of man, and devoted to music and matrimony," and in Act I that he was "aged 40, improved by age and circumstances, like whisky, which he likes." Nearly everything about Chanfrau was big: voice, body, limbs, method. He must have been a very handsome man in his younger days. I find also that I was cast for *Frau Pedders,* "an ancient production of Faderland." Skirts again! I had useful experience with them at the Museum. I was growing familiar with corsets and petticoats.

At one of the performances of Kit, Harry Meredith's pistol missed fire. He snapped and snapped, and Chanfrau besought the murderous bullets with oaths and lamentations: "Why don't you shoot?

Fanny Davenport   Lotta

John T. Raymond   Frank Chanfrau
as Colonel Mulberry Sellers   as Kit, the Arkansas Traveler

VISITING STARS AT THE WALNUT STREET THEATRE
PHILADELPHIA, 1878–9

Damn it, shoot!'' The actor must always think quickly. Meredith picked up a stage boulder weighing something like half a ton and hurled it at Chanfrau. The papier-mâche rock sailed over, struck the star's shoulder with the impact of a toy balloon, and dropped quietly, softly to earth. After the curtain had fallen there was a pistol-shot. It was the property man hurrying to the wings with a relief pistol, and the audience was delighted.

Some one has said that the reason the auditor is filled with satisfaction at the sight of perplexity, despair, rage, jealousy, thwarted love, or any emotional upset, tragic or comic, on the part of the character, is because of the elation he feels that he is not in a similar stew. The woes of *Lear, Othello, Shylock, Pierre* in THE TWO ORPHANS, *Uncle Tom,* nearly the whole tribe of stage unfortunates, give him a sense of superiority. That is why a stage accident always moves the laughter of an audience. In the streets we laugh at the man who slips on a banana peel, and at the fat woman rushing frantically out of the way of an approaching automobile. In the theatre we are ready to be tickled with a straw.

Next to feeling itself a sort of composite Nero, an audience loves best to be bullied. Witness how it always responds to the brutal woman-taming of *Petruchio,* the triumphant villainy of *Iago* with his sneer: ''I bleed, sir; but not kill'd.'' The accomplished stage liar hoodwinking perfectly innocent people; the glib politician twisting a nation around

67

his finger. I think it is one reason why I have loved to play rascals—*Philippe Bridau,* the *Harvester, Denis Roulette, Hajj, the Beggar, Anthony Bell-chamber.*

But to come back to the Walnut. Benefit performances were a feature of stock company contracts. The member would sign for so much salary, and one-half or one-third clear benefit on a certain night of the season. Mr. Smith's benefit would be announced and Mr. Smith's friends were expected to rally around their favorite and buy tickets. Canvassing for subscriptions was generally precedent to the event. Our rotund second comedian, Sam Hemple, a simon-pure Philadelphian, was a most persistent canvasser. Sam would begin about three weeks before his "night" to circulate the glad tidings among his supporters, and as the days of his liquid electioneering went by he grew mellower and more incoherent in his performances. He used to tell with great gusto how he had once been reprimanded by Mrs. John Drew at the Arch Street Theatre. "The Duchess had me up before her," said Sam, "and fixed me with her cold and glitterin' eye. 'Mr. Hemple,' says she, 'what was the matter with you last night?' Takin' off me hat with the grace of a Chesterfield, and layin' me hand on me stummick, 'Mrs. Drew,' says I, 'be God, I was drunk!'"

A benefit legend of the Walnut relates to the comedian who asked the comic of the Chestnut Street Theater to play the *Second Grave Digger* to his *First,* in order to strengthen the bill for his "night."

68

A GRAVE DIGGER'S INNOVATION

The rival was compliance itself: he was glad to do anything in his power for his brother actor: there was only one condition—

"Anything! Anything at all, my dear fellow!"

"I want my exit."

"Exit! Of course! Introduce all the gag lines you like."

"Not a line. Just my exit."

He could have anything on earth if he would appear. An eminent tragedian was playing *Hamlet*. The familiar scene of the two grave-digging clowns having ended with Number Two giving up the conundrums of Number One, Number Two was bid, "Get thee to Youghan; fetch me a stoup of liquor." The beneficiary's rival instead of taking the jug and going off L. S. E. made his exit *into the grave*. The audience was somewhat startled by this innovation, but their attention was diverted by the entrance of *Hamlet*. When the *Number One* got down into the grave with his pick and shovel, a smile spread over the faces of those in front; it grew to a titter when the bones and skulls were thrown out. *Ophelia's* body was lowered into the grave, and the laugh grew boisterous. Where was the *Number Two?—Laertes* leaped down to clasp his sister's body, and *Hamlet* leaped after him. Was all this atop the vanished actor? There was the grave; he was in it, or so it looked to the audience. The struggle between *Hamlet* and *Laertes* became burlesque. The culprit wasn't in the grave; he had slipped off the trap into the cellar, and fled from the theatre. He had ruined his rival's scene!

Tricks of this sort were legitimate sport of the stock company. There was one always played at the expense of the uninitiated utility man, sending him to a neighboring theatre to request of its stage manager the "key of the curtain" with the message that that of the sender was broken. If there were more than two theatres, the messenger would be passed on, and finally sent back with a large valise laden with bricks. Sometimes I think that actors never really grow up; years pass over their whitening heads and find them still *Peter Pans* and *Topsies*. Tragedians, of course, like the dyer's hand, are subdued to what they work in—or at least they were when they took themselves and their art seriously.

A vestal virgin who did not always take her art with seriousness was Mary Anderson. Never a tragedy queen, she was, at that time, more the boarding-school miss. She had splendid equipment in stature, face and voice—all of which were well-suited to *Juliet, Julia, Pauline, Evadne, Parthenia* —parts she presented at the Walnut to packed houses. At a performance of EVADNE, I have seen the curtain fall on the bloody issue of *Ludovico*'s treachery, with the entire group of stage folk giggling, and Mary Anderson herself snorting. The theatre was a playground to her; it was such a fine thing to look out over the footlights and know that the people were all loving her. Not until her visit to England showed her something of care and discipline did she gain smoothness and conviction. Who

70

can forget the vitality, grace and magnetism of her *Perdita* when she brought her production of A Winter's Tale back from London? The raw crude girl had, as by magic, been transformed into an artist; and then almost immediately withdrew into the privacy of domestic life, leaving thousands lamenting.

While an opera troupe was at the Walnut, our company went down into the coal towns on a week's tour of Henry VIII, with the two Walcots as *Cardinal Wolsey* and *Queen Katharine*. 'Twas a dismal trip—every day it rained, and at night the audiences were spiritless and sodden. As we were riding along with the rain beating on the car windows, Sam Hemple looked out on the wet landscape and moaned, "O be God! The rain of Henry VIII!"

Some of the people in the coal towns took the advent of this play seriously and brought with them the family copy of Shakespeare, as big as a dictionary, to use as a libretto. The acting version of Henry VIII is always a wide departure from the long original—whole episodes are cut out. Our version was still further compressed. This caused confusion among the good folk with their tomes of Shakespeare. They scarcely saw the play at all; just as they found the right spot in their books, the scene would shift, a transposition take place, and they would flutter the leaves back and forth seeking for light. As we carried no scenery and the stage manager had difficulty in adjusting local settings to the different scenes in time for quick changes,

especial perplexity arose when he would say to
Lord Sands and *The Lord Mayor,* "Go on again,
scene isn't ready." Back the two comedians would
stroll and play the *Grave Digger's* scene from HAM-
LET. Still the set behind wasn't ready, and Hemple
would return and speak the *Mock Duke's* speech
from THE HONEYMOON. It certainly was a mystify-
ing performance. At Pottsville, the orchestra was
a German band. It was necessary to have pathetic
music for *Queen Katharine's* death, and the leader
said, yes, he knew just the thing that was needed.
When Mrs. Walcot was lengthening her dying moments that night, the band struck up:

> "In the sweet bye and bye,
> We shall meet on that beautiful shore!"

the yellow clarinet being particularly agonizing.

Years later in Pinero's fine comedy, TRELAWNEY
OF THE WELLS, at the Lyceum Theatre in New York,
Mrs. Walcot was cast for "a faded queen of tragedy." When she spoke her line: "Ladies and gentlemen, I have played fourteen or fifteen queens in
my time—" she might have been reciting her auto-
biography. I had seen her play at least three-quar-
ters of them at the Walnut.

We returned to Philadelphia to support John
McCullough, who was one of the finest spirits that
ever came within my ken. "Genial John" was his
fitting sobriquet. It was rare to encounter a star
who could be so simple and unaffected. Dignity he
never lacked. The position he had won was never

hazarded by an unworthy act. Too often men of his rank were imperious in the theatre—vain and jealous of their accomplishments, and intolerant of opposition. It was rather remarkable that McCullough should not have resembled his fellows, for he was of that not infrequently unbearable type—the self-made man; moreover he had the blood of fighting Ireland in his veins. When little John was landed on these shores at the age of fifteen, he could read with difficulty, and he could neither write nor spell. To have met McCullough, as I did, at the age of forty-nine, was to have known a man of the world, and a gentleman; polished in manner, refined in conversation, kindly, modest and manly. If ever the educational influence of the theatre—of course, I mean the theatre at its best—had an exemplar, it was in John McCullough. His college was his professional life; his instructors, the men and women through whose ranks he climbed; his inspiration the golden words of William Shakespeare.

There was something paternal about McCullough, a tender and comforting quality. CORIOLANUS had been the bill for over two weeks. My unimportant characters, a double of *Sextus* and *Lucius,* had given me no trouble either to memorize or act—except for the care and thought I tried to put into every part I played—and I was sailing through seemingly calm waters when one night I stuck in a speech—stuck dead. I had on more than one occasion floundered through lines at the Museum with

73

the vaguest knowledge of what I was talking about; but here was a part I knew perfectly—and suddenly something had gone wrong with my brain. I know of nothing more painful and hopeless than the panic the actor feels when he is before an audience without the power to utter a sound. The scene was with McCullough too. He got me out of it, somehow, and I left the stage with the feeling that my career had come to an end. I was alternately sobbing and swearing like a trooper in the wings, when I felt a touch on my shoulder. "Don't mind," he said, "it's nothing. I've stuck dead in the last act of OTHELLO and had to ring down the curtain."

This episode has always been associated in my mind with another that happened four years later at the Cincinnati Dramatic Festival. McCullough was playing *Master Walter* in THE HUNCHBACK to the *Julia* of Mary Anderson. I fell over him in the dark, behind the scenes of the big stage. He was sitting on a trunk with his face in his hands, tears streaming through his fingers and his body shaken with sobs.

"Mr. McCullough!" I cried. "What is it?"

He reached out for my hand and said, "Oh, my boy! My boy! I can't remember my lines."

This was the first showing of the malady that poisoned his mind and body at the end. He died in November of the following year—quite mad—at the age of fifty-three.

I made my first appearance in New York with McCullough. The Walnut Company went over to

that city and appeared for a fortnight with him in
Coriolanus at The Grand Opera House. Coming
back to Philadelphia he made a revival of Sheridan's old play, Pizarro.

I used to envy Jack Mason's unusual memory;
he could swallow a part by reading it through two
or three times, while I beat my speeches into my
brain in pain. Sometimes I received better parts
than he, but now and then he would be cast for
something as good as or better than that falling to
me. Then I would feel sadly put out, and Maylin
and I would sit far into the morning at Zeiss's over
recurrent beers, telling ourselves how much better
actors we were than Mason.

The procession of stars brought Lawrence Barrett and Fanny Davenport in adjoining engagements. Each had a huge repertory, and I played
thirteen separate parts in two weeks. As strenuous
a task as this was for me, think what it was for the
leading people: exacting Shakespearean rôles to
memorize, rehearse, costume and play from night to
night. Of Barrett, I need say nothing here; a long
association with him came after this.

Fanny Davenport appeared as *Rosalind, Lady
Gay Spanker, Julia, Lady Teazle, Imogen,* and *Fanny Ten Eyck* in Daly's play, Divorce. Never a great
artist, she was a pleasant lady whose talent had
been developed by Augustin Daly, albeit she inherited much from her father, Edwin L. Davenport,
one of the foremost actors of the American stage,
and from her mother who, at that time, was the first

old woman of our company. Miss Davenport was a handsome woman, her business sense keen and her industry untiring. To these qualities rather than to her acting, she owed the later success in which she accumulated a fortune in her productions of Sardou's dramas.

Another group of stars was James Williamson and his wife Maggie Moore, in STRUCK OIL and THE EMERALD RING; Frank Bangs as *Marc Antony, Virginius* and *St. Marc;* and John T. Raymond as *Colonel Mulberry Sellers,* in the dramatization of Mark Twain's THE GILDED AGE.

Raymond was a droll man, irresistibly comic in his acting and with that true comedian's sense of incongruity that made his *Colonel Sellers* live. He was an incorrigible guyer; it was his delight to tangle everybody in deepest confusion with interpolated and irrelevant gags. He made me exceeding angry at the opening performance. I was playing the witness, *John Peterson,* who compromises the Hawkins case in his cross-examination. As I stepped from the witness stand, *Sellers* should say, "John, you've played the devil with this case;" instead, Raymond knocked every line out of my head by saying, "Skinner, you played hell with that scene." He laughed at my anger over being a victim of his joke, but he did not molest me again during the week. He was an inveterate gambler; matching for dollars was his passion. If an acquaintance happened to be sitting in the box or in the front row orchestra, Raymond wouldn't scruple in the least to lean over the footlights, take a coin from his pocket, slap it on the back of his left hand and say, "Heads or tails for a dollar," and if the man was not too full of confusion, he would call the coin. No respect for the illusion of drama or acting ever deterred Raymond from shattering it completely if he felt in the mood. He was like the comedian who, as *Peter* in ROMEO AND JULIET, walked back to the flat while *Romeo* and the *Nurse* were earnestly conversing down stage, and caught flies off the church steeple, painted in perspective a good furlong away.

There had been some engagements of minor importance. Various members of the company were busy with their benefit bills. That of Atkins Lawrence, the juvenile man, was unique. Emulating the example of the UNCLE TOM'S CABINS of the day with their five *Topsys*, three *Marks* and four *Uncle Toms*, Lawrence offered even richer fare: ROMEO AND JULIET with six *Juliets!* The composite *Juliet* had every qualification. She was young and old, short and tall, beautiful and plain, lean and plump, and her voice ranged from the hollow of the tomb to the shriek of a locomotive. Lawrence had a grand time; never had he been so multitudinously loved— and he looked like a glorified barber!

As the closing time came on, it occurred to some one that we ought to give Manager Goodwin a present. We had our photographs taken, set in a large frame and brought to the theatre. A halt in the rehearsal was called, and Goodwin, summoned from his office, appeared in the glory of his celebrated clothes. Walcot made a complimentary speech of presentation; Goodwin choked, emitted a sentence or two and then made this triumphant finish: "I do not know, ladies and gentlemen, if I shall have a stock company at the Walnut next season, but" (and here his eye brightened) "if we do meet again, I assure you it will be with the same feelings of pleasure as those with which I now part with you."

Some scattering engagements kept me in Philadelphia for a time after the closing of the regular season; the most important was at the Arch Street Theatre in a week of Old Comedy with Mrs. John Drew. For years Mrs. Drew had managed the gradually declining fortunes of the Arch with wisdom and stern discipline. She was a woman of overawing dignity, crammed with the traditions of her art, capable in stage direction, and the accredited and brilliant possessor, for a generation, of the parts of the heroines in the Sheridan, Coleman, Goldsmith and Farquhar comedies of manner. The annual revival of these pieces by Mrs. Drew was looked upon as an event of each Philadelphia season. Her selection for 1879 consisted of The School for Scandal, The Jealous Wife, Paul Pry, Wives as They Were and Maids as They Are, The Golden Farmer and To Oblige Benson. I was in all of them. Six walking gentlemen to play in six nights, and I loathed the "pretty parts." By Saturday my mind was so chaotic that all the characters were rattling about within it simultaneously.

The prospect of the week's work had so appalled the leading man that he disappeared after the first performance. His place was filled by a new leading man for each night, the most strenuous work falling upon the shoulders of John Drew. He arrived in town at four o'clock in the morning of Wednesday, returning from a long and disastrous tour of DIPLOMACY. He was met at the door of his home by his mother—play-book in one hand, candle in the other. She put the prompt book in his hand and said: "Don't go to bed, John. You play this to-night." John didn't go to bed, and that evening he spoke every line of *Mr. Bronzely* in Mrs. Inchbald's WIVES AS THEY WERE, a part longer than the moral law. Mrs. Drew's daughter, Georgie, who afterward as Mrs. Maurice Barrymore won a reputation as the best comedienne and the wittiest woman on the American stage, played *Maria* to her mother's *Lady Teazle* during the week.

With the ending of the dramatic year in Philadelphia, the old type of provincial, star-supporting company went out of existence in that city. It was disappearing everywhere: the public was growing tired of seeing the same people in the same clothes season after season, and welcomed the change that brought each week a set of new faces, fresh costumes and complete scene settings. The local scene-dock was still kept stocked with the familiar Gothic Chamber, Rocky Pass, etc., but the dust of neglect and decay was settling on the things of yesteryear.

Thus was slipping by a group of old fellows who met life with a laugh—sterling lads of ready wit and admirable equipment. Often they may have taken themselves over-seriously; but the Lord keep their memories green! They possessed distinction and they respected the King's English!

The fault of the old stock companies was that it allowed actors but little time for introspection. Efficiency it did give them—easy adaptability for whatever might be called for, but the true meaning of the character was very apt to escape them. Now and then, one would rise out of the ranks into greatness, but such a one would have succeeded, no matter what his obstacles. Yet the old stock company laid foundations not to be secured in these days of long runs and the specialization in "types" in acting. It put into the hands of the actor the tools of his trade, and it bred versatility and competence. He was always at work.

I am glad I was able to be in at the death and before the old system quite passed away; glad that my novitiate was one of hard knocks that compelled me to swallow my technique in great gulps; glad of the vast experience that gave me every sort of character—in two years I had played over one hundred and forty parts; glad of that compulsion of quick study and performance which renders the body supple and the mind obedient; and glad that my dramatic kindergarten was placed among men and women filled with the knowledge of their trade, and with honor for their calling—residents of a true Bohemia since changed for an estate of greater respectability and social recognition and less art.

I packed my trunks and went over to New York with a breast full of hopes, fears and ambitions—but with no engagement for the coming year.

CHAPTER V

A DARK HOUR AND MR. BOOTH

For me New York loomed forbidding, heartless and resentful. Among her crowds I felt a deep loneliness.

Here the door of opportunity is barred to the seeker after favor or advancement, and the heel of every passer-by is a juggernaut. What does New York know of Who's Who in Philadelphia?

I sought out the arbiters of the destinies of prayerful actors, the dramatic agents, and felt the joy of the Hebrew vender of collar buttons who, when kicked from each floor in his descent of the twelve-story building, exclaimed: "My God—vot a system!" Companies were forming by dozens each day and managers were seeking every grade of talent, but not mine. I was an unrecognized piece of jetsam in the scum of theatrical wash. There were four or five "bureaus" of these hucksters of talent on whose thresholds I paused each morning between ten o'clock and eleven-thirty, long enough to cock my hat a little to one side, infuse something of jauntiness in my pose and enter with an air. "Nothing to-day" was the best I got. The rounds once gone through, naught remained for the next twenty-four hours but to peer helplessly into the future

81

and behold—blackness. The temptation to write to
my father for aid cost me a struggle. The voice of
my needs cried aloud, but that of my pride thundered in the opposite ear. I could not, I would not
acknowledge defeat, but through that long summer
I knew the deferred hope that "maketh the heart
sick."

A companion in misery buffeted adversity with
me. Once we were sent to Augustin Daly. We
found him mounted on a pile of lumber and plaster
debris within the walls of Wood's Museum in
Broadway near Thirtieth Street which was being
transformed that summer into Daly's Theatre. He
read the introduction and said he'd send us word.
His message to the agent was brief and to the point:
"The two young men you sent up to me won't do."
Had he possessed the gift of prophecy, he would
have beheld, five years hence, my unworthy self as
one of the group of players at his theatre, and, in
view of his letter to the agent, I know the vision
would have disturbed him much.

It was fortunate that my newspaper brother
could afford to shelter me in his two small rooms in
Brooklyn. But one must eat, and my store of savings dwindled as daily journeys over the Williamsburg ferry took me to and from the herdings of the
unemployed in theatrical intelligence offices. On
one occasion I returned down through Broadway
and Grand Street, hating every stone of the pavement—as I always did—and over to our diggings on
Bedford Avenue to discover that I had forgotten to

take the door-key with me. It was late; the house
was black and silent. I rang the bell, but something was wrong with the bell-pull—there was no response. Whistlings, knocks at the door, pebbles
hurled at my brother's window were unavailing except to bring the policeman on the beat who doubted
my denial that I was a housebreaker. Perhaps
Charles had been sent by his editor on some all-
night assignment. It was terribly hot. I waited;
so did the policeman. One o'clock—and my bed was
no nearer. Another half-hour. Giving up in disgust, I moved away, trailed by the suspicious guar-
dian of the peace for some blocks. I consulted my
finances and discovered fifty-six cents. This would
buy a bed—a clean one at that. The prospect was
not appealing for the heat was still oppressive.
Feeling hungry, I went into an all-night place near
the ferry and ate copiously of clam chowder. A re-
past that with the addition of a cheap cigar brought
stimulation and a calmer view of life.—After all, a
bed is but a place of last resort.

I retraced my route to New York and strolled
leisurely through streets lighted by a slim procession of gas lamps. The Bowery was quite dark; no
elevated railway reared its structure overhead; the
quiet was like that of a country village. Strange de-
formed creatures came into the radiant circle of a
lamp-post and passed beyond. An occasional nymph
of the pave brushed by with her limp finery and
smell of cheap perfume. Sinister beings searched
ghoul-like for treasure in gutter or ash barrel. The

night reeked with odors. I reached Union Square, then the Rialto of disengaged actors by day, but now deserted except for the ghosts of heartaches and disappointed hopes. I shuddered and turned southward on Broadway—a furtive chasm of locked and shuttered buildings.

At Newspaper Row early editions of the SUN, HERALD, and TRIBUNE were thrown by bundles into carts which rattled off to outgoing trains at the Grand Central Station. Would future editions chronicling events of the theatre ever bear my name? Probably not. At the Battery the moon was dropping low, paving a track to Staten Island with gold, across which crept the silent rowboat of a river thief. I was tired and felt grateful for the first stirrings of the morning breeze. It was at the hour when vitality grows feeble. That June day I had become of age. Twenty-one years old! I had spent two seasons in the Philadelphia theatres, happy, busy, rejoicing in a few sincere friendships, beginning each day with a hope for the future, and now, from my man's outlook on the dramatic horizon, nobody appeared that knew me or wanted my services.

Over beyond Brooklyn Heights the sky was beginning to lighten. Another day was dawning; another day of dreariness and waiting. An odd couple approached and took the bench next to mine. The older was a man with a long white beard and hair that fell over his collar. He pointed out the various dark masses down the harbor and located the islands to the younger man who was evidently a foreigner. He told him that there was shortly to be erected on Bedloe's Island a wonderful new statue that France had presented to America, and it was to represent Liberty Enlightening the World. Before this pair departed I heard the old man's name—he was a well-known newspaper man—and before that week was over, I read of his death. His body was found floating in the East River—a suicide.

The East was flushing with the hot gleams of a humid New York morning. An early immigrant came stretching out of Castle Garden's round building to greet the day in his new-found country. A tenement mother brought her dirty babe to a near-by fountain and made the toilet of both with comb and soap. As the clouds over Brooklyn docks took fire, some one said, "Hello!" It was a young fellow I had known in Philadelphia.

"I'm stopping at a little place up yonder," he said, "and I couldn't sleep. Going to Europe to-day."

"What? How?"

"Got a job on a Cunarder. Work my passage."

"How are you fixed?"

"Haven't a nickel."

"Well," I said, "it's breakfast time. Suppose we go up-town." By now I had more than cut my supply of cash in half; that which remained sufficed for "coffee and sinkers" for two at a refectory on Newspaper Row that never closed. We wished each other luck and parted. I slipped the last of my pennies through the ferryman's wicket at the foot of Roosevelt Street, and reached Bedford Avenue as the slavey was taking in the matutinal milk at the basement door.

On the hall table was a letter directed to me which bore the address of a well-known agent. I scarce dared open the envelope. It was, in very truth, an offer. While I had lived my dark hour, this message had been waiting.

I was summoned to the office of Imre Kiralfy. The meeting was eminently satisfying to me, and when August arrived and with it a notice to appear at Niblo's Garden for a rehearsal of ENCHANTMENT, my long vigil ended.

The Kiralfy brothers—Imre and Bolossy—were dancers of Hungarian birth who, by industry and shrewdness, had become authoritative producers of spectacular ballet pieces in America. Their entertainment was a sort of forerunner of the New York Hippodrome. To see Bolossy at work with a stage full of ballet girls was to behold a pale excitable foreigner with a long stick with which he thumped the measure of the dancing steps, and his voice, hoarse with shouting and a chronic catarrhal cold, barking out: "Von—two—tree! Von—two—tree! No-no! Stop! Vot's de matter wit de back line? No please —please! Ladies! LADIES! Vonce more! Von— two—tree!" etc. Their old-line girls had been with the brothers for years, and a decent, domestic, hardworking lot they were; many of them bread-winners of families, good mothers and wives, and for the

THE KIRALFYS

most part bright and comely. There were no motor-cars waiting for them at the stage door; their shapely bodies were not clad in silks and sealskins; when they shed their pink tights and tarleton skirts and dressed for the street they looked like a company of milliners' workers. The ballerinas of the higher order were more gorgeous, but they took their work as matter-of-fact, spending two or three hours each day in the theatre, practising their steps and keeping their legs supple and muscular. Bolossy had a large placid wife who had once been a dancer but who had gone to flesh quite irretrievably. On the night of the dress rehearsal when the poor *maître* was beside himself with nerves, the lady planted her bulk in his pathway and purred: "Bolossy, you have not petted me to-day." "No, Elise," he cried, "I haf not had time!"

ENCHANTMENT, produced September 4, 1879, was a typical Kiralfy show, and my real début in New York was made amid gratifying conditions. My part of *Maclow* was a sort of compound of the *Black Crook*, the *Apothecary* in ROMEO AND JULIET, and *King Lear* compressed into one episode. I had a death scene which ended in my being dragged from the stage hurling expiring curses at my enemy.

One critic said the next day, "The best acting was done by Mr. Otis Skinner, a conscientious and feeling young actor new to the Metropolitan stage, but a valuable addition thereto if his last night's work may be taken as a sample of his style."

Nevertheless, all did not run smoothly on the

opening night. *Maclow* was old, with a hawk beak, scraggly beard, heavy eyebrows and claw-like hands. I was over an hour in putting on this heavy make-up with nose putty and crêpe wool. I had to be seized by John Studley—good old favorite of the Bowery—and hurled down from a lofty platform. It is a long distance from the top of a twelve-foot platform to the stage beneath—it has a dizzy look as you are about to jump. Kiralfy said I could use a dummy, but I said no; I would not spoil the illusion.

Our property man had a sympathetic heart and a groggy voice. Before the curtain rang up he came to me and croaked out, "Say, young feller, a little tip, it mayn't do any good, but it won't do any harm. To-night and every night, see? Just before you do that jump, you say a little prayer."

That shook me somewhat. I blinked, but I thanked him. If ever good advice was needed, I needed it that night. But alas!—"to dumb forgetfulness a prey," I jumped, prayerless, landed square on my heels on the mattress below and telescoped my spine. For a moment or two I was stunned by the shock, then I was aware that something clammy and corpse-like had fallen on my hand, which I presently realized was my putty nose; it had plowed down my face carrying an area of eyebrows and whiskers in its descent. In a dull way I knew that there was a long scene in which I was hauled out of the chasm of the rocks by the juvenile tenor, and died to shivery music. I slapped the mass of make-up, which looked like a defunct tropical spider, back on my face and finished the act with my back to the audience. The accident had given me a sort of delirium that proved effective, and thereafter I retained this manner for *Maclow* and blessed the mishap that gave it birth. When I reached my dressing-room, my mirror showed me a face looking as if it had been peeled, while my nose was sticking between my eyes upside down!

Studley, the wicked magician who hurled me from the cliff, was a man over six feet high, with a coarse furtive face and a voice whose depth and gruffness fitted him for the line of Bowery villains that gave him celebrity. He occasionally "crooked the pregnant hinges" of his elbow at the neighboring bar, and one night, completely helpless, he fell upon me on the precipice set and bore me to the platform's edge. I was bending back, wildly clutching the set rocks, unable to throw off his weight, and thought my end had come and his too, when my prayerful friend, the property man, scenting danger, ran up the ladder and rescued me by pulling off my antagonist in time for me to turn and leap.

ENCHANTMENT ran until late December, when it was succeeded by an Irish play called THE HEARTS OF STEEL, written and produced by George Clark, with a good cast and fine stage effects. I was especially engaged for a wordy and wicked old sinner who, I think, must have disagreed with the audience —I know he did with me. I was very, very bad in the part. The play failed and was soon withdrawn.

FOOTLIGHTS AND SPOTLIGHTS

A few weeks at Colonel William E. Sinn's Brooklyn Theatre in Bronson Howard's play, WIVES, Leonard Grover's MY SON-IN-LAW, and Kiralfy's BLACK CROOK filled my time profitably, and I made the pleasant discovery that the winter's work had given me a little reputation.

My part in the Grover play was the most ambitious of this Brooklyn group; it was the "name part," and had some excellent comedy opportunities, mainly love-making episodes—something in the manner of Schnitzler's ADVENTURES OF ANATOLE —with the different female members of the cast— five of them, I think there were.

There was a passionate affair with a fiery Spanish señorita which culminated in her dragging me off to the altar. The actress who played this character, (Miss F—— P——), boasted of her physical prowess, and thought it would be a novel and laughable piece of business if she *carried* me off bodily. I doubted this when she broached the idea at rehearsal, though the lady allowed me to feel her biceps which she said she had developed in rowing boats and training mustangs. To be sure, I didn't weigh much, and the Amazonian actress was full of confidence.

The stage manager allowed the innovation, and seizing me by an arm and leg, she did manage to get me clear of the exit door without mishap, and to the mirth of the audience. She was a bit breathed, however. The second night, though she had seemingly supplemented her muscular force by certain stimulants, she was less successful and we had rather a bad time of it at the door in getting off. At the third performance we didn't get even to the door, we were within several feet of it when she toppled— keeled over on her back, her head and shoulders off the stage, and my hapless and helpless self in a similar position squarely atop of her. I need not say that subsequent performances were given without this acrobatic "added attraction."

In the early spring an engagement presented itself that had much to do with shaping my subsequent career.

Edwin Booth in the year 1880 was in the flower of his artistry and at the height of his power. At the age of forty-seven he had not begun to exhibit that weariness of work which overcame him after his return from Europe. His ambition was dauntless; his body flexible and obedient to his will; his face, beautiful and melancholy, showed nothing of its later traces of lassitude, and the music of his voice which held to the very end, was never more harmonious. No actor of his time so completely filled the eye, the ear and the mind with an ideal of romantic tragedy as Edwin Booth. His *Hamlet, Shylock, Iago, Bertuccio, Richard II* and *III, Ruy Blas, Macbeth, Richelieu* and *Othello* became the criteria by which other actors were judged.

The opening given me as a member of the company engaged by Henry Abbey to support him in a season of ten weeks in New York and Boston was opportune and thrice welcome. His polished meth-

91

ods, the superb control of his resources, the perfection of his "attack" upon a character, the curb of his climaxes, and the imagination, power and eloquence of his acting were profoundly instructive. Extravagance never marred his work; his was a living illustration of *Hamlet's* advice to the players concerning the temperate smoothness to be begot in the torrent, tempest and whirlwind of passion.

The engagement in New York was at Booth's Theatre at Sixth Avenue and Twenty-Third Street, which had then passed from under his control. The building had been erected by the tragedian eleven years previously—the realization of a dream to be at the head of a playhouse where the plays he loved could be presented under his own direction. The misfortunes which attended that direction are well known. Ever a bad business man, as simple and credulous in financiering as a child, an easy prey to designing men, he was unable to bring a practicable working system to the theatre, and in five years, after having given to the public poetic and sumptuous interpretations of splendid plays, the enterprise was bankrupt. Far less worthy performances of Shakespeare have been given since then and have succeeded. Booth had the misfortune of being before his time in these matters.

Like all remarkable actors, he had the power of suggestion to the mind of the spectator; never losing his own personality in his assumption, he yet conveyed the impression that he *was* the character. It was never with the dominating force of Edwin

Forrest who is said to have exclaimed, "By God! I *am* Lear!" The alchemy of Booth's art was more profound and subtle. Although a small, even a frail man, I could swear that at times in *Othello* and in *Macbeth* he was seven feet tall. *Cardinal Richelieu,* as he presented him, was a physical giant, stately and statue-like, through whose majesty peered the playful Booth humor. But as *Shylock,* with the copious gaberdine he wore, his body appeared shortened to stumpiness. His *Iago* was small, lithe, dangerous and radiant with devilish beauty. In spite of his fine voice he could not sing, but as he rendered *Iago's* bacchanalian ditties, such was his command of suggestion, that he gave the impression of a trained vocalist.

I once asked him if he recalled his father's acting sufficiently to say how it compared with his own. He hesitated and then said: "I think I must be somewhat quieter."

A distinguishing feature of Booth's acting was the pantomimic action of his face, hands and body. It was highly illustrative and vivid. *Shylock's* line to *Bassanio,* "Would'st thou have a serpent sting thee twice?" was accompanied by a darting movement of the right hand—the finger-tips closed, resembling a serpent's head—forward and back on a flexible wrist. It was the striking of a snake. *Macbeth's,* "The crow makes wing to the rooky wood" was pictured by a waving of hand and forearm as undulating as Ruth St. Denis in an oriental dance. As *Richelieu,* when bated by *Baradas* at the end of

Act IV, he turned round at his tormentor with his upper lip drawn up, his teeth showing, and gnashed at him like an animal at bay. He told me he saw this action in a horse that turned thus on the brute that was beating him in the street. A nerve racking bit of business was the grinding of his teeth with a sound like crushing pebbles when he said as *Iago,* "From this time forth I never will speak word."

Booth was a man of infinite gentleness and tenderness, and like most men truly great, of sweet modesty. Not that he lacked a temper; I have seen him ablaze with wrath at some stupid mishap of a blunderer upon his stage, and after a few moments all but beg pardon for his anger. He was ever considerate of his humblest supporter; all he asked of that supporter was to show that God had given him a modicum of intelligence. The annoyances he was subject to from this source were, in a measure, the result of his own habit of indolence. The drudgery of his profession exasperated him. During rehearsals of his plays he would be absent. I frequently asked the stage manager, "What does Mr. Booth do here?" or "What is his business in that scene?"

"Don't worry," would be the reply, "Mr. Booth will find you at night."

Very reassuring phrase that, but the practise was scarcely conducive to good team work. The old charge frequently laid at his door that he selected bad actors was unfounded. The truth is, he didn't care—so long as he was not interfered with.

He was sorely tried during this short season. I

GURNEY & SON   FIFTH AVE. N. Y.

EDWIN BOOTH
as Richelieu, 1879

think his heart was not in the enterprise. He was on the eve of departure for European engagements, and his eyes were turned across the ocean to things of moment that waited him there. Mrs. D. P. Bowers was the leading woman, and to secure her valuable services the management was compelled to engage her husband, J. C. McCullum, for leading male rôles. Ill luck was forever at McCullum's heels. If he knew his lines—and it was a fearsome thing to get up a repertory of ten or a dozen pieces—something happened to spoil his best effects. If any one missed a cue, it was in McCullum's scene; stage hands and carpenters were at their loudest racket of scene-shifting during his impressive moments; he would commence *Macduff's* stirring speech rousing the sleepers in *Macbeth's* castle to shake off "downy sleep, death's counterfeit, and look on death itself!" and before his reward of applause came, an ass of a stage manager would send on the supernumeraries ages before their time.

I caused him a bad moment, and an instant of terror to myself in OTHELLO. I was playing *Roderigo*. McCullum, who, as *Iago*, had been steering through troubled waters, was weathering his gale when I drew him on the rocks. The Booth Theatre stage had an enormous curved "apron" in front of the curtain. During the action of the play, this space was utilized by the players who consciously or unconsciously stepped out of the picture below the proscenium level. I had died with fitting agony under *Iago's* rapier thrust, and lay on my back congratulating myself on getting through *Roderigo* with some credit, when, to my horror, I discovered I was too far down stage. I had time, however, during the ensuing action to hunch myself by imperceptible movements, out of the danger zone, as I thought, before *Iago's* spirited exit speech. I lay quite still when the scene ended and the curtain, a ponderous affair with a barrel roller, commenced to unwind. It became evident that I had miscalculated my distance by a fearful margin; the enormous weight was descending directly over my body. I wriggled faster now and forgot the audience entirely; it was a race between my squirms and the curtain. Just as the breath was about to be crushed from my body, the defunct *Roderigo* hurled himself over on his stomach with an all-too-visible flop, and *Iago's* exultant cry, "This is the night that either makes me, or fordoes me quite" bore a meaning quite new and original.—The unfortunate McCullum was certainly fordone.

Mrs. Bowers—no longer in the fresh bloom of youth—was very effective in the tragic parts. She guarded her dignity and her position jealously. Once, having been called for the act, she was ready, standing in the entrance, but the curtain did not rise. Impatient, she called out to the prompter, "Why this delay?" The prompter replied that the poet Longfellow was visiting Mr. Booth in his dressing-room.

"Humph!" said the offended star, "Longfellows make long waits!"

BOOTH'S ENCOURAGEMENT

I was delighted with the personal interest Booth took in my acting, especially as *François* in RICHE-LIEU. This part of the cardinal's page was some-times given to women on account of its demand for a youthful appearance and, fortunately for me, my spare figure presented no handicap. My nervous manner and raw enthusiasm amused him a little but he gave me every encouragement. The things he told me were, for the most part, little things—mat-ters concerning exits, entrances, pauses, etc. He would watch my work and wait in the wings until I came off and tell me of improvements I might make here and there. Occasionally he would send for me to come to his room, and would suggest different and more effective readings, and always he was quiet and gentle—never insistent. And that was a quality of his acting—gentleness; poetic symmetry.

A ludicrous thing happened at the Academy of Music, Brooklyn, in THE FOOL'S REVENGE. In one of the acts the jester's daughter is made the victim of a plot by the wicked *Duke Manfredi*—myself. Rep-resenting this sensual nobleman, I had to mount to a high balcony and receive in my arms the uncon-scious *Fiordelisa,* while her father (Mr. Booth) held the ladder beneath and danced with glee, think-ing the abducted one to be the wife of his dearest enemy. Miss Ellen Cummins, suddenly called upon to enact *Fiordelisa,* was a lady of some bulk. She looked up at the top of the high balcony and at my meager figure, and said: "Not for me! That man shall never carry *me* down that ladder!" We had to use a dummy—a stiff wire object, hastily requisitioned from a near-by millinery shop. This, swathed in a long cloak, might pass in a dark scene. The moment arrived, full of impressiveness; Mr. Booth was holding his audience in a spell. Assistant ruffians came over the top of the porch, sweating under the load of the dummy *Fiordelisa,* who weighed about fifteen ounces, and deposited her across my arms as I stood with both hands grasping the sides of the ladder at the top. These varlets gave me the lady a few inches off her exact center, and she shot down to the left quite alarmingly. To save her, I thrust out my left elbow, corrected her equilibrium, and away she tilted to the right. For a few dreadful moments the rigid feather-weight teetered violently; there was no stopping her, and when the draperies fell away from her wire feet, concealment from the audience was impossible— THE FOOL'S REVENGE became a farce comedy and Booth's tragedy was killed.

Before the season ended I asked Mr. Booth if I might have the influence of his spoken word. His reply was the following letter:

Hotel Brunswick,
April 16, 1880.

Otis Skinner, Esqr.,
        Dear Sir:
        Should it be desirable to refer to me regarding your ability for the line of characters you mention, do not hesitate to do so. It is a pleasure to me to recommend those who evince such decided ability and interest in their profession as you have mani-

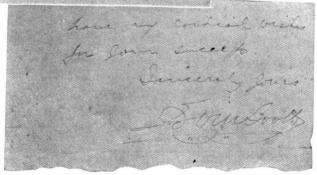

Hotel Brunswick
April 16th 1880

Chas Skinner Esq

Dear Sir

Should it be
desirable to refer to me
regarding your ability for
the line of characters you
mention do not hesitate
to do so.

It is a pleasure
to me to recommend those
who evince such decided
ability & interest in their profession as you have mani-
fested during the past
six weeks, and I

have my cordial wishes
for your success.

Sincerely yours

Edwin Booth

FROM EDWIN BOOTH

fested during the past six weeks, and you have my cordial wishes for your success.

Sincerely yours,
Edwin Booth.

The one regret I have of this Booth episode, is that it came to an end all too soon. I was destined to meet him again, professionally, but the finest memories I have of the man and of the actor belong to 1880. I like best to bring him to mind as *Othello* and *Macbeth*. True, they had not the celebrity of his *Hamlet,* but there was that about them infinitely human, and at the same time infinitely poetic and lovely—very much like Booth himself. There were flashes in them of alternating spirit and depression; sweeps of passion and depths of sorrow; levels of splendid dignity, and moments of uncontrolled weakness. His *Hamlet* had grown to be such a classic that it turned cold and mechanical at times. It was as if he allowed the part to play itself.

CHAPTER VI

THE following season I was established at the Boston Theatre in possession of the juvenile leads. After the three bustling years through which I had passed, it seemed like a time of stagnation. In the regular season there were but two plays produced: KIT, THE ARKANSAS TRAVELER, which had been a fall perennial with Chanfrau at the Boston for a long term, and THE VOYAGERS IN SOUTHERN SEAS, taken from a story by Jules Verne, and by D'Ennery made into a spectacular ballet piece. There were besides a few single performances given, among them NICK OF THE WOODS with the veteran actor, Joseph Proctor, as *The Jibbenainosay.* Mr. Proctor, stately, formal, of the Forrest school, was now practically retired but acted occasionally this rôle with which he was popularly identified.

The revival of KIT was, as I have said, traditional to the Boston Theatre as was Chanfrau in his part; so were Dan Maguinnis and Leslie Allen as the *Two Beats,* and their entrance upon the stage was a signal for yells of delight. As the juvenile part in KIT was about as bad as juvenile parts can be, I played instead, *Mr, Jerry Sleepers,* a gambler whose toughness was appalling.

100

TOO REALISTIC

Lord Glenarvon in THE VOYAGERS was somewhat better, but there was really no chance to do much more than stalk stiffly and speak bombast. Nothing mattered but the ballet and the scenery, which were of sufficient splendor to give the piece a long life in Boston and on a tour of a few large cities— Providence, Baltimore, Pittsburgh, Chicago, Philadelphia, New York.

What pleased me most was the excitement of travel and the big towns. An incident connected with the opening of THE VOYAGERS in Chicago has become a part of stage history—a companion piece to the legend of the British tar who, unable to endure the sight of the heroine in BLACKEYED SUSAN being evicted from her cottage, climbed down from his gallery seat to the stage and well-nigh murdered the miserly landlord. Our story had run along to the point where little *Jimmy Grant* (Miss Rachel Noah) is discovered on the ice floes of the Antarctic Sea, in the last stages of delirium, pathos and cold. The heavy villain, *Burck* (Mr. Jordan) who, during the previous acts had been doing his best to make sausage meat of the castaways, suddenly comes upon the scene, and finding little *Jimmy* alone at once starts to hack him up. Just as *Burck* had his hatchet raised for his sanguinary attempt, a man in the balcony circle shouted, "Hold on!" The words were no sooner uttered than he rushed to the boxes, climbed over from the balcony and dropped into a lower box, breaking a rail in his descent, and cutting an ugly gash in his forehead.

The accident stopped his progress but an instant. He gathered himself together, leaped upon the stage, seized the blood-thirsty *Burck* by the throat, and exclaimed: "Damn you, you shan't touch that boy while I'm here! This ain't no square deal." *Burck* tried to say in a stage whisper, "It's all right. Get off the stage." "No!" exclaimed the champion. (He was from Colorado.) "Damn your eyes; I wouldn't trust you." From astonishment the audience passed into uproar. They laughed, they cheered, they yelled, but the riot did not interfere with the purpose of the chivalrous gentleman from the plains. He tightened his hold on poor *Burck's* neck, and probably would have done him injury had not some stage hands rushed in and with difficulty dragged him off the scene and thrust him into the alley where, in a snow-drift, he had time for cooler reflection upon stage illusion.

The season was fraught with peril by reason of mechanical devices used throughout the piece. One of these abominations was the rockslide of a mountain summit. A group of us had to stand on a movable platform, counterweighted and made to descend upon slanting rails, disappearing from view behind a big padded bank. At Providence when this supposed crag was thus precipitated into the abyss, the structure flew down the incline so rapidly that we landed in a football jumble at the bottom, and it was,discovered that the butt of the rifle I carried on my shoulder had knocked out the false teeth of Leslie Allen who was playing the *French Pro-*

fessor. The poor man was sorely put to it to finish the performance. Another perilous night was on the stage of Booth's Theatre in New York, when the platform slipped out of its groove. My companions leaped on the padded rocks, but I, facing the chasm, saw no landing place but a strip of stage flooring a yard wide, buttressed on one side by a canvas set-piece while on the other yawned the open trap above the deep sub-cellar. I had no time to think: I made the leap and landed flat on my stomach. It was with shaken nerves that I looked over the edge of the trap to the cellar pavement thirty feet below!

Traveling through this play was like journeying around the world with Burton Holmes, to England, the Atlantic, Argentine, Patagonia, and by the time we reached the last act we were in Antarctic waters chasing whales. What motive this yachting *Lord Glenarvon* had in whale hunting, only the dramatist knew; but the titled harpooner hurled his lance and the monster of the deep rose and lay placid above the up-stage "set water" line. The whaleboat, a clumsy affair of half-a-ton weight, was pulled on with jerks that occasioned unseamanlike movements on my part, for I stood in the bow in much the attitude of "Washington Crossing the Delaware." The lines of the scene ran somewhat as follows:

LORD GLENARVON

Back men, for your lives! Back all! Stay! What is that sticking in its side?

103

BOATSWAIN

Rusty old harpoon, sir.

LORD GLENARVON

Ahead again! Steady! I have it. (*Plucks old harpoon from the whale's side—reads inscription on the shaft.*) Captain Grant—Balker's Island! Thank God, we've found them at last!

CREW

Hooray!

CURTAIN

The castaways had considerately left their names and addresses on the harpooned whale!

Awful things—stage boats. They taught me much profanity. I marvel that audiences ever stood them without uncontrolled laughter. No stage sailor was ever seen really to *row*. He thrust his oar straight down behind the level pieces of "set water" and his boat skipped like a kangaroo.

Once, in a western town, a touring company presented an Irish play in which the hero had dodged the *sojers* to visit his sweetheart who lived on a lonely island in the midst of canvas water. While he wooed her, his faithful henchman kept watch in the boat below. On this night the property boat was missing, but a cottage door hastily torn from a shabby scene sufficed, and the two patriots stood behind it as it was placed lengthwise on the stage and rowed out from the wings to the trysting place, the comedian holding the door frame with his fingers, and moving along with that shuffling of feet we used to call the "grapevine twist," while the hero, likewise gliding as he rowed, poked vigorously at nothing with his oar. After the agony of kisses and parting, and the hero swearing to die for ould Ireland, the two men had again to brave the perils of the deep. Mickey grabbed the door edge, and shuffled toward the wings, while the hero poked, but his sense of the picturesque overcame him. He paused to wave adieu to his colleen. Mickey, intent on his job, failed to see the action, and on went the boat leaving the pride of Ireland standing in the lake throwing kisses. But the actor was equal to the emergency—he took off his coat and swam!

In our stock company, which was an able one, Dan Maguinnis stood foremost in popular favor. His was the *vis comica,* and while Dan was always himself whatever he played, he was always funny. Tall and angular, he was the owner of one of the homeliest faces that ever topped an Irishman's shoulders. He was greeted everywhere by his sobriquet of "Handsome Dan," and was a prime favorite at banquets and little supper-parties for his stories and comic songs, the reputation for which was gained in his burnt cork days with Morris Brothers' Minstrels. His interpolated gags were ready and witty. In COSETTE, John Craven, the father of Frank Craven, played a vagabond with a red patch on his trousers, and Dan alluded to him as "a cautious old man with a danger signal on the rear platform."

In Quincy Kilby's HISTORY OF THE BOSTON THE-
ATRE I find mention of Dan's first contract with J.
B. Booth (Edwin Booth's elder brother) who was
the manager. Here it is:

Boston Theatre. Manager's Office
May 7, 1867
Memorandum of agreement between J. B. Booth,
lessee of The Boston Theatre and D. J. Maguinnis:
Said Maguinnis agrees to play general utility
business, also singing and dancing when required,
and to aid in preparing the Calcium lights, etc. The
said Booth agrees to pay the said Maguinnis twenty dollars per week for forty weeks more or less,
commencing about the 26th day of August. When
said Maguinnis is playing Demons, or parts where
the risk of being injured is incurred, he is to have
Ten Dollars per week more, and when playing in the
country, one dollar per day in addition to the regular salary.

J. B. Booth
Dan J. Maguinnis.

Dan died of a broken heart after the loss of his
only son, a boy of four years. His wife, too, had
died shortly before. He was only fifty-four, but he
looked an old man. Thousands attended his funeral
—people from all walks of life; his friends were
legion.

With the name of another member of that company, George Parks, a sadly romantic figure rises
to my mind. A Boston boy of excellent family, he
had brought to the stage an athlete's physique, an
unusually handsome face, a deep musical speaking

106

voice, a gracious manner and fair talent. Such gifts easily made a place for him in the theatre, and he found favor in the juvenile characters. Women sought him and wrote *billets doux* to him, but he bore his sentimental triumphs unostentatiously, even shyly. He left The Boston Theatre Company a year or so later and secured an engagement in Gillette's HELD BY THE ENEMY. One evening, after his season's close, he walked into the office of the Tremont House in Boston, handed a package to the clerk at the desk, saying: "Keep this for me, Frank, I'll call for it later." "It's heavy," remarked the clerk. "Yes, an old shirt of chain mail I've worn in the Shakespeare plays." He returned shortly before midnight, claimed his package and departed. Some days later his body was fished out of the Charles River. He had tied the chain armor to his feet and dropped himself over the rail of Harvard Bridge. No one ever found a reason for his strange deed; it remained a mystery.

In the career of every player there comes a time when his progress seems checked. He finds himself bewildered, and he is obsessed by the fear that he is deteriorating. Such self-consciousness came to me in this Boston year. I suppose it was the grind of repetition, the lack of change, and the leisure to think of the method by which I was expressing myself. For three years parts had been heaped on my shoulders by the wholesale. Lines and business had been hurriedly swallowed, and ill-digested. Now came a period of inertia. Acting hitherto had been an impulse, the art of the amateur. I had learned many tricks of the trade. I had seen great actors; acted with them; watched them thrill their audiences, but of the real art of acting I knew very little.

CHAPTER VII

Now there was opened for me an experience extending through three years with one of the most mannered men the American stage ever produced. From whatever source Lawrence Barrett may have gained his style I never knew. In effect his work was of a character wholly his own.

Lawrence Patrick Barrett was the son of an Irish tailor who had located in Detroit. The story forever cropping up in gossip and newspapers that the true family name was Brannigan, Barrett denied with indignation. Barrett senior, when I was a member of his illustrious son's company, was a tall erect individual, with frosty hair and "Galway" whiskers. On several occasions during the Detroit engagements, the old boy appeared in the front row of the orchestra seats where he sat like a judge on the bench. He would stalk out between acts that he might hear, as he passed up the aisle, the comment, "that's Lawrence Barrett's father." Some one once said to him in the lobby one night, "It's a great actor your son has become, Mr. Barret." "Why shouldn't he be?" came the assertive answer. "If I had gone on the stage, it's myself 'ud be twice the actor Larry is." These paternal

109

visitations were vexatious to the proud spirit of Lawrence Patrick.

Barrett's early struggles had been of the most strenuous character. He was born with a hunger after knowledge not easily gained through the meager advantages of his childhood home. One of his first treasures was a dictionary, and this he used to pour over night after night by the dim light of candle-ends, memorizing words and their meanings. The lack of gentle and educational influences during his childhood would account for much that was odd and marked in both his acting and his ''off stage'' manner.

His voice was of unusual range, and in the more robust Shakespearean parts, or the romantic heroes of the Victorian Bulwer Lytton and Sheridan Knowles dramas, it had a compelling and powerful effect. He was a man of medium height—quite vain of the curve in his back—and his features were attractive; a good nose, wide mobile mouth, deep-set and burning eyes, and a broad and thoughtful forehead. It might have been the face of a monk.

Too ambitious to take the world easily, ever lifting his vision to his star of destiny, impatient, sensitive, frequently suspicious and given to many moods, Barrett never seemed a happy man. His Celtic temperament sometimes led him into moments of playfulness, and again to hours of irritability and peevishness. His path to fame had been rough, but he had pressed on with courage and high resolve. When I joined his company he was making the last of a long series of payments on a disastrous venture in the management of the Varieties Theatre at New Orleans. Failure, however, had but served to feed the fires of his determination. His activity was never ceasing.

The stage of America owes more to Lawrence Barrett for his production of high-class plays than to any other of the tragedians of his day. The list is a long one, and includes the first presentations of YORICK'S LOVE, THE MAN O' AIRLIE, PENDRAGON, GANELON, William Dean Howells' THE COUNTERFEIT PRESENTMENT; revivals of Boker's FRANCESCA DA RIMINI, RIENZI, ROSEDALE, MONEY, DAVID GARRICK, besides the familiar Shakespearean and classic plays. It was owing to his initiative that Edwin Booth met with the crowning financial success of his later years, Barrett acting as director, organizer and supporting co-star for the greater actor.

That Barrett should have numbered among his personal friends men of intellect, position and worth, was a true achievement for the self-made Irish lad who had battled his way up from obscurity, weighted down by the handicaps of a suspicious nature, a temper that took fire like tinder, and an overweening ego. There was a tempestuous, torrential character to his acting in many of his parts that swept his audiences into enthusiasm. In a high pitch of nervous intensity he would often shoot through these parts like a race horse. *Richelieu* and *Cassius* were his most widely admired impersonations. Many identified him wholly with *Cas-*

111

sius; the "lean and hungry" one seemed to have stepped into life when Barrett stalked into the forum scene. But to me his one true masterpiece was his *Jamie Harebell* in THE MAN o' AIRLIE. The play, translated from the German, was one long sob almost from the beginning, but Barrett's Scotch poet, a kind of tragic Robert Burns, was infinitely tender and appealing. His usual mannerisms seemed to fall away, and his artificial elocution was thrown completely overboard. He became quiet, human and gentle; the Scotch brogue dropped from his lips with the sweetest delicacy, and his final picture of the mad old man, wandering back to his native village on the occasion of the unveiling of his own statue, remains a beautiful memory to me. The play, in spite of the tender portrayal, was never popular. I suppose that was because most American theatre-goers do not enjoy the spectacle of a suffering man. Women have exhibited their trials and heart-breaks on the stage from remotest times, and audiences have blubbered delightedly with them; they have flooded the stage with tears, and managers have waxed fat over the box-office takings, but it is difficult to coin the agony of the male into hard cash.

In Cleveland, where there was a large Barrett following, a demand was made for a performance of THE MAN o' AIRLIE. The properties required included a statue of Barrett in the character. To save expense of bringing on the original statue from New York, *Jamie* was painted in proper perspective on canvas by the local scene painter, glued to a thin "profile" board which was sawed along the outline, mounted on a pedestal and the whole held firmly in place by a stage brace from behind the figure, at about the waist-line, and covered with a sheet. The illusion of solidity was quite good, and after I (*Sir Gerald Hope*) had delivered the customary speech, extolling the supposedly dead poet, I began the unveiling. The orchestra was playing pathetic music; the moment was impressive, but the sheet stuck. I gave a tug; again it stuck! Plunkett, the comedian, pulled it from the opposite side; it stuck fast, caught by splinters of the sawed board. We came in front of it and pulled. The statue bent forward from the waist, but refused to shed its shroud. We went to the back, reversing our tactics, and the statue performed a rearward contortion. Barrett, as the mad poet who had returned unknown to the unveiling of himself, was fuming with rage and saying violent things *sotto voce*. Finally, in a crisis of agitation, we pulled—regardless of consequences. The statue bent double, the clutching splinters gave way and the sheet fell 'down over our distinguished star while the fragile statue flopped backward and forward like a hideous German toy, making profound obeisances to the hysterical audience.

I had quite forgotten about this play and the *contretemps* of the statue until one summer day in 1910, in the little city of Arles in southern France. We were in the museum there when we came upon the Provençal poet, Frederic Mistral, directing

some laborers in the replacing of his own statue—a
plaster replica of the bronze that stands in the little
square where later we again saw the handsome old
poet, looking not unlike our Buffalo Bill, sitting in
front of the café, sipping his *apéritif* and contem-
plating the tangible evidence of his own immortal-
ity, and the love of his Provençal compatriots who
had placed it there. To see a great man standing
before his own and well-deserved statue, is an emotion not to be forgotten.

Our repertory was large, our productions, so far
as traveling scenery was concerned, absolutely nil
and dependent upon the supply of the local theatres.
Our costumes, wigs, tights, swords, etc., all our
own. My wardrobe I had purchased from a Boston
costumer whose effeminate tastes had led him to
ornament it with much needlework floriculture.
Archeologically it was a freak, but it looked quite
gorgeous to the eye.

I had put in the entire preceding summer in the
study of my parts and before two weeks were
passed, after our Des Moines, Iowa, opening, I had
played ten of them. *Laertes, Cassio, Gratiano,
Buckingham, Julius Cæsar, Gaspar* in The Lady of
Lyons, *Veaudore* in The Marble Heart, *Malcolm* in
The King of The Commons, *Edmund* in Howells'
Yorick's Love and *François* in Richelieu. This
last part Mr. Barrett insisted on my playing because Mr. Booth told him that I had made good in
it, but I had plainly outgrown it—I had become
heavier and deeper in voice.

WHEN LOUIS JAMES PLAYED HAVOC

I was over-young for *Cæsar,* and I can not believe that I was convincing, but there was one feature in my performance in which I took great pride; it was my fall after the assassination. *"Et tu Brute!* Then fall, Cæsar!"* Old Joe Nagle had taught me that fall at the Walnut Street Theatre, and it was so successful that when I introduced it at my first performance the house applauded generously, and Barrett was so astounded he failed to object to it. It was a rigid backdrop, straight from the heels with arms extended so as to strike the stage simultaneously with my shoulders and save my spine and the back of my head. The whack on the planking never failed to shock the audience into applause. I know Barrett thought it inartistic, and he was right. Neither *Cæsar,* nor any human being before or since, ever died like that. It was pure trickery. I can not understand why my star didn't annihilate me for doing it.

The leading business of the company was in the keeping of Louis James, one of the most talented and capable men in the country, but his perfect health and boyish spirits were sometimes a menace to the artistry of his acting. He was the most inveterate guyer I ever met. When the eye of the star was not upon him, he would say and do truly atrocious things with such dignity and composure that they would seem quite a part of the performance, but they would play havoc with us. To go on as *Bassanio* with his wife's curling tongs stuck like a stiletto in his belt; to slip an iron bolt into my

115

hand in the second act of JULIUS CÆSAR where *Cæsar* meets *Brutus;* to scrape the Moorish-colored grease paint from his face with his forefinger and with it paint mustaches on the face of the dying *Desdemona* after he, as *Othello,* had strangled her, were among the least of his offenses. I've seen him drop a piece of ice down the neck of a toga-clad Roman in JULIUS CÆSAR. After playing a dramatic scene with me in RICHELIEU he parted from me, leaving in my hands an iron bar, three feet long, which he had been concealing under his cloak. We were never sure of Louis, and no one ever grew angry at his misdeeds.

Marie Wainwright, then in her heyday, radiated beauty and charm as *Ophelia, Desdemona, Alice* in YORICK'S LOVE, *Ada Ingot* in DAVID GARRICK, and *Pauline* in THE LADY OF LYONS. The last mentioned piece, with its perfervid sentiment, was a favorite matinée bill. One afternoon in Milwaukee a situation of delicacy arose in the last act that brought about a small storm. It was in the scene in which *Pauline* is about to affix her signature to the hated marriage contract, when the disguised *Claude Melnotte* darts forward, tears up the paper, clasps the suffering lady to his bosom to the discomfiture of the villain and the glory of the wind-up of the play. At this exciting moment Miss Wainwright should have gone down quite into the right-hand corner of the stage and have left the center to the star. Miss Wainwright knew that; but something had happened. The scene proceeded as usual up to the dra-

116

MARY ANDERSON

CLARA MORRIS

MLLE. RHEA

LEADING WOMEN OF THE CINCINNATI FESTIVAL, 1882-3

matic situation. *Claude's* speech of exultation rent the air:

"Peace, old man! I have a prior claim. I outbid yon sordid huckster for your priceless jewel. There is the sum twice told. There is not a coin that is not bought and hallowed in the cause of nations with a soldier's blood."

PAULINE

That voice! Thou art—?

CLAUDE

Thy husband!

(*Pauline runs up from corner R. into Melnotte's arms. Picture and chord from orchestra.*)

But Miss Wainwright stood stock-still in the middle of the stage. Our astonished and irritated chief acted all around her, and his lines were well-nigh incoherent. The curtain fell. "What is the matter with you, Miss Wainwright?" he shouted. "That's what is the matter, Mr. Barrett," she replied quietly, and lifting her brocade skirt she stepped out of something filmy and white, adorned with lace and ribbons—their name is not mentioned in polite society.

Before the close of my first year, I was given the part of *Marc Antony,* a circumstance that brought me great joy. *Antony* is one of those rare opportunities of sure fire that well-nigh defy the worst of actors. He is a very bad player who can not rouse the enthusiasm of the house into repeated curtain calls after the prophetic curse of Act II and the subsequent oration to the Roman populace. A season or two before I joined our chief he had been so impressed with *Antony's* seductive qualities that he was wont to change his costume after two acts of *Cassius*, slip on a blond wig, play the oration scene, get his reward of applause, then finish his part of *Cassius* in the succeeding acts. The poor chap cast for *Antony* had a sad life. He never knew when Barrett would take his oration away from him. Public criticism had condemned this inartistic practise, and *Antony* was now left unmolested. My predecessor in the part was a long lank individual, rather scant of breath and awkward of movement, whose attenuated figure was liberally upholstered with padding. Sometimes his leg symmetries would get twisted and a beautifully developed calf would travel around to the front of his shin bone, but notwithstanding his unfitness for the character, his gasps and pumpings in the oration, he rarely failed with his audience.

My first essay in the part at Leadville, Colorado, ten thousand feet above sea level, at which elevation the least physical effort is trying to the unacclimated, was nearly disastrous. My nervousness had sent me pell-mell into the stirring scenes with no thought of husbanding my physical resources. By the time I had reached the middle of the big speech, I was all in. The blood was pounding in my ears and in my temples, and my chest was heaving in asthmatic convulsions. I just did get through, and when the calls came I had only strength enough to fall out in front of the curtain and to fall back again. I soon learned that in *Antony* the race is not always to the swift. A few more performances served to set the pace right and leave me breath enough to finish, and shortly I found *Antony* a "property of easiness."

Leadville in 'eighty-two was a wide-open town, saloons, gambling houses, dance-halls and variety shows, all ablaze after night-fall. Roulette, keno and faro were to be found every few blocks on the main street in shabby establishments open as the day to the passers-by. In one of them, whose door was never closed night or day, there was an outer anteroom where prominent citizens of Leadville could meet and talk politics. On a table in the center of this room was a well worn copy of the Bible which some one, generally a lean and grizzled miner, was invariably reading, while from the hall at the back came the click of the marble in the little stalls of the roulette wheel; or the drone of the keno caller as he read the numbers: "Seventy-two—eight—eleven—twenty-four!" "Keno!" "Hell!"

The chief variety theatre was a tawdry affair, afflicted with much cheap gilt and bright paint, where sorry-looking "serio comics" in lurid dresses sang to an audience that threw silver dollars at their feet. These daughters of Danaë would ogle and nod as they sang and work very hard to start the silver shower, which, when begun, resembled a hail-storm. The ability of these nymphs to sing,

119

dance and pick up coin in simultaneous action was much admired. I saw one poor black-face banjo player bob and pantomime at the occupants of the bench rows without result until, either in pity or disgust, a drunken miner threw him a dime.

Another interesting place on our route list that year—San Antonio, Texas. Largely Mexican, it had a very Old World aspect forty years ago. Many of the streets were unpaved; there was an air of peaceful indolence about the plaza. Hotel accommodations were not the best. I have preserved the dinner *menu* of our hostelry; the chef had done himself proud in the dessert list. Here it is:

Cardinal Pudding
Richelieu Sauce.
In honor of the great tragedian, Mr. Lawrence Barrett.

Mountain Cake
In Honor of Mr. Louis James.

Peach Ice-Cream
In Honor of Miss Marie Wainwright

Strawberry Tarts
In Honor of Mr. Otis Skinner.

DOGS NOT ALLOWED IN THE DINING-ROOM

Notable in the season of 1882-83 was the Dramatic Festival at Cincinnati, which was held for a

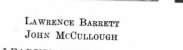

LAWRENCE BARRETT JAMES E. MURDOCH
JOHN MCCULLOUGH NAT C. GOODWIN

LEADING MEN OF THE CINCINNATI FESTIVAL, 1882–3

week in the Academy of Music. Rarely, if ever, has such a collection of American actors been assembled for regular public performances. The group included John McCullough, Mary Anderson, Lawrence Barrett, James E. Murdoch, Clara Morris, Mlle. Rhea, Nat C. Goodwin, John Ellsler and others, who appeared in Shakespearean and standard plays as one company. The general support was rendered by a combination of the Barrett and McCullough companies. The plays were staged in a way that made the occasion memorable. The big auditorium was crowded for the week.

The most interesting personality of the group, because of his age and the suggestion of palmy days he carried, was that of James E. Murdoch. No longer able to look the Prince of Denmark, he yet contrived to convey in his bearing much grace and courtliness, and his reading was a delight. In watching his *Hamlet* from the wings, I found myself shutting my eyes that I might not see the bowed back, lined features, and the unsightly wig he wore, leaving my ear to drink in the clarity and music of his elocution.

Modern methods disturbed him. In *Cæsar,* the mob scene was rehearsed in the manner of its usual presentation in both the Barrett and McCullough companies. Our youngsters who ''doubled'' as plebeians in the two companies worked with a will in vast rivalry to outdo one another in maniacal yells in response to *Antony's* appeals. The worried old stager stood this for a while, then lifting his hand he said: ''Gentlemen, I shall have to request you to

121

cease this tumult. If you do that to-night, you will knock every line out of my head.'' The scene, as planned, was a leaf taken out of the book of the Saxe Meiningen Company's performance in this country with Herr Ludwig Barnay as *Antony*—a tremendously effective piece of ensemble work, but our populace of Rome, for Mr. Murdoch's sake, remained as passive as gate posts, receiving *Antony's* stinging sarcasm and the news of *Cæsar's* munificence in bequeathing to every Roman citizen seventy-five drachmas, in dead silence. It was a splendid declamation, though it sounded a little like a lecture. The old gentleman's eyesight was not of the best. On reaching the close of the oration, he descended from the rostrum to the dead *Cæsar* on the bier with the emotional, ''If you have tears, prepare to shed them now,'' and with the burst of anger in which he was to tear the mantle from the covered figure, revealing to the mob the face of the great *Cæsar,* majestic and cold in death, Murdoch went to the wrong end of the corpse and uncovered only his *feet.*

Mary Anderson and Barrett seemed to regard Romeo and Juliet as an occasion of rejoicing, and played buoyantly, but well—albeit Lawrence was somewhat mature for the flower of Verona's youth.

The shadow of McCullough's doom was creeping upon him, but the sweetness of his nature remained to the end. He gave a good accounting of himself during this festival week, although he walked about as if in a dream.

What a noble mind was here o'er thrown!

CHAPTER VIII

THE EMOTION OF ACTING

ABOUT this time I discovered, to my alarm, that I had begun to lose the emotion of acting—that species of hysteria attendant upon a first performance. Nearly all of my characters, owing to frequent changes of bill, had been of short life and were withdrawn before the nervousness and excitement of novelty had worn off. In most actors this high tension effectually combats the self-consciousness that makes one aware of legs and feet and hands and arms; of swords and canes, of gloves and clothes; of every sort of stage property to be handled or worn.

Nowadays one has time in the period of long and careful preparation to free one's mind of doubts as to these things, but in the companies I had been with, dress rehearsals were almost nil. One got a general idea of exits, entrances, of the *mise en scène*, with the injunction to give the star the center of the stage and keep out of his way. A few rehearsals with speeches rattled off, stage business agreed upon, and we were ready for the performance, leaving sets, music cues, curtains on the acts, "shouts outside," etc., in the hands of the poor devil of a stage manager who was sure to let something go

123

wrong and, in consequence, be hauled over the coals by the star. First nights were visitations of terror. Under these conditions one has little time to develop his technique: things are moving too rapidly. When a man is escaping from a charging bull he doesn't stop to think if he is running in true athletic form; his one idea is to get to the fence. There was an old saying, "Twelve o'clock is sure to come." I now had a chance to cool off on the other side of the fence, but what had become of my freedom and my *feelings?*

As *Laertes*, in HAMLET, I found myself in such pain of inhibition that the mere effort of walking across the stage became disagreeable. I felt the condemning eyes of the people in front. *Laertes'* earlier scenes are in the first act of HAMLET and then he disappears from view until, toward the close of the play, he comes rushing upon the scene to demand of the *King* what has become of his father, The long stupefying wait in the bad air of the dressing-room—over an hour and a half—robbed me of every particle of spirit. I employed violent callisthenics just before the scene of fury, in an attempt to fling off the leaden weight, and set my blood flowing, but after a few experiments the process became ineffective. Then I tried stripping myself of grease paint and costume and leaving the theatre for an hour to walk the streets. That was more successful. I renovated my lungs with fresh air, at least,

One biting winter night, in Cincinnati, I suddenly realized that I was an incredible distance from the Opera House, and in a state of nervous panic. Suppose I should be late! What if the chief had decided to hurry his performance and get through —he sometimes did that! I was away from the lights of the business section of the town. I began to run, and came panting to the Opera House fully half an hour too soon. I think I must have played *Laertes* that night, at least, with spirit.

I was learning the lesson that every actor must learn in his storm and stress—that an emotional debauch is not an expression of feeling in acting. That he should feel the emotion of his scene is unimportant if his audience remains unmoved. They are the ones to supply the emotion; his the art that supplies the suggestion. I have known actors who could not speak a line of poetic beauty or of pathos without flooding their faces with tears, and yet the spectators looked on unmoved. I have seen old Madame Janauschek, after a tragic scene, turn up stage, carefully arranging her drapery, and speaking a flippant aside to a supporting player, while the audience sat spellbound. Clara Morris had the gift of weeping copiously in *Camille, Alixe* and *Miss Multon,* but her tears were a trick—something she could turn on and off at will. She never lost her control and, like Fanny Janauschek, she could quietly laugh with her stage companions while sorrow swept the auditorium.

Art never becomes perfect until the artist has mastered his medium. As the painter uses his pigments, so the actor uses his capacity for emotion, deliberately, carefully, even mathematically, begetting by his reserve that "temperance" which our Shakespeare commends.

James A. Hearne and I sat up one night till the small hours talking shop. We were speaking of this emotion in acting, and Hearne cited the case of the story he told as *Uncle Nat* in SHORE ACRES; the story of his father's death at sea that never failed to move the audience deeply. "Mrs. Hearne opened my eyes to its possibilities," he said. "I was turning on the tear taps at rehearsal and working the pumps pretty hard when Mrs. Hearne, who was watching from out in front, said, 'Why are you working so; why do you cry? Aren't you going to leave some of that for the audience to do?' If I had played *Uncle Nat* the way I had played similar parts as a young man, I should have sobbed and suffered and had a terrible time. Now, I tell the story quietly, recalling the memories with a little smile. It's wonderful how you can pick an audience up into your arms that way."

The whole secret lies in suggestion. If your acting fails in this quality, you may have the grace of Booth, the romanticism of Fechter, the strength of Salvini, and the soul of Keats, but you would far better drive a street-car.

But how to discover the secret of this quality! No text-book can lay down a hard and fast rule for acting. The process of one individual can never be the process of another. Talent is but crude stuff—raw material until it is beaten into shape by infinite

126

labor and a thousand failures. I had been relying on my impulse and my feelings for five years. It was high time I was discovering a method. I had taken stage conventions for granted; it was unnecessary to examine into this and that way of doing things. That was the way they were done. Now came the time when these conventions were challenged! What matter if they had been done that way forever and a day! Did that make them right? These questionings; these doubts; these struggles of self-analysis and self-expression come to painter, writer, musician, actor when his youthful enthusiasm subsides in the face of stern experience.

During the second season I had the chance to play *Antony* in Boston—within two miles of my birthplace in Cambridge. The audience at the Park Theatre included many personal friends and friends of my family. Call after call came after *Marc Antony's* two strong scenes, until finally my conscience smote me. Louis James came out of his dressing-room and stood generously smiling as the curtain went up and down. In nervous fear that I was appropriating a reward never meant for me, I seized him by the hand and led him out with me. While the subsequent "tent scene" of *Brutus* and *Cassius* was proceeding, Mr. Barrett's dresser came to my room and said that the chief wanted to see me. He was sitting bolt upright in his Roman armour.

"Sit down, sir," he said.

I sat.

"Mr. Skinner, I wish first to congratulate you on your success to-night."

"Thank you, Mr. Barrett."

"Now let me tell you something, young man. You have done one of the most unprofessional things to-night I've ever encountered. You have patronized my leading man. Patronized, sir! Led him before the audience! If you arrogate to yourself that privilege, where am I?"

In vain I tried to tell him that my action had been prompted not by effrontery, but by confusion.

"Pooh, sir!" he answered. "If you had had fifty calls, they would all have been for *Antony.* That's what *Antony* is for, sir, to get calls."

I felt myself growing smaller and smaller.

"Look at me! Who cares for *Cassius!* My only reward is the artist's reward. They never call for *Cassius.*"

Just then the dresser rushed in hastily. The tent scene was over. "They're calling for you, Mr. Barrett!" he cried.

The offended tragedian forgot his rage. He fairly ran out to take his call.

He was human after all.

On the fourteenth of September, 1882, at Haverly's Theatre in Philadelphia, Barrett made the most noteworthy revival of his career—George H. Boker's FRANCESCA DA RIMINI. This play had lain on library shelves for years. Written in the early 'fifties and presented for the first time at The Broadway Theatre, New York, in September of 1855, it had received comparatively few performances, and records do not show that it attracted much attention. Barrett, always alive to the value of unusual plays, had seen its great merit. It has the fateful, inevitable movement of Greek tragedy, and it contains many scenes of tenderness and beauty. It remains, after years, one of the outstanding American plays.

Boker was a man of affairs in Philadelphia, a lawyer and a politician. He was a social leader as well as a poet, and had been appointed to ministerial posts in Turkey and Russia. He had not found it easy to come to an understanding with Barrett about the stage version of the tragedy. Barrett's sense of acting values found much reason for elimination and transposition, but the white-haired aristocrat of the Union League was stubborn. The children of his brain must not be molested. Barrett raged secretly and openly. At the rehearsals, with the author present, we heard some stormy arguments. Boker's views of the actor's proceedings had an air of tolerance and condescension which made our chief writhe. But Barrett prevailed, and the play was produced as he had directed.

Barrett, with his volcanic elocution and strenuous methods, carried his scenes effectively. His *Launciotto* roused the house to enthusiasm repeatedly. Francesca da Rimini grew steadily in favor on tour, and was presented for a run of several months at the Star Theatre, New York, commencing August 27, 1883. I was cast for *Paolo*. This was my first

Metropolitan opportunity for an appearance in a leading juvenile part. I felt that the swing of circumstances had brought me around to the chance I had been waiting for.

Before our engagement at the Star Theatre was over, Henry Irving and Ellen Terry took possession of the stage to rehearse with their company for their first American tour. I dropped in to the theatre now and then to watch Irving at work. His method was a revelation to me. Such care and insistence on the smallest detail I had never seen. He would sit in front, slumped in an orchestra chair, his long body so far down as to leave no vestige to the observer behind except a high hat covering a thatch of long hair. From this spot he would drone out his directions. One day he lost his temper, suddenly shot out of his seat and scrambled to the stage. The play was THE BELLS, and in the dance of the Alsatian peasants one particular dancer was so stiff and ungraceful that his awkwardness finally got on Irving's nerves. He seized the offender and danced with him, forcing the awkward one's body first to right, then to left as if he were administering a set of Swedish Movement exercises, and crying out in well-known Irving gutturals, "Bend, my boy, bend! Take the stiffness out of your bones. Show a little grace! Great God! You're made of wood! Swing! Bend!" The unfortunate youth was reduced to limpness. Irving's impatience was spent and he stalked, vigorously refreshed, to the orchestra seat again.

HYPNOTIZING FRANCESCA

Previous to opening for a week of Francesca in Washington, Barrett had an idea. He discovered, all at once, that the love scene in the garden between Miss Wainwright and myself (*Francesca* and *Paola*) was immodest and suggestive. He could not countenance such an exhibition. It must be changed. A rehearsal was called.

The original termination of the scene was a frenzied declaration of love between the guilty pair, and the resolve that nothing should stand in the way of its consummation, and they left the scene, locked in each other's arms.

Barrett decided that this must all be discarded. There should be no embrace after the fatal kiss. I was directed to meander up to the arbor and pluck a rose. *Francesca,* at the same time, to turn to the center of the stage, pick up the book containing the story of Launcelot and Guinevere which the two had been reading, then advancing, we were to come face to face and stare at each other as if we were strangers. I held out the rose as our eyes met, and then proceeded to back off the scene while she limply followed after the extended arm as if hypnotized. The whole thing was false, mock-sentimental, horrible. Nevertheless, we did it.

A certain Professor Carpenter, hypnotist, had been occupying the theatre for a fortnight prior to our coming. His especially amusing exhibition was to place his subjects in an hypnotic trance in which they did absurd things, following him about the stage like a flock of geese, his extended forefinger held within a few inches of their noses. He woke his subjects from their trance by snapping his fingers in their ears, and saying, "All right!"

Miss Wainwright and I had begun our slow exit; she had spoken her concluding line: "Come, love! We'll hear the voiceless future when its turn arrives." I had just reached the entrance, holding out the rose to the following *Francesca*, when an entire row of young fellows on the front seats arose as one man. A little broadside of finger snaps and a half-dozen voices called out, "All right! all right!" We never repeated the business; it was for one night only.

My earlier doubts began to gather once more. What was to be my future? I had been working steadily for seven years without developing a method of my own. I had grown into an imitation of Barrett, although this imitation came from no admiration of his methods. His style was something by which he had been able to express himself with eloquence and conviction, but it was laden with mannerisms dangerous to copy. I used to discover myself reading a speech like him, making a gesture like him, and then I would take myself aside, quite in rage, and endeavor to undo what I had drifted into. I seemed able to find no other way than his way. It mattered little that my companions in the company were doing the same thing—we were all lesser editions of our chief—that didn't console me or make my struggle easier. It was a natural result —the consequence of the dominant stage direction

132

of a mannered star. The same thing was observable in other companies. McCullough's people were all like him, and there were young Irvings and Jeffersons and Wilson Barretts.

In the midst of my perplexities an offer of great importance came to me. Barrett regarded my leaving him as an affront, and became immensely angry, but I knew that a longer association with him would not help my work. And yet I owe Lawrence Barrett much: opportunity, advancement, the benefit of his experience, and the example of his high ideals. Many found him difficult to get along with. I did not. In spite of his stormy nature, he had been very patient with me. I took away many faults from him, but I carried away the memory of a remarkable man. His peculiarities were many, but so were his virtues, and in his character there was much that was exalted. The profession of acting has been the richer for his example.

CHAPTER IX

WHEN Augustin Daly fixed his name to a three-year contract for my services I felt like a spent swimmer to whom a life preserver has been thrown. Five years before I had gone to him to ask for a hearing, and the word he returned to the agent who furnished my credentials was that *I would not do.* Now he had come to me, but I needed him far more than he needed me. If any man was capable of beating the tricks of exaggeration out of me, it was Daly. His company was composed of expert comedians; his theatre was one of popularity and of fashion and his productions the most talked of in New York. Several wrecks of managerial ventures lay behind him, the Twenty-Fourth Street Theatre, the Fifth Avenue Theatre, and others, but he had defied failure and was now reaping his reward.

First nights at Daly's were such sought-after events that he could select his audience from the representative names in town. All Gotham was sure to be there. He invariably stood at the ticket taker's wicket, with a word of greeting for the illustrious ones. At his back was the inviting lobby, hung with paintings, engravings and historic play bills, warm and homelike, where well-groomed peo-

134

ple kept up a buzz of talk. Expectation stood tip-
toe. The programme gave announcement of old
favorites in new parts. Widmer's orchestra dis-
coursed excellent music. The lights were subdued
and the curtain went up. There was a little flurry
of music to bring the members of the cast on the
scene, and each received his greeting as an old
friend. It was all very much like a huge family
party, well ordered, sympathetic.

Augustin Daly was a tall man who carried himself awkwardly and wore the same peculiar stiff
black hat year after year, giving an annual order to
his hatter for a new edition. No martinet was ever
more strict in discipline and cast-iron rule. While
he had able lieutenants, he left little but the veriest
drudgery to them. He ran the entire establishment
from the ticket office to the stage door, He was
ubiquitous. At one moment he was on the paint
frame, criticizing the work of the scenic artist, then
in the property-room issuing orders for furniture,
draperies and bric-à-brac, and his trail could be followed into the costume workshop, the carpenter
shop, to the business office whose windows over-
looked Broadway, and then plunging back again
into his own private den in the rear to labors of
play-writing, work with his translator, and the
thousand and one things that were crammed into
each of his twenty-four hours, His capacity for
work was limitless.

Habitually self-centered, Daly's manner was ordinarily repellent, and yet there were times when

he would break into boyish glee over a foolish antic or a funny story. There were other days when gloom and temper claimed him for their own. His hobby was the perfect running of the machinery of his organization. Suspicious of the loyalty of those about him, he was absolutely blind to the virtue or merit of a contrary view to his own. There could be but one method of accomplishing anything; that was the method of Augustin Daly.

Religion with him was a matter of ever-present obligation. He gave much to the Catholic charities of New York. A hobby of his was his collection of books, engravings and art objects. On some of his books he spent a small fortune in extra illustrations.

Essentially was he a city man. Nature made little appeal to him, and flowers were of no value except at the florist's. The sky was a region where rain and snow came from. The rattle and crash of the city streets were music to his ears.

My engagement began with the close of the New York season in 1884 when the company went on its spring and summer tour. This summer it was to venture across the ocean for an attack upon London, and the entire organization was thrilling over the prospect. My first appearance was in Philadelphia in a slight play called RED LETTER NIGHTS, a kind of semi-farce with musical numbers. There was little for me to do except to wear good clothes, and as I had squandered riotous sums upon a fashionable New York tailor, I trusted to his skill to see

AUGUSTIN DALY
From the Collection of Miss Elizabeth Daly

that they *were* good. They proved to be almost too good, as I found out a few nights later in SEVEN-TWENTY-EIGHT. *Paul Hollyhock* in this comedy was a nice harmless sort of a part. In the third act, I had to appear as returning from the opera with my young and frivolous wife. I was clad in one of the creations of the fashionable tailor; in fact I was clad in two of them; an evening dress suit and a top coat. I then began to divest myself of my immaculate top coat, but horror seized me when, as I gave a tug at the left sleeve, I found that the sleeve of the dress coat, being of light material, clung to the outer garment with a grip of awful tenacity. Carrying on a line or two of the dialogue, I changed my tactics and tried the right sleeve. An area of white linen at the shoulder, and an exposed waistcoat showed me that this side, too, was fast. The audience discovered my plight, and grew both visibly and audibly amused at my expense. Daly was in the prompt entrance, where he always stood on first nights, watching his new juvenile man, and probably, at that moment, not thinking very well of him. I tried many different kinds of squirms to rid myself of the dread thing, but it was a veritable robe of Nessus. Meanwhile, though I was still carrying on the scene, the audience was having a fine time. Not so the "Governor" at his post of observation in the entrance; he was fairly writhing. To have played that scene in my overcoat, now, would have been to cover myself with ignominy. There was but one way. I deliberately stopped in the dialogue and stripped myself; the accursed objects clung together and came off as one. There was a gasp out in front. I thanked the Lord my haberdashery was blameless. As I separated the garments, the sleeves of the outer one turned *inside out!* It was becoming a conjuring trick. Then as I put the top coat in order and resumed the dress coat amid a breathless silence, there came a round of applause. I was considerably shaken, but Daly performed contortions of delight in his sentry box.

Besides the two comedies mentioned, the repertory included others adapted by Daly from German sources. The two "old" comedies in the group were THE COUNTRY GIRL and Colley Cibber's SHE WOULD AND SHE WOULD NOT. None of the modern plays was of great substance; they were, however, excellent vehicles for the exploitation of the company with a background of attractive stage settings and the fine clothes. The dressing of the women had become famous. Daly's skill as an adapter was considerable; the original German characters under his hand became credible Americans and said and did amusing things, but the great delight to our patrons was the company. *Place aux dames!* Ada Rehan headed the list, buoyant, scintillant, with a manner unlike other women, a voice that melted and caressed as it drawled, an awkward grace, an arch expression, a look of mischief in her gray Irish eyes, she was a young goddess of laughter—a modern Peg Woffington. She had a sense of the incongruous that sometimes caused her to go to pieces with suppressed amusement. An accident on the scene, a peculiarly read line, a grotesque face seen out in front, almost any unexpected thing would render her well-nigh helpless with mirth. Some one wrote of her:

"Your laugh would make a dying world rejoice.
You speak, and Shandon's bells are in your voice."

Mrs. G. H. Gilbert's dear old ladies, foolish virgins, and peppery viragos were perennial in their welcome. She had a brusk and garrulous habit of speech, bred of her stage Xantippes, that might have suggested to a stranger a temperament composed largely of vinegar, but two minutes' talk with her would have shown him a sweet, tender, lovable old soul who made a place in every one's affections.

Daly sought his material wherever it could best be found. Reputation meant nothing to him, personality meant everything, whether he found it in a variety troupe or a fly-by-night band of strolling players. One of his ladies had been a bareback rider in a circus. He discovered May Irwin at Tony Pastor's variety theatre, singing comic songs and doing sketches with her sister Flo, and saw at once the comic genius that later made her famous on the legitimate stage. She was altogether a new species to the decorous Daly company, and if, during rehearsal, a little group was seen in a remote corner giving out smothered peals of laughter, it was pretty sure to be May Irwin, all curves and plumpness, entertaining her hearers with her negro songs, an imitation or a bit of drollery.

Virginia Dreher and May Fielding were comely, clever women whose appearances were hailed by a circle of admirers, and there was a small army of pretty maids whose heads were filled with dreams of the day when they should push Ada Rehan from her pedestal.

Longest in his service to the House of Daly among the men was James Lewis, eccentric comedian, character actor, what you will, but in whatever part you will he was always James Lewis. Dry of speech, with a crackling sort of voice and a fussy little manner, he held his own in every piece. Mostly he was coupled with Mrs. Gilbert as a rowing, cantankerous old pair. He was above all an actor of modern parts. The annual revival of old comedy was a period of chastisement to him, especially if the comedy chanced to be by William Shakespeare. "Heh! Shakespeare is no friend of mine!" he would exclaim as much in sorrow as in anger. He was a lean little man, generally nursing an illness real or fancied. Superstition with him amounted almost to religion. He had a whole menagerie of theatrical superstitions. Quotations from MACBETH were presages of calamity, and to sing the music of the witch scenes of the play was to sound the trumpet of doom. One had but to mention the mere title to bring out Jim's "Heh! That settles it!" But no one took Jim's odd grouches and pet aversions seriously; the more he kicked the better we liked him.

As Lewis was coupled with Mrs. Gilbert, so John

JOHN DREW NEVER FAILED

Drew was generally paired with Miss Rehan, and they wooed and quarreled, and fenced and fondled, danced, adored and spat their way through many a comedy, old and new. John was looked to always to furnish perfect light comedy, perfect manners, and perfect clothes, and he never failed in his duty. There was another perfection of his that was not so much in evidence—perfect *camaraderie,* but that was for his fellows, not for the public. Accomplished, hospitable, generous, a good acquaintance, a splendid friend, a capital raconteur, there was no circle where John Drew did not find the warmest welcome. When, in later times, Charles Frohman plucked him forth and made a star of him, there were no heartier rejoicings over his success than those of his old comrades in arms.

Our *père noble,* as the French stage would catalogue him, was Charles Fisher, sometimes referred to tenderly as "the old bird." Fisher had size, appearance, distinction and an aristocratic manner. Old comedy was very much in his line. He wore his costumes with an air and displayed the graces of the period of Sheridan and Farquhar as though to the manner born.

Charles Leclercq, a member of an English theatrical family, and W. J. Gilbert, of an American one, played eccentric and character parts, and William H. Thompson, who afterward made a name for himself, did character "bits."

The acknowledged butt of the company was George Parkes, who specialized in fops, mutton-headed dunces and blithering idiots. Why he chose such a line of work I can't conceive, but such was Parkes' skill in it that Daly often wrote him into the comedies. A part which he made quite his own was that of *Sparkish* in THE COUNTRY GIRL.

These were my companions, and this was the troupe of Americans who in July, 1884, sailed from New York on the Guion Line S. S. *Alaska* to storm the dramatic citadel of London.

There are but few emotions in my life comparable to that of setting foot on England's soil for the first time. It was with a feeling of wonder that I listened to the Westminster chime of the Abbey, the deep boom of the Parliament clock and the sound of Bow-bells. England the land of Shakespeare, Dickens and Thackeray! London, the town enshrining memories of the rogues and heroes of romance! Here lie Newgate Prison where Jack Sheppard, Dick Turpin and Claude Duval started their last earthly pilgrimage to Tyburn Tree; Drury Lane and Covent Garden amid whose stuffy shadows stalked the ghosts of David Garrick, John Phillip Kemble, Sarah Siddons, Peg Woffington, Sheridan and Edmund Kean. The Law Courts reverberating with the echoes of the interminable suit of Jarndyce *vs* Jarndyce, and near by the little graveyard where *Joe* saw *Lady Dedlock* with her hands clutching the iron gate palings; London bridge telling of *Fagin, Nancy* and *Bill Sykes;* the dark Thames by the Tower where *Rogue Riderhood* plied his trade of river thieving. A bit of the an-

142

cient Marshalsea Prison over in Southwark eloquent with the woes of *Little Dorritt,* and not far away the Old White Hart Inn with memories of *Pickwick* and *Sam Weller.* I stumbled across the ruins of the Fox Under the Hill on the Thames Embankment, and thought of *Pendennis* and the hilarity of the Waterman's Tavern nights. It all seemed too good to be true.

To a city whose theatres held records of celebrated runs and noted actors, a city bristling with tradition and insularity, the challenge of a troupe of American comedians smacked of the audacious. There was a vague feeling of resentfulness in the air, and outspoken objection in certain theatrical circles. What right had we to take the bread out of English actors' mouths? The reflection that English actors had for years been filling their mouths with American bread in our country did not, perhaps, occur to them. Nevertheless our greeting from the London public was hospitable when our bow was made to it, on the night of July nineteenth at Toole's Theatre. The occupants of the stalls and balcony were largely American, but in the pit lay the area of suspicion and apprehension; we had heard much and read much of the merciless London pittites and their habit of booing and hissing on first nights. Mrs. James Lewis and Mrs. John Drew, sitting in the back row of the stalls and only separated by a rail from the front row of the pit, overheard derisive remarks from the crowded benches long before the curtain rose. One burly chap exclaimed, as he took his seat, "Well, 'ere's 'alf a crown thrown away!" a remark not calculated to promote pleasant anticipations in these ladies' minds. As the performance progressed, however, their fears and ours gradually lessened. There was little hissing; there would have been none at all had our countrymen not been so demonstrative in their welcome. As each of us entered, there was a hullabaloo of greeting from friends which grated on the fine sensibilities of the pittites. They stood it patiently for about three appearances, then they turned loose and drowned the friendly handclapping with vigorous jeers and boos. After that all was peace. The Britons approved of us.

Never was a knot of actors more nervous and apprehensive. We went into battle with white faces and trembling knees. The play was SEVEN-TWENTY-EIGHT, but an English producer having pirated that caption a month previously, Daly couldn't use his own title and called the piece CASTING THE BOOMERANG.

THE TELEGRAPH's reviewer said:

"Mr. Augustin Daly's Company of Comedians would seem to have been selected with special care and fitted with characters precisely suited to their histrionic capacity. Not merely is a remarkable completeness thus obtained, but separate claims to distinction are advanced and readily admitted. The most subordinate personage in the comedy is a New York postman, having only a few lines to speak and no further purpose to serve than the delivery of a packet of letters on a stormy night, yet so naturally

144

acted was this small part that there was a general
turning of the playbill toward the light to ascertain
the name of the representative. Where there is no
weak link in the chain, the whole may be safely
trusted.''

For more than six weeks the BOOMERANG was
cast from the stage of the grubby little theatre in
Chandos Street into increasing popularity. Augustin Daly had gambled with fate for his London
venture, and won.

On October 9, 1884, in one of the milk and water
cubs that Daly invented as especially suited to my
style, I made my bow in the home theatre in something called A WOODEN SPOON which was typical
and frothy, polite farce. Playing opposite me, and
making her New York début, was Edith Kingdon,
discovered by Daly in the Boston Theatre Company. The future Mrs. George Gould was a slip of
a thing—vastly pretty—to whom such things as
wealth and luxury must have seemed as far away
as the moon. Enrolled as a member of the famous
Daly Company, what more could she ask? A fate
filled with vast fortunes and titled connections was
a thing that happened in fairy tales. Neither of us
had more to do than simper in parts that might as
well have been cut out of the piece. Brighter things
were in store for us both.

A new comedy by Pinero, LORDS AND COMMONS,
was put on to follow our opening bill, but
proved to be too English to be understood. Something had to be substituted at once and nothing new

was ready. Here came one of the striking examples of Daly's resourcefulness. Among his stock of German comedies was one by Stobitzer which was renamed LOVE ON CRUTCHES. Though it was not completely translated we were called to rehearse this piece next day, and for two weeks we practically lived in the theatre. The master director was never more effective than when he was running under forced draft; alert, nervous, inventive, insistent in perfecting the smallest gesture and the subtlest modulation of voice (I have known him, on occasion, to be dissatisfied with the crook of his leading lady's forefinger and to straighten it out, to adjust the pose of her head and the turn of her foot), he went over the first act again and again, impatient when we didn't grasp his unexplained meanings, and then laughing like a schoolboy over a spark of unexpected comedy. We had a rather foggy idea of the piece; it was being adapted as we went along. I never knew a time of greater confusion and hysteria. All day we worried through the painful rehearsals. At night, and twice on Wednesdays and Saturdays, LORDS AND COMMONS struck its apathetic note to diminishing audiences, while succeeding acts of the new comedy came from Daly's private office where, through the midnight hours of the deserted theatre, he worked unwearied. Then came the night rehearsals, to which the day rehearsals were as recreation. We got but little sleep. When Broadway was opening its shops we were at work; a half-hour for lunch or a sandwich

146

A NIGHT OFF

John Drew   Charles Leclercq   Otis Skinner
    Ada Rehan   Virginia Dreher   May Irwin
    James Lewis   Mrs. Gilbert

LOVE ON CRUTCHES

Edith Kingdon   Ada Rehan   Mrs. Gilbert
    Otis Skinner   James Lewis   John Drew

REPRESENTATIVE PRODUCTIONS AT DALY'S THEATRE

and cup of coffee brought in to us, a hasty dinner, the evening's performance, becoming more flabby and weak-kneed at each repetition, then midnight and nerves, aching feet and atrophied spirits that failed to respond to the goad. Sometime before daybreak an excuse for sleep, a cold bath and we were at it again.

We felt horribly abused, but the chief never stopped his drive, and while for an hour or so we did get a chance to tumble into bed, for all any one knew *he never slept!* Finally the last act was written. The pace became quicker. Monday: all day in the theatre, stopping in time to act the Pinero play in the evening; midnight; at it again until four o'clock; Tuesday: same thing, day, evening, midnight; Wednesday: run over the lines in the theatre lobby; afternoon: matinée of LORDS AND COMMONS, and the *première* of the new piece *that night.*

If the play had failed—but it could not fail: our very desperation would have "sent it over." It was one of Daly's supreme achievements. The opening night was notable for the suprise of Edith Kingdon's hit in a capital part. We two were paired off as before, but in more sympathetic rôles, and yet Miss Kingdon nearly threw the piece on the rocks. At the most critical moment of the third act she forgot her lines completely, and nobody was able to throw her the missing word. But there wasn't a vestige of dismay on her part. Calmly fanning herself she strolled up to Jim Lewis, saying *sotto voce,* "What's the word?" Jim failed to rescue her. She sauntered over to Mrs. Gilbert. "What's the word?" Collapse on the part of Mrs. G., and general inane cackle from all the characters. Sleepy old Moore at the manuscript came to his senses and threw her the line from the prompt stand, but it was lost in the buzz of the impromptu talk. With charming indifference she wandered toward the prompt entrance, caught the line and resumed without turning a hair. Everybody on the scene showed panic, but not Edith Kingdon. After the act cries of "Kindgon! Kingdon!" were heard. The little actress had gone to her dressing-room, the call boy flew after her and in a few moments the curtain was pulled aside and she peeped out rather disheveled with a rag of a kimono pulled over her.

In the old comedies I found myself once more at home in costume. Tailor's creations were fetters to me and I had not subdued a stride that took me from one side of the "set" to the other in half a dozen lopes. *Harcourt* in THE COUNTRY GIRL isn't such a bad part, either; breezy, frank, buoyant and engaging. He laughs quite a bit at the others and that helps. When old-comedy young men engage in their blithesome tasks they usually laugh like hyenas—always at their own jokes. It sends things along, but you aren't always sure that the audience is overcome with mirth.

On the heels of the old comedies came the production of a riotous farce, A NIGHT OFF. The parts were all good. Mine, *Harry Damask*, a young doctor with a wife jealous of his pre-nuptial love-affairs, was quite worth while. Leclercq, as *Marcus Brutus Snap*, a barnstorming tragedian, had opportunity to show his quality, and May Irwin was extremely funny as a romantic servant girl. Drew and Rehan, Lewis and Mrs. Gilbert fell into line with the same kind of parts they had always played. The piece was tremendously liked both in New York and on our summer tour which extended to the Pacific Coast.

Daly's faith in Pinero was unshaken. We began the following dramatic year with one of the best comic plays ever written, THE MAGISTRATE, and it ran joyously for over three months. I had a deal of difficulty with my part, *Captain Horace Vale*. I couldn't quite get the bored and impassive English military swell at rehearsal. I tried the stupid Lord Dundreary method and found it leaden and meaningless; I imitated some of the English actors in our company and the result was worse. Pinero had come over from London to direct his piece. The rehearsals progressed sloppily and without spirit, lacking the goad of our martinet director. One rainy morning Pinero was somewhere in the gloom of the parquet. There had been a long and ominous silence out there when suddenly we were called down unmercifully in a disconsolate wail by the suffering author. It was a high-pitched voice, full of pathos, even agony. "I say, you up there! Farther down the stage everybody! We *must* have quicker action or we won't get anywhere. Please! Please!" The man seemed about to dis-

149

solve in tears. Higher and higher went his voice until it reached pure falsetto. "My heavens!" I thought, "here is my military swell—Pinero! He's *IT*." Thereafter I sought opportunities for little meetings and talks with the author. I waylaid him on every possible occasion—stalked him like a footpad in his hotel and at the theatre, thinking up excuses for conversation that I might absorb the inflections of his high-keyed voice and imitate it. I got it at last. To be sure I exaggerated and perhaps my imitation was, after all, a bad one, for Pinero never recognized it, and I had nothing but the warmest thanks from both him and his wife on the night of the first production.

When it came to the traditions of the old standard plays, Daly, wholly irreverent, never hesitated to cut, transpose, introduce unprecedented action and even to rewrite. The old playwrights must have turned in their graves at his ruthlessness. In THE COUNTRY GIRL, as we gave it, one of the most effective scenes had been lifted bodily from another play. Shakespeare's lines were no more sacred to Augustin Daly than those in the original text of his German farce writers. He was perpetually assaulted by the critics for what they termed his vandalism. However in THE MERRY WIVES OF WINDSOR he introduced no startling innovation unless it were mechanical and electrical effects, which seemed to offend some of the gentlemen of the press but which have been far outdone since his day by stage directors seeking for sensation.

CHAPTER X

AT the close of the New York season of eighteen eighty-five and eighteen eighty-six we made our second pilgrimage to London. It was a far different band of players that made its bow at the Strand Theatre in May from the frightened actors who had appeared two years before at Toole's. We felt sure of our London public now. Perhaps this attitude of ours was somewhat fatuous, but there was a feeling that we were among friends. For ten weeks the little Strand Theatre was filled to its limit, the engagement being divided between A NIGHT OFF and NANCY AND COMPANY. King Edward—then Prince of Wales—came to see us, and talked in an abominably loud voice in his box during the performance. Daly was in high feather and engineered little excursions, and a special journey to Stratford-on-Avon on the Fourth of July for a week-end. He was like a youngster on a picnic. We went out for an evening row on the Avon and he took Ada Rehan, Drew and myself into his boat with strict injunctions to John and me at the oars to keep in the van. He became most excited when some of the others tried to crawl ahead and laughed in triumph as we shot into the lead again.

151

Some one had told him of a legend that the swans of the river always swam after the boats of the good actors. He watched them eagerly. Presently three or four of the big stately fellows detached themselves from the flock and came our way. "Here they come!" he cried. "You're good actors! You're good actors!" He fairly crowed with delight. It was another Augustin Daly. The awkward, moody, domineering manager was having his play day.

The ten London weeks at an end, we went to Edinburgh and Glasgow, where the effect of our farces on the dour Scots was very curious. Our smartest speeches and funniest situations met with a grimness that tried our souls. Then suddenly all was changed. Like the breaking up of ice in a spring freshet their coldness and caution were swept away on a flood of laughter. We had passed the test, we were funny.

On the last night in Glasgow our house had been especially uproarious over A Night Off. The performance over, we had packed our trunks and emerged into the blackness of the dirty alley upon which the stage entrance opened. May Irwin came along and we walked together toward the lights of the street beyond. Suddenly, from a niche in the blind wall of the building, a figure projected itself and was silhouetted against the distant street lights. I couldn't see the face in the gloom, but the figure was marked; it was tall and had powerful shoulders. I looked for trouble, for Saturday night in Glasgow was a time of wassail, the night when the hard-headed Scot absorbed enough "dew of Ben Nevis" to last through the tight-shut, godly *Sawbath*. Brawls were not infrequent and I saw myself at the beginning of one. It would not do to stand still in this deserted passage; we moved on, so did the figure; it faced us, walking backward, giving ground slowly. For a number of seconds there wasn't a sound but our footsteps echoing against the brick-walls. Then he spoke thus:

"Uz Teule a ber-rer actor then yeou?"

"What did you say?" I returned.

"Uz Teule a ber-rer actor then yeou?"

There wasn't any sense to it; surely the man was drunk.

Then a light dawned on me and I got the meaning of his mystic inquiry. *Is Toole a better actor than you?*

By this we were out into the lights of the shops and I could see the man wasn't drunk at all. He was a respectable mechanic in his Sunday clothes. The grasp on my walking-stick relaxed.

"Oh, no!" I said with perfect seriousness, "not at all!"

The man looked puzzled.

"He's considered gret guns aboot here," he remarked. "It's a gret peety ye air goin' awa the neet. Y' ought to stay anither week."

No, we had to go.

The hotel where the company stayed lay near the Theatre Royal. I took Miss Irwin's arm and started to steer her through the stream of vehicles and tram-cars, but no farther than the curb—I was whirled about like a top.

"Gi' us a grip o' yer hand, sir," said the tall fellow.

I submitted to a squeeze that nearly made jelly of my fingers. I thanked him and again attempted to cross over. His big paw shot across my chest and tapped Miss Irwin's shoulder.

"Gi' us yeours, Miss."

May's hand was pressed flabby, then we were suffered to depart.

John L. Toole was an idol of the Glasgow public, the most comic figure it could conceive, and here were *farceurs* who drew as much laughter as Toole —perhaps more. He couldn't figure it out.

There were more worlds for Daly to conquer, Germany and France. We jumped from Glasgow to Hamburg, where we appeared for three nights and then on to Berlin for a week. The Germans knew our plays; we were carrying coals to Newcastle. The valet who was allotted to me at the Wallner Theatre in Berlin acknowledged that these American comedians were capable. *"Aber, ach!"* he exclaimed, "you should see *our* actors in these plays." This valet of mine led a double life. At night he was a theatre dresser, during the day he was a tailor. He was John Drew's valet as well, and took great interest in our clothes. In one of the scenes of Love on Crutches John had to stand in profile just inside a door, left entrance, and overhear a conversation. The tailor-dresser,

154

following him about, discovered, as he stood there, that his coat collar was pulling away from his neck, and the audience was amazed at the sight of a long arm emerging from the doorway adjusting the recalcitrant collar while John said unprintable things.

It was terribly hot that summer in Berlin. A few natives came to the Wallner Theatre, moved, perhaps, by curiosity, the critics of course, some visiting Englishmen and all the American tourists and residents who had courage to brave the heat. The press was condescending and tolerant. But our spirited comedy went for nothing, the harder we worked the less the response.

How we welcomed the seidel of cool Meunchner at the Franciskaner Garten when the evening was at an end!

The Berlin week pulled its hot and humid length through to a finish. There was no money for Daly in the foreign invasion and I presume he expected none, but at home his daring was received with tremendous éclat.

Our appearance in Paris had been well advertised and aroused considerable interest. French ideas of an American performance had hitherto been gained through Buffalo Bill's Wild West Show, or of a Yankee importation at a *café chantant,* and there was general disappointment when it was discovered that we wore no eagle plumes, and did not break into scalp dances and war whoops. But to the Frenchman there is but one city—Paris, and but one art—that of France; and who were these

155

American comedians that Paris should concern itself about them? And they had such barbarous
customs! They kissed their women on the lips in
sentimental scenes! No French actor would be
guilty of such bourgeois, indecent display; even in
the most risqué farces a chaste salute on the cheek
was the nearest approach to boudoir familiarities
permissible. And they had music played while they
acted! What had music to do with comedy? The
French stage, unlike the English, has never made
use of incidental music for dramatic action, except
in musical farces and certain of their melodramas.
The *Théâtre du Vaudeville,* in spite of its name,
was without an orchestra or even an orchestra pit.
The *entr' actes* were without music and the curtain
rose, as at the *Français,* with the ominous and sus-
pensive three thumps. Now Daly was wedded to
his musical accompaniments. There was something
swinging and non-committal to take the curtain up,
the principal characters had a lively measure for
their first entrance, played softly at first, and
growing crescendo to their appearance, there were
"hurries" for quick action, chords for climactic
speeches, and ballads *con sordini* for sentimental
scenes. For this essential accompaniment to our
plays Daly engaged an orchestra and planted them
behind the scenes with cues and prompter. When
we made our entrances the audience, hearing the
music, thought *we were going to sing!* However,
no fault could be found with our reception nor the
enthusiasm evoked.

A TOUR UNPARALLELED

During the three evenings prior to our opening I saw enough good acting in the Paris theatres to inspire me tremendously. The ease, the eloquence of gesture, facial expression and attitude, the freshness of manner, the spontaneity of action which was yet under complete control, the clean clear diction and, above all, the perfect *mise en scène* were object lessons of inestimable value. What do we not owe to France for the beauty of her theatrical art!

From Paris we trekked across England once more, playing for a week at Liverpool to appreciation and profit, and then to Ireland. Dublin was cordial, was demonstrative, was, in short, *Irish*. The farces went with shouts and the comedies with approval. The press was enthusiastic. The ancestral strain of Irish blood in Daly's veins reacted to the warmth.

When our Cunard steamer bumped her nose into the dock at New York and people and press had made much of our welcome home I felt I had been living through the adventures of an Arabian Night. Five foreign countries in four months—a tour unparalleled in the history of the American stage.

In midwinter of the ensuing season Augustin Daly achieved his highwater mark in the production of THE TAMING OF THE SHREW. Not in the memory of any playgoer had this play been given in its entirety in America. We became, as it were, the "creators" of the characters in a play by Shakespeare. The quaint "induction" was restored, the episode of *Bianca* and her lovers, and many scenes the lines of which had never been spoken to American ears.

Rehan's *Katherina* in a blaze of terra cotta brocade, wigged in a wreath of curling red hair, was a gorgeous thing to look upon as she dashed storming upon the scene at her first appearance. Drew's *Petruchio* was his best Shakespearean performance. Lewis, always miserable and downcast when the old plays were put on, was, nevertheless, amusing as *Gremio,* and the entire company, Fisher, Leclercq, Mrs. Gilbert, Frederick Bond, Joe Holland, Miss Dreher, in fine fettle.

It is interesting to note the name of Master W. Collier in the cast; this is none other than our own William Collier. Willie was our call boy, a prankish youth who little dreamed of the golden fate the years were bringing him.

My part of *Lucentio* did not trouble me seriously. Daly generally allowed me my own way in Shakespeare and the old comedies.

It was during the run of this play that I first saw Doctor Horace Howard Furness. An outsider behind the scenes was an untoward event in Daly's Theatre, particularly as a spectator in the wings, but Daly had made an exception in the case of the eminent Shakespearean scholar on account of his deafness, and had planted him and his ear-trumpet in the prompt entrance where he viewed and heard our proceedings with evident pleasure.

In later years it was my privilege to know

THIS EVENING, TUESDAY, JANUARY 18, 1887,

First Representation in America of

Shakspere's

Comedy, in Five Acts and AN INDUCTION, slightly modified and re-arranged, for the present
occasion, by Mr. AUGUSTIN DALY, entitled:

The Taming of the Shrew.

.The NEW SCENES by Mr. JAMES ROBERTS and Mr. HENRY E. HOYT. The NEW HISTORICAL
COSTUMES by Messrs. ARNOLD & CONSTABLE, from designs by E. Hamilton Bell, Esq.;
and the original and selected INCIDENTAL MUSIC by Mr. HENRY WIDMER.

Characters in the "INDUCTION."

A LORD..Mr. GEORGE CLARKE
CHRISTOPHER SLY, a drunken tinker.........Mr. WILLIAM GILBERT
THE HOSTESS..Miss M. SYLVIE
A PAGE, representing a lady.......................Master W. COLLIER
HUNTSMEN............Mr. PATTEN, Mr. IRETON, Mr. MURPHY, &c.
PLAYERS....... ....Mr. BOND, Mr. WOOD, Miss HADLEY

Persons in the Comedy.

BAPTISTA, a rich gentleman of Padua............Mr. CHARLES FISHER
VINCENTIO, an old gentleman of Pisa.................Mr. JOHN MOORE
LUCENTIO, son to Vincentio, loving Bianca..........Mr. OTIS SKINNER
PETRUCIO, a gentleman of Verona, suitor to Katherine..Mr. JOHN DREW
GREMIO, an old gentleman...... } suitors to { ..Mr. CHARLES LECLERCQ
HORTENSIO, a young gentleman } Bianca } ....Mr. JOSEPH HOLLAND
A PEDANT, an old fellow, set up to represent Vincentio..Mr. JOHN WOOD
A TAILOR...Mr. GEORGE PARKES
GRUMIO, serving man to Petrucio........ ....Mr. JAMES LEWIS
BIONDELLO........ } servants to Lucentio { ....Mr. E. P. WILKS
TRANIO........ ,,. } {..........Mr. FRED'K BOND

Guests, singers, servants, &c.

KATHERINE, the Shrew.............................Miss ADA REHAN
BIANCA, her sister..............................Miss VIRGINIA DREHER
A WIDOW, who marries Hortensio.............Miss JEAN GORDON
CURTIS, of Petrucio's household..................Mrs. G. H. GILBERT

THE INDUCTION.

Scene 1.—Before an Alehouse on a Heath (ROBERTS).
Scene 2.—A Bedchamber in the Lord's House. .(ROBERTS).

THE PLAY.

ACT I.—*Scene:* Padua. A Public Place. (ROBERTS.)
ACT II.—*Scene:* A Salon in Baptista's House. (ROBERTS).
ACT III.—*(Same scene.)*
ACT IV.—*Scene 1.* Before Baptista's House. (ROBERTS)
    Scene 2. A Hall in Petrucio's Country House. (ROBERTS.)
ACT V.—*Scene 1.* Before Lucentio's House. (ROBERTS.)
    Scene 2. Banquet Hall in Lucentio's House. (HOYT.)

*** The song, "*Should He Upbraid*" (music by Sir HENRY BISHOP), which will be given in the
final tableau, is sung by MISS ST. QUENTIN and a choir of boy voices.

I TUNE MY FIDDLE

Doctor Furness in his own home in Wallingford. An evening there was an unforgettable occasion. In his library one night after dinner he read aloud to us, in his rich mellow voice, Maurice Baring's "diminutive drama," THE REHEARSAL. He laughed over it until at times he had to stop reading. We laughed too, but no one could visualize the scene as he could—this rehearsal in the time of Shakespeare with the temperamental Burbage as *Macbeth*. It has always seemed to me that the consolation in deafness must be in being spared much that is commonplace. To speak into that gleaming ear-trumpet of Doctor Furness's was a privilege that brought forth one's best efforts—mental and vocal.

In the fall of 1887 the theatre was opened with DANDY DICK, a racing play by Pinero. In it I had to *play the violin,* and I do not and never could, play the violin! The illusion, however, was well managed. I tuned my fiddle and was accompanied by Effie Shannon—a charming actress—upon the piano. I bowed the instrument pantomimically against an opening in the window curtains, behind which Widmer, our leader, played MY PRETTY JANE, with great sweetness. Heaven knows how many times we rehearsed it. Miss Shannon didn't play the piano any too well, but she had really to play and she was nervous. I was praying that the audience would not detect the trick and jeer at me. It was fearfully difficult for we had lines to speak through the music. The trick finished, I was astounded at receiving an insistent encore. We could not repeat, without repeating the scene, lines, business and all. The house had taken the bait and believed it real. I bowed repeatedly in an agony of deprecation, while Daly was tying himself into knots of mirth down in the front entrance. Widmer had been altogether too good!

In January we gave A MIDSUMMER NIGHT'S DREAM ornamented with electrical effects, music, songs, dances, a panorama, fire-flies, chirping crickets and general prettiness. Lewis was intensely funny as *Bottom*—Shakespeare's super-clown, in spite of his favorite protest that the poet was "no friend of his."

With March came the historic blizzard of 1888. The city was buried in vast snow-drifts, people were imprisoned in their houses, traffic annihilated, railroads blocked and food supplies stopped; telegraph and telephone connection cut off. Many people perished from cold and exposure. New York looked out that morning upon arctic desolation. About mid-afternoon I fought my way through the drifts from my lodgings in Washington Square to the Lambs' Club, where I found food and warmth, and later, buffeting the swirling snow I reached the theatre. Our presentation was largely one of understudies before a handful of forlorn people— many of the cast were snow-bound and one member, Leclercq, was held prisoner on Long Island for four days. Besides ourselves, and Irving and Terry down at the Star, only one other theatre in all New York opened its doors.

THE YOUNG LAMBS

Not the least factor in the theatrical life of the 'eighties was the swirl that drew some of us off the stream of Broadway down Twenty-Sixth Street to the old Lambs' Club. Its inception had come from Wallack's leading man, handsome Harry Montague, and it became a cherished meeting-place for the English theatre folk engaged in New York. In time its popularity spread among our native actors. It was not the splendidly prosperous club that to-day preserves the name of The Lambs, but a coterie of a few men of the stage and men about town who affected the theatre. Its furnishings were not sumptuous; we were a poor club, but I can not bring to mind a membership that included Charles Coghlan, Maurice Barrymore, Osmund Tearle, John Drew, Ned and Joe Holland, Robert Mantell, Kyrle Bellew, Digby Bell, DeWolf Hopper, Richard Mansfield, Tom Whiffen, William H. Crane, Nat Goodwin, Henry Dixey, Marshall Wilder, Clay Greene, Augustus Thomas, Steele Mackaye, without the glow of good company stealing about my heart.

Lester Wallack was a sort of perpetual *Shepherd,* being continually reelected to office. Monthly dinners were served with as good food as our resources could command, and in the long list of guests appeared the names of Irving, Wilson Barrett, W. H. Kendall, Chauncey Depew, General Horace Porter, General Sherman, E. S. Willard, William Winter, Edgar Saltus, Buffalo Bill, and many more in honor of whom the fonts of wit and eloquence were tapped.

161

An afternoon at the Lambs would sometimes find Steele Mackaye, tall, spare, emotional and eloquent, looking like a more stalwart Edgar Allan Poe, holding forth to a knot of listeners on some theory destined never to be realized, some dream never to become articulate. He was always magnetic and compelling.

And one would be pretty sure to find Joe somewhere about—Joe, the well-beloved—the youngest of the sons of that Holland whose funeral service made the fame of "The Little Church around the Corner."

There was a shout from adoring Lambs whenever Maurice Barrymore entered. This founder of the house of Barrymore was English-born, Herbert Blythe—preeminently a man's man, and beyond question a woman's man, of a wit so telling and yet so good-hearted that even the objects of his keen satire, joined in laughter at their own expense. On the stage he was always a picture—in private, an Apollo in a slop suit. Amateur champion middleweight boxer, narrator of a thousand stories, quick in resentment of an insult, generous to a foe, burner of candles at both ends, Bedouin of Broadway, this was the Barrymore that I knew.

A sinister figure in the sporting life of New York at this time was Jerry Dunn, a promotor of boxing matches and athletic tournaments, familiar to frequenters of race meets and affairs at Madison Square Garden. Dunn had shot and killed Jimmy Elliott, a prize-fighter, and though acquitted on the ground of self-defense was said to be pursued by the face of his victim and would never go to bed in the dark. His nights were his days. When cafés closed their doors, he would wander forth in company or alone, but never to bed. Now and then going to my Washington Square lodgings toward the morning hour, I would catch a glimpse of the solitary figure of a bearded, faultlessly dressed man smoking a cigar, standing in the recess of a Broadway entrance somewhere above Twenty-Third Street. It was Jerry Dunn waiting for the dawn.

The third European trip of the Daly Company began in May at the Gaiety Theatre, London, with THE RAILROAD OF LOVE, which met complete and instant failure. The favor which the London public, famed for its fickleness, had bestowed upon the organization in 1886 at the Strand, went glimmering. There were thirteen weeks laid out at the Gaiety and no new plays to fill the time. The prospect was black. There was, however, THE TAMING OF THE SHREW, but Shakespeare in the English capital by American actors? It seemed a temerity. Our comedians had established a reputation in modern farces and the lightest of old comedies, but when it came to Shakespeare a still small voice said, "Hands off!" The one point of vantage lay in the fact that the piece had not been known in London since the days of Samuel Phelps at Sadler's Wells Theatre, and few critics and scarcely any laymen could remember anything about it. But the air was filled with omens. To cap the forebodings of the opening night our leading lady flew into a rage over some fancied injustice, and refused to go on. It was a full half-hour after the advertised time before the curtain rose. Success or failure hung on a hair. Every one was keyed up. The events of the first act were viewed without objection, but when Ada Rehan, all fire from her late tantrum, tore into view like a tigress, the house capitulated and the story was told. The big Gaiety Theatre was crowded until the end of the engagement. We even went to the birthplace of the poet and acted his comedy in the Memorial Theatre.

This occasion was made joyous in my companionship for the day with William Winter, poet and critic. Winter loved his Stratford. We wandered about the village, and talked of delightful things. We crossed the fields to Anne Hathaway's cottage at Shottery. As we passed through the gate and over the stones of the flower-edged walk, old Mrs. Baker, long custodian of the place and a descendant of the Hathaways, was standing in the doorway.

"Why, it's Mister Winter!" she cried, and thereupon he was as welcome as a prodigal son.

While passing through the Shakespeare Inn where the sleeping-rooms, instead of being numbered, are named after plays, he pointed to that labeled, Love's Labour's Lost, and with a chuckle remarked, "They call that the bridal chamber."

In spite of the air of dejection and melancholy he habitually wore, he was possessed of a humor which now and then flavored a delicious anecdote.

One he told of piloting Joseph Jefferson to the Shrine of Shakespeare on the occasion of Jefferson's first visit to England.

"We walked through the quiet streets," he said; "it was at the evening hour when Stratford is soft and dreamy in the twilight. A lark was winging its way up into the heavens and sending down a shower of melody upon us. Presently we turned a corner and stood before the house in Henley Street.

" 'Joseph,' I said, 'this is the spot.'

" 'The birthplace, Willie?' he asked.

" 'Yes, Joseph; the place in which our beloved Shakespeare first saw the light.'

"Joseph raised his hat. We stood silent. And I thanked God at the time, and I thank God to-day, that Joseph had the sense to keep his G— d—n mouth shut."

(Willie was a little afraid of Joseph's quick and ready wit.)

Paris was again visited for a week. Press comment was mixed; though generally favorable, one paper pronounced THE TAMING OF THE SHREW to be crude and brutal. An English provincial tour, Dublin once more and then home on the Cunard S. S. *Servia*.

In the stream of receptions and refections tendered to our members, was a delightful supper in the old Beefsteak Club room of the Lyceum Theatre where the grave and gentle courtesy of Henry Irving, the warmth of his greeting, the sincerity of his praise for the work of our chief and of our own efforts, the grace and infectious spirit of Ellen Terry, the speeches from noted men in the world of literature and art, the mellow atmosphere of good fellowship, stand vividly in my recollections of many hospitalities. Another occasion was a dinner tendered us by John Hare at the Garrick Club. Literary, dramatic, scientific, musical, artistic, political and titled England were represented there. Besides ourselves there were other Americans present, among whom was Bret Harte, a voluntary exile from his California—almost an expatriate. Rosy-faced, white-haired, few would have taken him for anything but a Briton.

About the walls hung protraits of the Kembles, Siddons, Garrick, Macready and other lights of the stage painted by Sir Thomas Lawrence, Hogarth, Reynolds, Gainsborough. It was a night of comradeship, brilliant in wit. About four in the morning, William Winter, replete with good cheer, bathed in sentiment and suspiciously moist about the eyelids, said to me in a dreamy sad tone:

"What a night! What a wonderful night!" then in deeper woe: "But *they never asked me to speak,*" and waving his hand to the framed masterpieces lining the walls, he added: "And what I *could* have said with these faces looking down on me!"

The strange part of this occasion was the absence of Augustin Daly. John Hare had extended the invitations to us individually, and because they did not first pass through his hands, Daly hid in his Achilles' tent and made no sign.

166

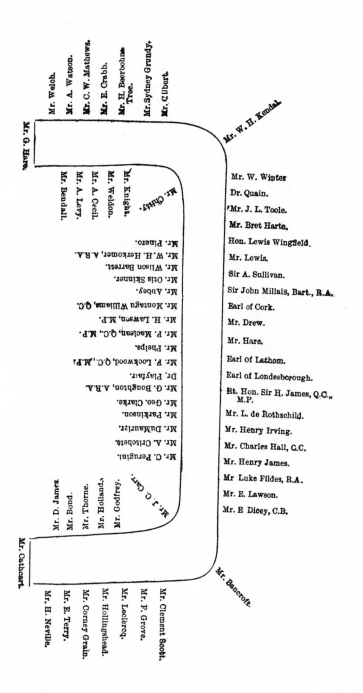

Mr. Welch. Mr. A. Watson. Mr. C. W. Mathews. Mr. E. Crabb. Mr. H. Beerbohm Tree. Mr. Sydney Grundy. Mr. C. Ubert.

Mr. G. Hare.   Mr. W. H. Kendal.

Mr. Bendall. Mr. A. Levy. Mr. A. Cecil. Mr. Weldon. Mr. Knight. Mr. Chitt.

Mr. Pinero. Mr. W. H. Herkomer, A.R.A. Mr. Wilson Barrett. Mr. Otis Skinner. Mr. Abbey. Mr. Montagu Williams, Q.C. Mr. H. Lawson, M.P. Mr. F. Maclean, Q.C., M.P. Mr. Phelps. Mr. F. Lockwood, Q.C., M.P. Dr. Playfair. Mr. G. Boughton, A.R.A. Mr. Geo. Clarke. Mr. Parkinson. Mr. DuMaurier. Mr. A. Critchett. Mr. C. Perugini.

Mr. J. C. Carr.

Mr. W. Winter
Dr. Quain.
Mr. J. L. Toole.
Mr. Bret Harte.
Hon. Lewis Wingfield.
Mr. Lewis.
Sir A. Sullivan.
Sir John Millais, Bart., R.A.
Earl of Cork.
Mr. Drew.
Mr. Hare.
Earl of Lathom.
Earl of Londesborough.
Rt. Hon. Sir H. James, Q.C., M.P.
Mr. L. de Rothschild.
Mr. Henry Irving.
Mr. Charles Hall, C.C.
Mr. Henry James.
Mr Luke Fildes, R.A.
Mr. E. Lawson.
Mr. E Dicey, C.B.

Mr. D. James. Mr. Bond. Mr. Thorne. Mr. Holland. Mr. Godfrey.

Mr. Cathcart.   Mr. Bancroft.

Mr. H. Neville. Mr. E. Terry. Mr. Corney Grain. Mr. Hollingshead. Mr. Leclercq. Mr. F. Grove. Mr. Clement Scott.

FOOTLIGHTS AND SPOTLIGHTS

There were glorious nights, *and mornings,* at the Green Room, the Savage, the Arundul and kindred clubs, and my recollections of Du Maurier, Sir Frederick Leighton, Whistler, George Boughton, Edwin Abbey, Comyns Carr, cheery and vociferous old Joe Knight, the critic, Justin McCarthy, Toole, Bancroft, Wilson Barrett, Beerbohm Tree, Sir John Millais, are still keen.

I can speak but little of my last year at Daly's Theatre. The governor and I had a quarrel of a personal nature, and our relations became strained. I appeared infrequently—only in revivals, and we parted, after five years' association, without a word. My memory of Augustin Daly is that of a very unusual man. His theatre was his shrine as well as his workshop; his labors therein so fierce and incessant that, when new managers in the field were disputing his leadership, his forces weakened and the machinery of his mind and body, long overtaxed, wore itself out. This strange, moody, iron-willed man carried many secrets to the grave, not the least of which was the story of a broken heart.

He crossed my horizon at a critical hour of my career. Greater than to any one man I have ever known is my debt to Augustin Daly.

CHAPTER XI

ONE late winter day, during my last season at Daly's, I ran into Lawrence Barrett. In the stream of pedestrians on Broadway I saw his top-heavy head with its accustomed tall silk hat floating my way, and remembering his pique at my leaving him five years before, I prepared myself for a frosty greeting. Nothing of the kind! His deep gray eyes lighted, a smile spread over his tight-shut lips, and he fairly opened his arms to me.

"I suppose, Mr. Skinner, that you're a fixture up there at Thirtieth Street; bed of roses, eh?"

I lied like truth. "Oh, yes, Mr. Barrett," I replied, "I'm extremely happy."

At the end of our chat he said, "Well, if you ever *do* leave, I want you to know there's always a place with me."

I was so delighted that nothing but diplomacy prevented my telling him that my job "up there" was very far from being a fixture. After a few weeks I wrote to him that I was free, and he replied at once, offering me a list of parts with Edwin Booth, with whom he had been co-starring, many of which, *Laertes, Macduff, DeMauprat, Bassanio,* he himself had been playing. He was sundering this

169

association for the ensuing year, though he still held the management of Mr. Booth, and was coupling him with Helena Modjeska, then in the very height of her popularity. In addition to the parts I have named, I was to play *Mortimer* in MARY STUART, and *Don Cæsar* in DONNA DIANA—two favorite, pieces in Madame's repertory.

Before the season opened I went to Chicago and produced a play at the Grand Opera House. While I had been drawing my weekly stipend through the previous months at Daly's, and rendering but little service for it, my brother Charles and I busied ourselves in writing a play treating with questions of labor. The piece was frank melodrama—blast furnaces, trip hammers, strike riots and general unpleasantness—had stir and sensation and was well acted by a company which I took out with me; but I can not say that our first effort marked an epoch in playwriting. It struggled against heat and a particularly ugly street-car strike, and after two weeks of life, it lay down very quietly, very resignedly and gave up its ghost.

Hic jacet THE RED SIGNAL!

I took my medicine with what philosophy I could command, and sucked consolation out of the few pleasant comments in the papers,—THE TRIBUNE saying that it was "a melodrama of ideas and a creditable essay on an American theme." All of which was no dampener on my enthusiasm over the coming engagement with Booth and Modjeska.

Of Madame I shall have more to say in a later

chapter. Her consent to this joint starring tour which, after all, had some of the features of "especial support," had been gained not only through a contract for a large certainty, but because of her great admiration for the artistry of Edwin Booth. I was to have the stimulus of the acting of two of the foremost artists of their day, and the tonic of the big plays once more. I had been spending overmuch time with the magnifying-glass. Breadth was what I needed now. Breadth and vigor, the music of ringing verse, lofty passions, vital action.

The Edwin Booth I found now was a different man from the one I had known. Ten years had dug devitalizing claws into his strength, his spirit and his ambition. It was more the shell of the great actor; symmetrical still, but with the echo of youthful inspiration growing fainter. His impersonations had been gone through so many times that he had almost forgotten the days when he hurled himself into them, hot-blooded and uncurbed. He had wearied of his life of turbulence. A success beyond measure had been his, and he had known the bitterness of defeat and bankruptcy. Death had early taken his first and greatest love—Mary Devlin—while the days of his second wife—Mary McVicker—were clouded by illness and mental collapse. His brother, John Wilkes' crime, his father's insanity, the malfeasance of trusted employees and friends, the excesses of a riotous youth that had swung him between the poles of ecstasy and despair—these things had left on him a weariness and a sadness that had but little of bitterness. Many things had been printed about him the reverse of favorable. "I suppose," he remarked to me once, apropos of newspaper vituperation, "no one on the stage has had more abusive articles written about him than I have. It is the penalty I've paid for good things."

Through all his reverses, and his periods of soul agony, he never lost hold on his ideal. With such gentleness as his it was singular that his greatest effects should have been made in parts of sinister and diabolic character—*Iago, Richard, Bertuccio, Macbeth, Pescara, Shylock.*

In MUCH ADO ABOUT NOTHING, we made our first appearance together, he leaning on my shoulder, as *Benedick* and *Claudio.* He generally arrived at the entrance some minutes before the cue, and I loved the interval of gossip, especially if he happened to be in a pleasant mood, which, as *Benedick,* he frequently was, although he disliked the part. "This fellow is a lover," he said, and his lip curled in contempt. "I loathe the whole pack of them. Always did. Even as a youngster I loved the villains."

The world in which he lived apart from the publicity of his stage appearances was a small one, measured by his few close friendships, but those friendships were so fine and strong that they made his world one of vast beauty and true companionship, peopled with the imaginings of the artist and the dreamer. His benefactions were many. His purse always opened to a tale of woe from an un-

1894

1889

fortunate member of his craft. It was his fondness
for his fellow players that gave to them the club
house, books and treasures that stand for a conser-
vation of the art and tradition of the English-speak-
ing theatre—The Players, in Gramercy Park.

A tale I have heard him tell illuminates the
much-discussed question of how far, and how
keenly, the actor should feel the emotion of the
parts he plays.

"One night in THE FOOL'S REVENGE I became
aware that my acting had gone beyond a merely mechanical performance of the *Jester*. It was all real
to me. I was *Bertuccio*. The love and tenderness
I expressed for *Fiordelisa* were my own love and
tenderness; it was my own malevolence that I spat
out against the *Duke*, and my own anguish which
shrieked at the discovery of my daughter's betray-
al. It was an entirely new experience. I came off
the last scene with tears streaming down my cheeks,
and my body racked with emotion. While I was
recalling myself in a kind of wonder that it had
truly happened—in a theatre—before an audience,
my own daughter who had been watching the play
from a box, came running up in some alarm. She
put her hand on my forehead, felt my hands and
said: 'Father, what's the matter with you?' I was
pleased indeed. She had felt it too. 'I did play it
well, didn't I?' I cried. 'Play it well! That was
the worst performance of *Bertuccio* you ever gave
in your whole life!'"

His rare frolic-mood broke out one night at Vincennes, Indiana, where a large guarantee had secured the appearance of the Booth and Modjeska Company in HAMLET on an absurd little stage over a harness shop. Our scenery couldn't be squeezed into the building, so the local outfit was used. The quay at Elsinore was represented by a modern lawn on which was painted a set of croquet wickets and a pair of brick gate posts one of which was surmounted by a *feather duster*. Down in front of the footlights was a white reflecting board displaying in large black letters this startling admonition: DO NOT SPIT IN THE TROUGH! Mr. Booth had been on some time before he saw it, then, in the soliloquy, I noticed he was shaky in his lines. His face was twitching as he galloped through the remainder of the scene at top speed. When he came off he gasped: "Did you see it? Did you see it! It's worse than Mark Twain's

> 'Pink trip slip for a six cent fare
> Punch in the presence of the passenjare.'

What would the audience have thought if I had said: 'To be or not to be—*Do not spit in the trough* —that is the question. Whether 'tis nobler in the mind not to spit in the trough, or to take arms against a sea of troubles and, by spitting in the trough, end them!' " He went to his dressing-room chuckling.

The repertory was for the most part, HAMLET, THE MERCHANT OF VENICE, MACBETH and RICHELIEU, though MUCH ADO ABOUT NOTHING was occasionally given, and two double bills—THE FOOL'S REVENGE with DONNA DIANA, and DON CÆSAR DE BAZAN with MARY STUART, which gave each star an opportunity.

In November, 1889, they appeared for the first time together in MACBETH. I was cast for *Macduff,* one of the most grateful of Shakespearean rôles. Barrett had been playing it the season previous. The fight in the last act had been a rather perfunctory affair, Booth's physical weakness increasing always toward the end of the tragedy, and Barrett going very gingerly with him. It now became necessary for him to rehearse the combat with me. After a few minutes of what seemed to me but gentle exercise, he sank panting into a chair, saying: "My God! I haven't worked as much as that for twenty years." I had thought our taps with the broadswords had been quite lovingly tender but Booth was near collapse. The catastrophe, however, was reserved for the night. I was nervous and over-keyed for my first performance. We came to the fight. The first meeting of the combatants is where *Macduff,* seeing *Macbeth* about to fly, rushes at him with uplifted sword, crying: "Turn, hell-hound, turn!" A down-swinging blow accompanies the line, and is parried by *Macbeth.* In a surge of excitement, I rushed at Booth and our heavy broadswords crashed; the swing broke through his guard, his wrist crumpled like a child's, and my sword caught him straight upon the *crown of his head.* A sick feeling came over me. I turned giddy. For an instant Booth swayed—then he whispered, "Go on!" We fought to the end with blows that children's sticks might strike in a game. The curtain fell: I helped him to his feet, but I haven't the least remembrance of the incoherent apologies I babbled. Lifting his wig, he disclosed a bump as big as a chicken's egg. His head covering had saved him. He wore a thick red wig as *Macbeth*, over that a cap of chain mail, while about his head was a circlet of steel in the form of a narrow crown. These stood between him and catastrophe. He smiled over the affair, but my feelings were too frenzied to describe.

His lack of care for his health was reckless in the extreme. For years the only exercise he took was the physical work of acting. He scarcely ever walked; he moved about slowly, and the constant companions of his hours at home and of the waits between acts in his dressing-room were his pipe and his long black cigars. I used to go to his dressing-room to call him for our entrance together in the first act of THE MERCHANT OF VENICE, and he rarely laid aside his book or paper and rose to his feet without being seized with a vertigo. He would reel like a drunken man, and his first steps would be quite uncertain.

"Why don't you try exercise?" I once asked him. "I think it might benefit you."

"That's what Joe Jefferson told me," he answered. "I tried it—went out every morning and walked up and down the street. I got completely tired out for my pains, and it ruined my acting at night."

One night, during our Cleveland week, he was passing through the dirty railway station, returning from the theatre, and spying the lunch counter, deserted, bleak and unappetizing, he decided he would go in. It was useless to remind him that in his private car was an abundant supper, carefully prepared and wholesome; no, he was obsessed by the lunch counter. There was nothing for his business manager, Arthur Chase, and me to do but accompany him into the dingy room, watch him perch on the high stool in his long ulster and devour hard boiled eggs, doughnuts and railroad coffee.

We had forebodings. It seemed impossible for one who ordinarily depended on liquid preparations of beef, iron, etc., to assimilate that mass of indigestibles. We were anxious for his appearance in the morning. He arose unusually alert, declaring that he'd had a beautiful dreamless sleep, and although the car had been bumped by switching engines in freight yards all night long, he hadn't had such a peaceful night in years.

One glimpse of Booth's brooding spirit was given me after his death by an old property man who began life as a basket boy at Booth's Theatre. Mr. Booth was very fond of this lad, Garrie Davidson, and employed him frequently in his personal service.

It was well known how terrible a blow to the tragedian had been his brother's assassination of

President Lincoln. For a while it was feared that it was affecting his reason; he was abnormally sensitive to the remotest reference to it.

At some date prior to the tragedy at Washington, the theatrical wardrobe and personal effects of John Wilkes Booth were alleged to have been confided to the care of John McCullough, for between the two men there had existed a sympathetic acquaintance, and conveyed by him into Canada. There was never a suspicion that McCullough had the remotest knowledge of the fanatic's purpose in wishing to remove his wardrobe from the country. Presumably, after threats of vengeance arose against all sorts of real and alleged conspirators, McCullough abandoned the trunk.

Only a few years ago, Harry Hawk, who played in OUR AMERICAN COUSIN and was on the stage at Ford's Theatre speaking the lines of *Asa Trenchard* at the moment that President Lincoln was shot, came to my house at Bryn Mawr for lunch. He talked of the tragedy and of the fact that not only were all the members of the Laura Keene Company placed under arrest for forty-eight hours, but so were all the actors in Washington. A cry went out for the arrest of the whole profession. John Wilkes Booth was not in the bill at the time, but he was in and out of the theatre, and it was said that among his theatre acquaintances there was a suspicion, and perhaps a knowledge, that some sinister plot was afoot, but there was no evidence, Hawk said, of either sympathy or assistance from Booth's fel-

178

low players. He was generally thought to have con-
templated the *abduction* of the president to a point
well beyond Mason and Dixon's line.

It was not until 1873 that Edwin Booth located
the whereabouts of the trunk, and had it forwarded
to him, by McKee Rankin, the actor, then engaged professionally in the Province. The story of
the disposal of the trunk and its contents, I put here
in Garrie Davidson's own words:

"Mr. Booth, you will remember, had a suite of
rooms over the stage where most of his time was
spent between his hours of business and acting. On
leaving his dressing-room this night, about twelve
o'clock, he gave me orders to wake him at three in
the morning. After the lights of the theatre were
out, I lay on a cot in the property room, but of
course I couldn't sleep. The day had been stormy;
sleet was beating on the window-panes and strange
sounds came from every part of the big empty theatre. I was glad when the time came for the call;
the three hours from midnight had been the longest
I ever knew.

"I mounted the stairway to his apartment, and
made him some strong coffee over a spirit lamp in
the library. This done, I opened the door to the
bedroom. He was lying partly dressed and in a
dead sleep. Mr. Booth had one peculiarity—he was
confused and irritated if suddenly wakened from
sleep; sometimes he would throw the nearest article
at hand at the one who roused him. As a precau-
tion I removed the pipe and book with which he had

179

smoked and read himself to sleep; his tobacco jar
(he was a great smoker)—and all the movables
from the reading-stand beside the bed—even his
boots I put out of the way, then I shook him gently
and told him it was time. As I expected he sat up
in a daze, and reached for something to throw at
me, but it was only a flash. For a minute or two he
sat sort of studying the bedclothes, very thoughtful.
I fetched the coffee. After drinking two cups of it,
he asked:

" 'Still snowing, Garrie?'

" 'Yes, sir.'

"I helped him into his coat.

" 'Where shall I go, Mr. Booth,' I asked.

" 'To the furnace room,' he said.

"Taking the lantern I had left outside his door I
led the way across the black stage and down to the
furnace room. The fireman had banked the fires
and gone home for the night when the performance
was over, but soon the drafts in the old-fashioned
heater were roaring again. I lighted a gas-jet, but
it didn't do much good. Over near the furnace
there was a large trunk, like a packing-case, tied
with ropes. He told me to get an ax. I cut the
cords and knocked off the top of the box which was
rickety and old. There lay the costumes of John
Wilkes Booth, all musty and smelling of camphor.

"There was no tray in the trunk—the things
were just packed up solid, and on the top of the pile
were some swords and wigs. These, after a moment
or two, he laid aside on the overturned trunk cover,

and commenced taking out the costumes. The first was a Louis XVI coat of steel-blue broadcloth. *'Claude Melnotte!'* I thought and was aching to ask, but I held my tongue. He turned it about at arm's length as if he were trying to picture his brother's figure in it, and remembering when he had worn it last. Then he handed it to me. 'Put it in there,' he said, pointing to the heater. I opened the door. 'Twas a shame to destroy anything so handsome! I looked back at him; he was as still as a statue, waiting. There was no help for it. I shoved it in. It settled down on the blaze with a sort of hiss—a bit of lace at the sleeve caught, and the coat was in flames. A satin waistcoat, a pair of knee breeches, and several pairs of tights followed the coat. He didn't spend much time over these; merely handed them to me, and motioned toward the fire. Some of them had J. W. B. on the lining in marking ink.

"There was a black-beaded *Hamlet* hauberk which Mr. Booth turned about curiously before passing to me. It didn't need much guessing to know how hard it was for him to part with it. Then there came some 'shape' dresses—Elizabethan— silk stockings and velvet shoes. They may have been worn for *Iago*—he had played the part. There were cavalier's costumes like those used in THE HUNCHBACK and THE DUKE'S MOTTO. These had seen service and showed their wear, for John Wilkes' most successful performances, with the exception of his *Richard III*, had been in the romantic plays. One, particularly fine, was a cut-leather jerkin with slashed green velvet sleeves, a sword belt to match, studded with steel nail heads, velvet trunks like the sleeves, and a broad-brimmed hat with an ostrich feather. These, with a pair of cavalier boots, went to the funeral pyre. Then his Roman things for *Marc Antony*, the velvet coat and gray trousers he had worn for *Raphael* in the MARBLE HEART; his costumes for *Romeo, Shylock,* and a gorgeous robe for *Othello* made of two East Indian shawls, so fine you could have pulled them through a bracelet.

"Done up in a cloth was an Indian dress—genuine thing—with a photograph of John Wilkes in the same costume, dated Richmond, Virginia, 1859-60. I guess that was *Metamora.*

"It was awful to watch him sit there without a word, inspecting each article, touching it as if it were his own flesh and blood before handing it to me to be burned. Sometimes a draft sent sparks through the furnace door into the cellar until it looked as if the building might catch. He didn't notice them; he was staring into the flames.

"He came across a package of letters, wrapped in a handkerchief, and tied with an old ribbon. As he examined their addresses, I shot a glance over his shoulder and saw that they were directed to Wilkes in a woman's handwriting. He had looked at only a few, when his eyes flashed, and setting his jaws, he stepped over and threw the package on the coals. 'Twas like the way he'd blaze out in *Othello.* But it was over in a moment—temper was always

182

that way with him. Since that night I've often wondered who had written those letters. No one will ever know.

"Presently he drew out a long, belted, purple velvet shirt, ornamented with jewels, and an arm-hole cloak trimmed in fur. Both garments were creased, and worn in places. He sat down on the trunk with the things on his knee, and for a while he didn't move—just sat looking at the costume; then he broke down and cried like a child.

" 'My father's,' he said. 'Garrie, it was my father's *Richard III* dress. He wore it in Boston on the first night I went on the stage as *Tressell*.

" 'Don't you think you ought to save that, Mr. Booth?' I asked.

" 'No, put it in with the others,' he said.

"By and by it was nothing but ashes. I felt as if I had assisted at a crime.

"He didn't linger so long now except, maybe, to pause over a costume as if he were puzzling his brain to recall what part it had been used for. He was eager to see every fragment destroyed. I turned the flaming stuff so constantly with the long furnace poker that my face and hands were scorched with heat. Sometimes he took the iron rod from me and did the work himself.

"At the bottom of the trunk we found a couple of daggers—they were beauties—scraps of stage jewelry, some odds and ends, and a pair of woman's satin dancing slippers. These were thrown on to the coals with the wigs—and even the swords, they would melt and break before the fire would die down. He had me knock the trunk to pieces, and that, with the ropes that bound it, was the finish. We stood watching the snaky rims running through the ashes, then he told me to shut the furnace door.

"'That's all,' he said very quietly, 'we'll go now.'

"I looked at my watch; it was nearly six.

"The morning was still black and stormy. Somewhere a loose shutter was banging against the side of the building, and booming through the empty galleries.

"Whatever feeling he had shown down in the furnace room was gone now. As we were crossing the stage he said, 'Thank you, Garrie. You needn't come.'

"'Good morning, sir,' I replied, but he just nodded, and I stood at the foot of the stairs with my lantern until I heard the door shut in his rooms.'"*

It was written that Madame Modjeska should, while we were filling an engagement at The Academy of Music in Brooklyn, step on a treacherous plank and twist her ankle, and that, in consequence, I should have a chance to play *Petruchio.*

---

*In an article by H. H. Kohlsaat in *The Saturday Evening Post* of February 9th, 1924, Mr. Kohlsaat quotes a letter written by Edwin Booth to President Andrew Johnson, in 1869, requesting that his brother's body be delivered to him at Baltimore for interment in the Booth family burial lot. The letter also refers to a trunk of John Wilkes Booth as being held by the national authorities. This, I assume, contained private and personal effects and should not be confused with the trunk mentioned in Garrie Davidson's story.

I WEAR BOOTH'S CLOTHES

On Monday evening in Philadelphia, Mr. Booth said to me: "I'm going to ask you to help me out. You know we no longer are a two-star team. Madame Modjeska will be out of the bill for three weeks. They want me to give THE FOOL'S REVENGE on Wednesday. Now, I can't do that and another play as well, and THE FOOL'S REVENGE isn't long enough for an evening. Could you get up in *Petruchio* by Wednesday? I'll furnish you with my costume and do anything to help."

Certainly I could and I would, even though the version of *Katherine* and *Petruchio* was Garrick's cut-down old farce, and I should probably be pretty bad with but two days to memorize the lines. Minna Gale, who had been hastily summoned to replace Madame Modjeska, was in a similar plight; she had never played *Katherine*.

I wore the Booth clothes, did the traditional Booth business in the part, and we got through.

When it was over, a newspaper friend came back to see me with some kindly remarks, and the usual compliments. But, he added, "You certainly speeded it up. What was your hurry?"

"Good lord! I never dared stop," I replied.

It was a singular fate that at the sale of the tragedian's effects after his death, Volney Streamer, the Players' Club Librarian, knowing that I was out of town and that I would value a souvenir, bid in for me the Booth *Petruchio* costume, which I had worn. And a few years ago, my daughter, Cornelia, wore it for *Petruchio* when the dramatic club f her girls' school at Bryn Mawr gave THE TAMING OF THE SHREW.

The thirty weeks passed quickly, leaving their inheritance of gain. I got back my breadth again. I attempted, at the first, to express myself in terms of colloquialism, but soon found that blank verse and commonplace, natural expression ran badly in double harness. Mr. Booth said one night, when the curtain fell on the melodramatic finish of the attempted assassination of the *Cardinal* by *De Mauprat* in RICHELIEU, "Mr. Skinner, I think that end needs more lift. It has to be rather strong and noisy, or it doesn't get over." I had enough strength and noise, heaven knows! All I need do was to turn them on.

I have ever cherished my recollection of this truly great actor and lovable man—happy that my acquaintance did not cease at the termination of our business association, but went on through his declining days at The Players' Club. He had hosts of acquaintances, and a world of worshipers, but few people *knew* Edwin Booth. He was fond of a small knot of professional friends with whom, over a cigar, he could lapse into gossip and anecdote of the past. I have often watched his eyes—the *Hamlet* eyes—that were wont to hold a world of pensive suggestion, slowly brightening under the influence of genial talk; little upward lines would appear at their corners, the brows strike a humorous angle, the ends of his thin-lipped mouth commence to twitch, and I knew that these were a prelude to a

186

quaint recital of stage life—perhaps of his days of vagabondage—and that the tale would be voiced in a low, somewhat tired tone. His quiet chuckles noted how keenly he enjoyed living over these episodes of humor—little springs of joy that overlay a bruised and sensitive soul, and which we guessed at only. There were few to whom it was ever frankly revealed,

At The Players the room in which he died is kept intact. The bed, the furniture, the portraits on the walls, intimate surroundings of his hermit life, are as he left them. His pipe lies on the mantel, and under a glass case is the book of verse open at the page he was reading when he fell asleep for the last time.

Once a year the room is thrown open for the reception of "Ladies' Day," and once every month, the directors of the club gather there for their business meeting in the interests of the benefactions bestowed upon his fellow players by Edwin Booth.

CHAPTER XII

OF the engagement that followed the memorable one I had concluded, I always speak with mixed feelings. It took me across the water again to England—a stormy passage in June, 1890, on the *City of Chicago* of the Inman Line—to play *Romeo* to the *Juliet* of a young woman, said to have been the wife of a wealthy man in the paint business, who had laid out a considerable portion of his profits for the purpose of introducing the lady to London in the character of Shakespeare's love-lorn heroine.

The event took place at the Globe Theatre, situated in a little tangle of streets off the Strand, since swept away by the opening up of one of London's great highways.

The presentation was not without merit. It was stage-managed with care, and enlisted the services of some seasoned legitimate actors who took the importation of an American *Romeo* with what grace they could command, albeit I was conscious of an unspoken protest against the deed.

Our star was possibly the very last person in the world one would picture in the character of *Capulet's* daughter—not that she was lacking in comeliness, but that she suggested the full-blown peony

188

rather than the passion flower, and was further handicapped by a lisp that robbed the lines of their melody, which latter defect the uxorious husband-manager-press-agent, with woeful lack of imagination, explained away in an official statement on the opening night as being occasioned by a gum boil. Juliet with a — No! Shades of Fanny Kemble and Adelaide Neilson! I can not bring myself to repeat it.

I viewed with some dismay the queue of shabby, sad-faced "sandwich men" shuffling along in the traffic of the Strand, their front and rear elevations armored with boards announcing the star's name and mine black-lettered on a lurid background of red.

The attendance was sparse; nevertheless, for eight weeks the woes of *Romeo* and *Juliet* were held forth to the delectation of certain curious ones who found their way down Holliwell Street to the Globe Theatre. Herman Vezin, an American who had foresworn his native land and had become one of the bright ornaments of the London stage, wrote me a very nice letter, commending me as "a graceful, poetical and a very fervent lover" and (good stickler for Shakespearean accuracy) made several helpful suggestions about the reading of certain passages.

There was a picturesque relic of other days (palmy and convivial ones), who had once stood high in his profession and had adorned the blank verse of Shakespeare with a voice of music, and his characters with a presence of majesty, but who had looked upon the wine when its colors were iridescent far, far too often. This old boy played *Friar Laurence,* and played it well for a period of five or six nights—and then the blight fell on him. At the first his *Friar* was as sober as a friar should be; then a spirit of dreaminess came over him. The first note of devastation was in a slight disarray of costume; his monk's gown was strangely mated as to buttons and button holes, his sandal lacings hung loose, and his friar's hood assumed a jocund angle. The next night his memory played him tricks and he had a hard time with the rhyming ends of sentences. But his resourcefulness came to his rescue—he said things that weren't Shakespeare but they sounded just as good. One of his ingenuous interpolations I recollect was the couplet he substituted for,

"Lo, here upon thy cheek the stain doth sit
Of an old tear that is not wash'd off yet."

The old stager got to the end of the first line, but he finished with the wrong word. He said:

"Here upon thy cheek the stain doth *stay*"—

Then he stopped and reflected; what would rhyme with "stay"? He had it!

"Of an old tear that's not yet washed away."

He went on forgetting and substituting, but always in meter and always in rhyme. He actually faked Shakespeare verse—and good verse! He was pro-

fuse in apologies; quite grief-stricken. The night
following was his Waterloo. He floundered; he
weaved at perilous angles; "affliction was enam-
ored of his parts, and he was wedded to incoher-
ency." I threw him cues; I even spoke his lines
for him; he was hopeless. Just at our exit, he found
a lucid moment. I was hurrying through, fairly
shoving him off the stage, when he pulled himself
together and held me away with a rigid arm. Fix-
ing a glassy eye upon me, he said:

"Wisely and slow; they stumble that run fast."

Then he had a fit of coughing—the most artistic I
ever saw. He went into spasms, demonstrating to
the audience that it was a bronchial affection that
had made him dumb, and having accomplished this
good piece of acting, he collapsed and I threw him
off.

He wept tears of concentrated alcohol on my
shoulder in the wings, and swore he had ruined my
scene. I told him that the audience probably hadn't
noticed anything out of the ordinary. He was in-
consolable.

"Oh, my boy! My boy!" he cried. " 'Sawful!
Parfec'ly awful!" (I offered a consoling "Don't
worry.") "No! No! Forgi' me! 'Sawful! But my
brother—only brother I got in the world. Sick! Dying! Been with him all day an' all night—can't live!
'Sawful! Forgi' me!"

He wrung my hand. Presently he was telling
his woes to Mrs. Calvert, the mother of that excel-

lent actor, Louis Calvert, whose death in New York is announced as I write these lines. She was playing the *Nurse*.

"Too bad about K—— isn't it?" she said to me later. *"His sister is dead!"*

"Oh!" I replied.

The next night poor old K—— was replaced.

My old companions of the Daly Company had revisited London. They were then at Irving's Lyceum Theatre doing As You Like It with Rehan's romping *Rosalind*.

My return to New York was almost precipitate: The very next day after the close of Romeo and Juliet I sailed from Southampton. I had made a contract to support Margaret Mather for a tour in a repertory of Shakespeare and standard plays, commencing in September.

Margaret Mather! What a picture of pathos rises in my mind with that name. In all records of the theatre there is no sadder figure than hers. Born Finlayson, and coming at the end of a brood of children of poor Scotch-American parents, her childhood was passed in surroundings humble in the extreme. It is said that as a tiny urchin about the streets in Detroit, she did her bit for the family support by selling papers. Perhaps in the surge of humanity and strife about her, her imagination first found its pictures of drama. In that little soul there was packed a passion that one day was bound to find its outlet. She had at no time, when I knew her, much conversation. Behind her silence was a chaos of fancy, ambition, sympathy, generosity, jealousy, timidity—all ill-adjusted and treading each upon the other's heels. Here was material belonging by right to the theatre; to the portrayal of emotion. I never could learn from her the period that separated the baby street waif from the first steps in her public career; but it must have been animated by a never-ceasing desire to do *something* —to be *somebody*. There was no control, training, and little schooling to direct the wild turbulence of her nature. It grew to maturity like one of those trees sprawling upon the hills of the California coast that are twisted into grotesque shapes by the blasts from the Pacific Ocean.

Scraps of her history that came in rare recurrences of a chatty mood, revealed that while in Detroit, she discovered her ambition for the stage too strong to suppress, and packed up bag and baggage for New York where she placed herself under the tuition of George Edgar, an actor of the old school who made an appearance now and then in RICHELIEU, OTHELLO, MACBETH, supported by a company recruited mainly from his pupils.

Little Margaret was put through her paces as *Pauline, Juliet, Rosalind,* etc., and it was while playing *Cordelia* to Edgar's *Lear* that her talents were discovered by J. M. Hill—at that time manager of the Union Square Theatre. Hill, a man of business methods, after securing Miss Mather under a long contract, withdrew her completely from public appearance and practically put her to school.

Realizing that a course of intensive culture would be of great aid to her vagrom imagination and unschooled mind, he prepared an elaborate plan to bring her out as a full-fledged Shakespearean star, and to this end he placed her in the home of his friend, John Habberton of the NEW YORK HERALD staff—author of HELEN's BABIES—with the understanding that she was to be mentally scrubbed down, introduced to the works of great authors and the amenities of deportment.

For a year her brain tied itself into knots in the attempt to understand many strange things, while her fancy was fed by the wonders of the mimic world to come. Meanwhile Hill's press-agent was busy with announcements, and his invention dripped with romantic stories of the newly discovered genius.

In due time, Hill brought out his fledgling as *Juliet,* and the advance agent went through the land taking much space in the advertising columns, and covering bill-boards with lovely lithographs. That the new star did not quite fulfill the expectation aroused by this heralding was to be surmised. She was greeted by large houses, and given liberal applause, but proved to the wise that stars may acquire a vogue, but they can not become artists in a single night. (This not withstanding the almost instantaneous success achieved by Mary Anderson, or the remoter Fanny Kemble, neither of whom passed through an apprenticeship to her art. But, after all, the cases were not comparable.)

MANAGERIAL CONTROL

Later Hill presented Miss Mather as *Rosalind,* *Pauline* and *Leah, the Forsaken.* The new luminary had impulse, power, intensity, but it was all unrestrained. And although she made the judicious grieve, she was lovely to look upon, and her youthful freshness covered a multitude of sins.

Margaret Mather was continually changing managers, her suspicious nature detecting unfairness in the handling of her business. To escape from Hill she married the leader of the orchestra, Haberkorn. When I met her, she was under the direction of T. Henry French. During his term of management, she essayed *Jeanne D'Arc* in a translated piece of the same title by Jules Barbier and Emil Moreau which had been used by Bernhardt in Paris with music composed for the play by Gounod.

For the year following, her lawyer, General Horatio King, suggested that as her constantly shifting managers had been unsatisfactory, I should take the managerial control, and that our names should be coupled in the advertising. This I did. My hands were full! In addition to playing many parts, I was obliged not only to book time, engage people, make contracts, order printing, but to plan the production of several plays new to both of us: THE LOVE CHASE, MEDEA, THE HUNCHBACK OF NOTRE DAME, and a double bill, NANCE OLDFIELD, the rights of which I secured for her from Ellen Terry, and THE VIOLIN MAKER OF CREMONA, (a translation of François Coppée now in the classic repertory of the Comédie Française).

195

My sorrow's crown of sorrows, however, was the task of holding my star in order. I might as well have tried to manage a cageful of wildcats. She could never learn the lesson of restraint. The stress of her acting would often react upon her physical strength. I have seen her coming away from the "Curse" scene in LEAH THE FORSAKEN, waves of hysteria passing over her; her fingers would snap; nervous laughter on her lips, and the pupils of her eyes dilating to an entire blackness. Then, in a moment, her body would be stretched upon the floor of her dressing-room, rigid as iron, and unconscious. The condition would last five or ten minutes, then she would come out of it as weak as a kitten.

The season was, to say the least, tumultuous. When it was half over, I served notice upon her lawyer, dissolving the partnership, although he and his client offered an equal share of the profits for me to continue. But human nature had its limits.

She married a few months after this and retired from her profession. It was a union of short duration. She emerged from her retirement, and was again seen in her old parts to which she added *Imogene* in CYMBELINE.

And now comes the last scene of all in this strange, eventful history. Six years had passed since the dissolving of our partnership. On Easter Sunday morning in 1898 I was journeying to Detroit to fill a week's engagement at the Opera House. Half an hour away from town, my advance agent, Leffingwell, met me on the train.

MARGARET MATHER
as Joan of Arc

TEMPESTUOUS TO THE LAST

"I don't know if you will approve of what I have done, Mr. Skinner," he explained, "but I had to act on the moment. Margaret Mather died two days ago in Charleston, West Virginia. They have brought her body to Detroit, and they're waiting the funeral ceremony until you reach the city. They wish you to act as a pallbearer."

It was a warm spring day. My traveling clothes were not of "the customary suits of solemn black" befitting the occasion, but I was rushed from the train to the cemetery where the mortuary chapel was surrounded by an idle mob of men, women and children—at least five thousand of them. The driver of our carriage dug a slow line through the mass that blocked the approach. Within the chapel lay all that was mortal of Margaret Mather. A few friends were present as mourners, and a row of her immediate relations, among whom sat her old father, gaunt, rugged and erect, his black suit rusty and his collar without a tie.

A minister with self-righteousness stamped upon every feature of his countenance began his funeral address with: "My friends, it is not for us to judge or condemn the faults of the deceased." After this pious *Mr. Chadband* had finished his painful exordium, a quartette from The Geisha Company made sad work of ROCK OF AGES. Then the coffin lid was removed above the dead woman's face. Peace had come into it after years of tempests. She lay clad in her white-beaded *Juliet* gown; she had no other for she died practically
197

penniless. When her trunk was opened not even a change of underwear was found; her stage costumes and small belongings were all that were left.

It had been understood that the public might have a view of her face, and by the time the service was at an end the mob had pressed closer and closer to the chapel door until women were fainting and confusion reigned. The doors were thrown open; a fight ensued for precedence; hats were knocked off, garments torn, elbows were thrust into faces, and screams rose from the seething crowd. The mistake was obvious, and a struggle followed to bar the way again. In closing the doors somebody's fingers were crushed. We got out only with the aid of the police. The crowd tore over hallowed mounds, regardless of decency, and by the time we reached the final resting-place of Margaret Mather's body, much of the spruce lining of the grave had been stolen for souvenirs.

The whirlwind had pursued her troubled path to the very end.

CHAPTER XIII

MADAME MODJESKA

HELENA MODJESKA CHLAPOWSKI, Countess Bozenta, was past her bloom of youth when I became
her leading man. My late star had, in a fit of spite,
called her an old woman. Old she was not; not
even in years or appearance, and in her art she
was at her very heydey. The dominant characteristics of her acting were eagerness and joy—particularly joy. There was joy in her laughter as
Beatrice; there was joy in her dark ambition as
Lady Macbeth; there was joy in her mischievous-
ness as *Rosalind;* there was joy in her feverishness
as *Magda;* there was joy in the intensity of her love
as *Camille;* there was joy in the humor of her
Portia, and even in *Mary Stuart,* at the moment of
her farewell to the world under the shadow of the
headsman's ax, there was joy in her exaltation of
resignation. It was joy always striking a different note, a joy restrained and admirable in execu-
tion; the great joy of artistry.

As a youngster I had succumbed to the spell of
her *Camille,* when her first manager, Harry Sar-
geant—known as "Scarf-pin Harry"—brought her
out from California.

At that period she was a wraith of a woman with

a voice whose every cadence contained a caress. I
know no better way to describe her *Camille* than to
say it had a fragrance. So winning and appealing
was the *demi-mondaine* of this fragile Polish woman
that Puritan mamas were apprehensive of its effect
upon their sons, declaring that it had that sem-
blance of purity that lent to the portrayal a seduc-
tion and danger much to be feared.

This was the Modjeska I had first seen in the
'seventies. In their gift of outline to the woman I
met now, the years had been liberal, but she was
not one whit less attractive. She had grown in power, and in victory over the handicap of her foreign
accent.

An opulent production of HENRY VIII opened
the season at the Garden Theatre, New York. Madame's *Katharine* was conceived and acted with fine
sympathy, though the character was less adapted
to her Polish accent and personality than other
things in her repertory. She was always the artist,
however; and while *Katharine* was never one of
her distinguished successes it had flashes of splendid dignity; in the trial, she rose to the full eloquence, scorn and majesty of the injured queen,
and in the death scene she was piteous in the extreme.

I was cast for the part of *Henry VIII*, that of
Wolsey going to John Lane, a veteran actor whose
elocution was unimpeachable.

I made up for the part on the assumption that
Henry, in his youth an athlete, a skilled horseman

OTIS SKINNER
as Henry VIII

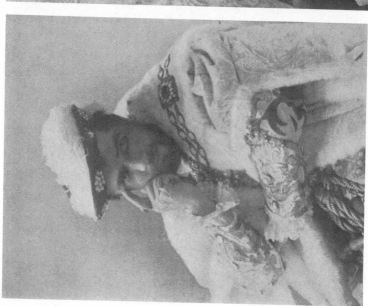

OTIS SKINNER
as Shylock

and a gay young blade, was in his early thirties at the time of his divorce from *Katharine of Aragon*. The gross butcher of the Holbein portrait was of a later date when much matrimony had driven *Bluff King Hal* to flesh.

Our stage manager was Beaumont Smith. He was something left over from another period. Like the thespians of the palmy days, he always acted whether in the theatre or out of it. His order to the waiter for his morning bacon and eggs sounded like blank verse. He combined the duties of stage management with those of a responsible player and he was the *Duke of Buckingham* of our production.

Buckingham has a splendid emotional opportunity in the episode of the farewell to the populace on his way to the scaffold. He meets his doom with fortitude and leaves his blessing on his country, his friends and his king. The people kneel sobbing, *Buckingham* turns to his guard saying, "Lead on, o' God's name! . . . I have done." He clasps his hands reverently before the crucifix, held by the monk before his eyes, and the lights dim out on the effective picture to which the audience reacts with sympathy.

On the opening night of HENRY VIII, Beaumont had lived quite up to the possibilities of this scene; he had the house with him, but just before the dramatic finish as he turned to the uplifted crucifix, he scarcely had his hands raised in prayer when the electrician, mistaking his cue, turned out the lights.

201

Then out of the darkness came the oratorical Beaumont Smith's voice booming in wrath, and the ears of the startled audience were assaulted with: "Lead on, o' God's name! Who the hell turned out those lights? Lead on, I have done. You blankety-blank idiot! O' God's name, lead—I'll show you who is running the stage. Lead on! Lead on!"

Before we concluded the New York engagement, we had given the season's repertory of plays. They were all presented practically within one week, and when the closing performances had seen me through the part of *Benedick* in MUCH ADO ABOUT NOTHING, and I could look back on *Macduff*, *Posthumous*, *Orlando* and *Sir Edward Mortimer*, played and out of the way, I actually fell upon my knees in gratitude, whereat Madame embraced me most sympathetically. It was a cruel week. CAMILLE came later in Philadelphia, so that *Armand Duval* was not added to my New York woes.

There had been two parts in the Booth season that Madame acted, one of which she loved and the other she loathed. *Ophelia* and *Julie de Mortimer* in RICHELIEU.

The bombast of Bulwer Lytton was an unpalatable dose for her. In my scenes with her, she would guy the lines under her breath. The passage she especially ridiculed was her speech to the *King*:

"Cast me to that grave
Of human ties, where hearts congeal to ice,
In the dark convent's everlasting winter."

MARVELOUS POISE

"What does that mean?" she would cry, quite agonized. " 'The dark convent's everlasting weenter?' Nobody freezes in a convent. They are verree nice!"

Of her *Ophelia* I have a most haunting memory. Infinite tenderness and simplicity were its dominant characteristics: it was an overwhelming exposition of betrayed maidenhood. Her madness was so real that it sent a shudder through me when I looked into her eyes, repeating the line of *Laertes*:

"O rose of May!
Dear maid, kind sister, sweet Ophelia!"

and she replied, singing:

"They bore him barefac'd on the bier;
And on his grave rains many a tear,
    Fare you well, my dove!"

Our life on the road was intimate. It was spent very largely in a private car, and not only did we meet constantly in the theatre for performances and rehearsal, but in the small hotel on wheels, lived, ate, and slept as well as the thunder of passing trains and the banging of switch engines in railroad yards o' nights would permit,—Madame, her husband, the business manager, Buckley, and myself, as well as Madame's indispensable Polish maid, Nascia.

With marvelous poise, Madame Modjeska played the hostess. It was no small matter to adjust one's moods and irritabilities, that come with morning coffee after a sleepless night, to the close

203

intimacy necessarily ours for an unusual number of meals per diem (the most vital business on that car was the business of eating), but Madame's temper seemed serene.

"I don't always feel pleasant," she said, when I asked if she was never ruffled. "I used to lose my temper very often, so did Mr. Bozenta, but it was not wise for both of us to be excited at once, so we agreed that but one of us should lose his temper on any occasion while the other keeps calm."

"And does it always work?" I asked.

"Perfectly," she laughed, "you see Charlie is excited all the time."

That her self-control was not infallible is verified not only by her confession, but by a legend of her first appearance in London. Adopting American methods of advertising, her managers were posting on hoardings, stray barrels and boxes, curbings, any place where space could be bought or stolen, the mysterious word

MODJESKA

Very few who saw it had the least notion of its meaning. Its appearance was puzzling and disturbing.

Her leading man, at that time, was Maurice Barrymore, noted for his ready wit, and his atrociously bad "study." On more than one occasion he had brought his star to the verge of tears by being hopelessly at sea in his lines. One night after the mystery of MODJESKA had been elucidated for the

A RETORT AND A CANARY

London public, Madame, upset over one of "Barry's" mental lapses, rated him roundly, quite hysterical and unnerved.

"Mr. Barrymore! Mr. Barrymore!" she cried. "You are insulting, you are ungrateful. You owe everything to me. I have given you your position. I have made you!"

"Made me?" echoed Barry, not the least fazed, "why I was known in London when people didn't know whether you were a woman or a tooth wash!"

Then there is the episode of her first night in New York at the Union Square Theatre as *Camille.* The stage had been set with unusual care and elaboration, and as a pleasant surprise, the property man had hung in *Camille's* boudoir a cage containing a live canary. When the curtain rose, the little creature, excited by the lights and the animation, piped up with vigor. For a while Madame went on with the scene, and then her nerves shattered completely; seizing the cage she tore it from the hook, and hurled it with its offending serenader into the wings. She had gone quite blind and deaf to everything but the irritating trill of the canary that was ruining her great third act. She was quite unconscious of her action and deeply contrite in a public apology.

It was a pleasure to watch her at the many receptions tendered her about the country. She had the diplomatic faculty of remembering names; a faculty which made her a welcome guest and brought joy to the heart of many a hostess. Her benefactions were numerous, particularly to her compatriots, among whom she had found and early encouraged the art of Ignace Paderewski, of the novelist Henry Sienkiewicz—who won the Nobel prize in 1905—of Jean and Edouard de Reszke. Her charities were never ceasing. I have known her to go on Sunday night to a squalid Polish settlement in Chicago and give all that was best of her art in a dirty, ill-ventilated hall, reeking with odorous humanity, in order that her fellow countrymen might once more hear their native tongue spoken on the stage, and a few homes be cheered by money gained in aid of their needs.

On the eve of the New Year in Milwaukee, I gave a little supper party to the company which proved a convivial affair. Everybody added his quota of story, song, improvisation. Madame's contribution was unique. It was after things got going, and we were in a jovial mood that she arose and said she knew a little recitation in Polish that might interest us. A note of suspense and drama was struck at once. Her liquid voice became by turns melancholy and gay, impassioned, tragic, light with happiness, and blighting with bitterness. Laughter rang through it, and now sobs and moans. There was not a note in the gamut of emotions she did not touch. She finished with a recurrent rhythm, fateful and portentous. We were clutched by the spell. We didn't know what it was about but we knew it was something tremendous. In the silence after she had ended some one asked:

MODJESKA as Ophelia

A PRACTICAL JOKER

"What was it, Madame? What was it?"

"I merely recited the alphabet in Polish," she answered.

Later she regaled us with a tale of one of her brother's pranks in their early days in Krakow. At the theatre to which they were attached, a spectacular play was being given with goblins, fairies and the monsters of Never Never Land. Two humble extra men were put inside lions' skins that were sewed together at the middle, and were made to drag on the princess' chariot, to which they were harnessed by gilded and jeweled traces. Before being sewed up into the stifling hides the supers stripped to their underclothing. The sight of the chariot, the princess, and the lions waiting calmly in the entrance for the cue was too much for the prankish brother. Hastily obtaining a hammer and two heavy nails, in the noise and confusion of the changing sets, he nailed the two tails firmly to the flooring of the stage. Then he waited; so did the unsuspecting lions. The cue came: the citizens of Fairy-land were welcoming the approach of the princess with shouts; the band was playing its loudest. The two lions leaped ahead, then fell back with a jerk. The hapless beasts strained at their moorings but the tails held. "Go on," shouted the stage manager, jabbing the pair with a spear. There was a duet of shrieks from the monarchs of the jungle, the sound of parting threads and ripping cloth: Two nondescript bodies leaped into the air, and goaded by a second thrust of the spear, tore on the scene with the princess thrown from her seat and sprawling in the bottom of her chariot.

What the shocked and amazed audience saw then were two perfectly good lions down to the ragged waist-lines but below that two perfectly good pairs of human legs blazing in red flannels.

During the season, Mr. Bozenta and I worked over a translation of Suderman's HEIMATH (MAGDA), Bozenta having secured the American rights. He made the direct, literal translation, and together we put it into colloquial English for Modjeska's use.

That summer I was hastily summoned from a country sojourn to play *Orlando* in an open-air performance of AS YOU LIKE IT at the World's Fair in Chicago. By doing a Marathon I managed to get to New York, dig out my *Orlando* costume and catch Monday's "Limited" for the West. Arriving in Chicago on Tuesday morning I was expecting to open the next evening in a Fair Ground enclosure called "The Sylvan Dell." Sylvan it was: three scrofulous willows and a sickly oak, and under their shade a stage, camouflaged by artificial shrubs, had been erected. An "all star" cast had been advertised and much ceremony planned for the opening performance, including an address by the Mayor of Chicago, Carter Harrison.

But now it was discovered that many of the "star cast" had failed to materialize, the only important actors visible to the naked eye being Rose Coghlan for *Rosalind* and E. J. Henley for *Jaques*,

INDIGNANT SANDOW

Sandow, the physical marvel, who had been announced for *Charles, the Wrestler,* had declined the part with vociferous thanks. He was running an athletic show at the Trocadero in town. When the proposition was put up to him, he warmed immediately to the idea.

"Me? I act; I play anyt'ing in de worl'."

Then, rather suspiciously: "Who I wrestle?"

He was told the *Orlando* was an actor named Skinner.

"He's strong man?"

"Well, not exactly. You see, in this play you and he have this bout, and he throws you, and—"

"He what! !"

"He throws you—it's in the play."

"Look 'ere! See dose people?" and Sandow pointed to a long queue at the Trocadero box-office. "Who dey come to see? Me, Sandow, stronges' man in de worl'. Nobody can t'row me."

"But that's the way it's in this play."

"Dat's all right. You change de play—I wrestle." That was why Sandow did not appear as *Charles.* The managers postponed the opening.

The next day I was conning my lines near the entrance gate when a human gorilla came shuffling up. His neck and chest and shoulders were so expansive that they seemed out of drawing.

In a husky voice he asked for the manager. Apprehension crept over me. Was this a *Charles?*

I asked the nature of his business.

"I hear dey want a wrassler," he replied.

209

"And who are you?"

"My name's Lewis: Evan Lewis, the Strangler."

I looked cautiously about. No one was watching us.

"I'm sorry," I said confidentially, "but we've just engaged a man for the job. But I know where we can get the finest glass of beer in the grounds. Come with me."

After two foaming seidels I expressed my delight at the honor of meeting him and my regret at the misfortune that had deprived us of his services and left him.

Strangler Lewis! Horror! A former dresser of mine was finally pressed into service as the wrestler.

I have encountered some notable *Charles's*—including that of the redoutable William Muldoon now New York State boxing commissioner. It was in Baltimore. The Elks had bought out the house for the performance of the Modjeska Company in As You Like It, and Muldoon had volunteered as an added attraction.

All day I was as nervous as a cat, seeking Bill in every possible place he was reputed to frequent that I might get him to rehearse the encounter with me. He was nowhere to be found until toward evening when I discovered him surrounded by a party of friends. He thought it too late to go over the business then, so I suggested his coming early to the theatre.

I was there at seven o'clock but Bill sauntered in at ten minutes before the orchestra went in, by which time I had reached the conclusion that the wrestling bout was doomed. And even then he said it would hardly be necessary to rehearse the thing.

"What do you generally do?" he asked.

I showed him.

"Oh, I don't know," he remarked. "I tell you; when you see me put my shoulder down on the stage you fall on me."

"Is that all?" I asked.

"That's the finish."

What, in the name of Hercules, was I to do for the rest of the scene?

He laid down the cigar that he was calmly smoking, brushed his short hair until he looked as though he had just come from the barber's shop and threw his cloak over his athlete's tights.

When the fight began he stood in a waiting crouch. I hurled myself at his massive frame and to my amazement found myself bounding back from him as if I were a rubber ball. Again! I was lifted, gently waved in the air and set down carefully on my feet. Then I began to get boiling mad. I tackled him from every side and seized every portion of him. Gibraltar would have been as easy to move.

I heard Madame say, "Oh, he will *keel* him!"

Who was to be killed I couldn't tell. I *wanted* to kill Muldoon but I couldn't. I couldn't even muss his hair. Finally I felt myself at my last gasp.

"Finish it! I'm all in," I whispered.

Giving me a strange look, he lumbered down on the grass mat and deliberately put his shoulder on the floor: I fell on his chest, quite vanquished.

Then the body of the unconscious *Charles* was borne off the scene.

When I reached the dressing-room Bill was sitting on a stool calmly smoking his relighted cigar—not a hair ruffled.

After a moment he said quietly, "Skinner, you got some of the damnedest holds on me I ever saw."

My first *Charles* was in the Margaret Mather season, a semi-professional prize-fighter who worked in a Pittsburgh rolling-mill. For a number of days this man and I regularly went through the tricks and falls of the stage encounter. At one time I was hurled completely across the stage and found the wrestler atop of me. At another I had him by a neck hold over my shoulder, at which juncture he obligingly did a back somersault landing full length at my feet, thus giving *Orlando* his victory.

Considerably racked by the fierce rehearsing of the week, I reached the front of the theatre on Saturday night before the performance. There, displayed in big black letters on an advertising stretcher was this startling announcement:

THE WRESTLING CONTEST

TO-NIGHT

WILL BE BETWEEN

OTIS SKINNER OF NEW YORK

AND

JAMES DUNKELLY OF ALLEGHENY

BOTH MEN BEING SKILLED ATHLETES

James was not all his admirers had hoped to see. His one line: "Come, where is this young gallant that is so desirous to lie with his mother earth?" was spoken with a penny-whistle voice that evoked a smile from the audience.

However, we went at it, fiercely circling each other—foot-to-foot with hanging arms and waiting hands. When I was thrown ten feet across the stage an expectant thrill moved the auditors. But when, at the finish, James obediently placed his hands on my hips from behind and aided by my tug at his bull neck did his parabola over my shoulder and fell in defeat before me, a voice from the gallery sang out:

"Aah, Jimmie, I could do you myself!"

Next season I was to have my opportunities as *Shylock* and *Macbeth*. *Shylock* had been a familiar figure to me for many years. He was the first character in the drama that had attracted me, and I had memorized all of the lines; but during the summer as I studied the part I saw not *Shylock* himself, but Booth's *Shylock*.

> It was the Jew
> That *Edwin* drew.

I found myself reading speeches with the Booth cadence, using the Booth gestures, attitudes and facial expressions, in short, giving a rank imitation. The ghost of the dead actor rose between me and the part. Each day I strove to exorcise him, and each day his figure grew more distinct and impenetrable. I nearly lost my nerve in trying to find

213

myself and my own *Shylock*; but he came through the mists to me at last, and the old spectre faded, growing less insistent every day, until he was a mere memory.

It was Booth's conception of a grasping, blood-thirsty *Shylock* that had stood in my way. In spite of his genius and his artistry I could not find myself agreeing with him.

To me this Jew is a much-maligned and outraged individual. It would almost appear as if Shakespeare had, in a Bernard Shaw manner, ridiculed the Jew-baiting practises of his age under cover of the romanticism with which he clothes his Christian characters. They are certainly a group of weak members when you analyze them. The sentimental *Bassanio,* moralizing over the gold, silver and leaden caskets, is really a fortune-hunter seeking to recoup his depleted purse by marrying *Portia* for her money.

The very loan of three thousand ducats which *Shylock* makes is for the purpose of supplying *Bassanio* with the means of arraying himself in gorgeousness to dazzle the eyes of *Portia.*

The noble *Antonio,* although he reviles and spits upon *Shylock,* does not hesitate to bargain with him and then invite him to dinner,

Lorenzo is the unlovable youth who plots and executes a robbery, aided and abetted by the degenerate minx, *Jessica,* who had no scruple in breaking her father's heart and swapping her mother's ring for a monkey. *Gratiano* and the other friends of

A PERSECUTED JEW

Antonio, Bassanio and *Lorenzo* behave like village rowdies, and indeed all these gentry are in the plot of the jewel theft; *Antonio* and *Bassanio* invite *Shylock* to supper in order to clear the way to this deed.

Even the head of the state, the learned *Doge of Venice,* before whom the trial takes place, possesses but little qualification as a judge. Faced by a few clear and logical arguments of *Shylock,* his jurisprudence fades away and he acknowledges he hasn't the ability to decide points of law until *Portia* expounds them for him.

Can Shakespeare have had no sympathy for this persecuted Jew who in return for a really generous loan, the forfeiture of which he could not have dreamed of being able to exact when it was made, finds himself the victim of a vile plot?

I never could quite understand the prejudice that exists among Jews against THE MERCHANT OF VENICE.

Once at a large public school for girls—the Washington Irving School in New York—I was asked by the principal if I would make an address to his pupils. I told him that I would prefer to read them the trial scene from THE MERCHANT OF VENICE.

About three hundred assembled for this reading and when they filed into the hall I was dismayed to see that they were mostly Jews. At the commencement of the reading I was conscious of the coldness and apathy of my audience, but as it continued the exposition of *Shylock's* wrongs wrought them into enthusiasm. At the conclusion the pupils were eager to ask me questions. One of the first was:

"What is your opinion of *Shylock?*"

I replied that I thought him the only gentleman in the play.

We opened at Buffalo, and at the end of the week we gave THE MERCHANT OF VENICE and I played my first Shakespearean star part. My Jewish gown and gaberdine had been the labor of love of a really artistic costumer, Barthe in London. Old velvets, brocades and sables had been used in its construction, and though it was brand-new, it looked as if it had been worn for generations.

The night was unforgettable for me. It was one of the occasions, such as come in nearly every actor's life, that I love best to remember.

Madame's *Portia* was a thing of radiance and fascination, her quibble over the rings in the last act a romp of playfulness.

To *Macbeth* I did not bring a like enthusiasm. The part of the murderous Thane of Glamis and Cawdor had a quality too rugged and primitive for me to digest easily.

Anyway I never did like kings. Of course one always excepts *Richard;* he is a fellow of craft and fascination, and a limp and a hump help tremendously.

Later on MAGDA was given its first American

performance. Madame had set her heart on this play, and put her last ounce of enthusiasm into her acting. Her *Magda* was temperamental and buoyant; her broken English much less a handicap to her than in her Shakespearean performances.

It was curious the psychological effect that my part of *Major Schwartz* had on me. He is a hard-headed, domineering, bigoted, passionate old Prussian with a paralyzed left arm. The play is a clash of two wills—the daughter's and the father's, and he dies of a stroke at the final curtain.

I felt far too youthful for the part in the first act, but as the action progressed, age overtook me rapidly. By the middle of the play, I had arrived at the years of the *Major,* and before the end, I was a tottering centenarian. The pall of tragedy descended like a physical weight. I always welcomed the escape from my make-up, out into the night where I could breathe with the joy of relief.

The season closed and Madame bade me good-by, to return for a year to her native Poland, wishing me success in my following season, which was to see me as a star in my own right. I had been preparing for this during the previous months, after Madame's Polish visit had been decided on. She and her husband had shown great interest in my venture, even offering financial backing.

From the diary of my wife who as a young girl began a stage career in Madame Modjeska's company and who later passed a summer at the Modjeska ranch, "Arden," among the California hills,

I am privileged to quote excerpts that illuminate
the character of the Polish actress.

* * * * * * * *

"Toronto, November 10th: We played MAC-
BETH to-night. Madame became fearfully angry at
Mr. Rose, the stage manager. He always manages
to get things wrong. He does the *First Witch*, in
addition to running the stage. When he had rung
up on the blasted heath and given the cue for the
thunder and lightning, he came tearing on.

"Simultaneously with his, 'When shall we three
meet again,' he was secreting the prompt book
under his witch's rags, but in his frenzy, he had
forgotten to remove his gold-rimmed eye-glasses
about which the stage lightning played with cruel
brilliancy. I don't believe there can be a record of
a witch ever before wearing gold-rimmed *pince nez*.
Some one had told Madame about it. Just before
the Cauldron scene, she, already dressed in the
white gown for her sleep walking, appeared. 'Hold
the curtain,' shouted some one. She walked to the
center of the stage and called out in her deepest
tragedy tone, 'Mr. Rose! Mr. Rose!'

" 'Yes, Madame,' said the perspiring witch,
stepping forward obsequiously.

"For a second it seemed as if her fury knew no
bounds. She couldn't speak, and then, after a silence that lasted an age, she said in a quiet voice,
'Mr. Rose, you are an idiot. Good evening!' With
that she walked back to her dressing-room, and
closed the door."

"She never reads in her dressing-room, but plays innumerable games of solitaire. She uses very small cards which can be laid on a lap-board. When the act is called her maid takes away the board with the unfinished game, gets her into her heavy robes, and then, the act ended, back she goes to her cards. It is incongruous to see her in her red wig and head-dress of *Queen Katharine of Aragon,* wrapped in a Japanese kimono, and smoking a cigarette as she silently lays out the patience cards. She is the first woman I ever saw smoking, and it shocked me at first. It was as if I had broken in upon an unfortunate habit which I must never reveal. But the other day, in proffering a cigarette to a dressing-room visitor, I heard her say, 'You know, you break bread with an Arab, and smoke with a Pole.' "

* * * * * * * * *

This from the diary kept during the summer at *Arden*:

"Last night when we played whist, Taddy, a young man from San Francisco, was even more absent-minded than usual. Mr. Bozenta and I had won the rubber. We started a new game; Taddy plays awkwardly; he was sleepy, and not paying attention. Madame was shuffling the cards, apparently calm, when, without warning, she rose, threw the two packs across the table at the poor boy, saying—'Taddy, you are a dunce!' and straightway she went off to bed. . . .

"Johnny, the Polish boy Mr. Bozenta has trained to become the overseer of the ranch, has had a birthday, and we had a barbecue, Mexican fashion. All the ranch people for miles were invited. We had a wonderful time under the sycamore trees. Hosts of people and so much to eat! The meat, strung on poles (a sort of primitive spit), was twirled over a low hot fire by two Mexicans. They liked it—the Mexicans; but I couldn't eat it, and I burned my throat with the red stuff they ate with a spoon; it was chile made into a purée. After dinner we danced on the veranda. Madame danced with those silent, handsome Mexican boys who live on the ranch between here and El Toro. They wore trousers with silver stripes down the sides, and their sombreros had heavy silver braids. In waltzing they revolve like tops. After a while we taught them a Virginia Reel, and then Madame and Mr. Bozenta danced some Polish dances, which Mr. Bozenta did better than Madame for she was tired from the spinning waltzes with the Mexicans."

* * * * * * * * *

"We are just back from Santa Ana where Madame gave a benefit entertainment for the library. She took as keen an interest in this simple and half-amateur affair, as if it had been of vital importance. For two whole days she and Nascia went through the wardrobe trunks sorting out things in which to costume the *Tableaux Vivants*—posed for by the young people of the vicinity. One girl held up the dress rehearsal by running off to the photographers when I inadvertently mentioned that the costume she was to wear for *Rebecca at The Well* was one of Madame's *Imogen* costumes which she had not only worn in the part but had made herself. This was too good a chance for *Rebecca* to miss.

"For the final number on the programme Madame and I played a little comedy—A FAIR ENCOUNTER. It has been a very helpful thing for me to watch her study her part. She never learns it by rote, but by always going through it, 'suiting the action to the word, the word to the action.' Only at the very last did she run through the lines without the business.

"She scolded me rather sharply the other day when she found, in studying *Juliet*, I was using her prompt copy. She insisted on my studying the full text and then making my own cuts before comparing them with any other acting version."

* * * * * * * *

"Johanna Tucholsky is staying with us. She is the young woman who taught Madame to speak English. Their enduring friendship through all these years is beautiful. She tells of helping Madame get her first hearing before Barton Hill, the stage manager for John McCullough in the California theatre, when Madame did scenes from *Camille*, while Johanna, this slip of a girl of eighteen, played alternately *Armand Duval* and the *Father*. It is an amusing story now, but it was desperately serious then. She has given me a pencil sketch of

Charles Coghlan as *Hamlet* made one night by Sienkiewicz as they sat with Madame in a box watching the performance."

* * * * * * * *

"The Mexican cook, Jesu, has got drunk and gone away. For three days Madame has cooked the dinners. Delicious Polish things we have had to eat. Wonderful woman! She can do everything! In these two months I have seen her gardening, acting, painting, playing the piano, sewing, and now cooking! She is an artist in everything, but I believe most of all in her great warm heart!"

CHAPTER XIV

THE venture of managing my own company was now ready to be launched. I opened my tour on September 22, 1894, at Rockford, Illinois, in HIS GRACE DE GRAMMONT, a four act, Charles the Second comedy of manners by Clyde Fitch. Associated with me, and a partner in the enterprise, was Modjeska's former business manager, Joseph Buckley, and six of her old company made up the nucleus of mine.

Fitch's play was a natural successor to his BEAU BRUMMELL, then in the repertory of Richard Mansfield. The period responded to his love for the fantastic, and in the oaths of the *Chevalier de Grammont, King Charles* and the beaux and belles of the Court, he could gratify his penchant for "Odd's blood!" "Odd's life!" "Odd's fish!" and other Restoration expletives. Led by his love of colorful costumes, wigs, frills and furbelows, he induced Percy Anderson of London to make the designs,

DE GRAMMONT was written for Henry Miller, but he was loath to leave his comfortable New York berth where, as leading man of the Empire Theatre, he was much in favor with his public and manager. His plans for starring were not fully perfected.

Miller, my friend for many years, wrote: "I am glad the play goes to you; not only because I believe in it, but because I have faith in you." He further presented me with the music score he had commissioned William Furst to compose.

I had no opportunity of meeting Fitch before the opening of my season in Chicago; he was abroad and I found the time of preparation too filled with the thousand and one cares with which I as an actor-manager was to burden myself for the rest of my life, to worry about this since he and Miller had thrashed out the manuscript until it only remained to put it into rehearsal. But the shower of letters from abroad! It has been said that Clyde Fitch had an infinite capacity for friendship. He had indeed. He had also an infinite capacity for detail. At first it was rather stimulating to try to decipher his letters; but after a while the arrival of fat envelopes stuffed with cryptic characters, used to fill me with such dread that I never summoned courage to read them. They were all about the play. Anderson had designed the costumes from the Lely portraits at Hampton Court, and I gleaned enough to know it was about these that Fitch had most anxiety. "The lace must be coffee-colored—NEVER WHITE! . . The women's hair must resemble the flappy ears of the King Charles spaniels! ! . . The pink must be *deep rose*—never pale! !"

He saw the play for the first time at Christmas in Philadelphia and was apparently pleased, but he fretted a bit because the women's heads did not look

Otis Skinner
as His Grace de Grammont

enough like the King Charles spaniels. He transformed himself into a *perruquier* after the final curtain, and, armed with a comb, his mouth full of hairpins, he proceeded to arrange each woman's wig as he thought historically correct, explaining how important it was that they should look not natural but thoroughly artificial.

Ten years later, when Fitch had become the most popular of American playwrights, I revived this comedy with lavish expense and a company of high-salaried actors. Fitch spent much time in revising it. He wrote me from Germany that he had cribbed an excellent idea from Reinhardt's production of A MIDSUMMER NIGHT'S DREAM, where *Helena* and *Hermia* almost tore the clothes off each other in the quarrel. This business we transferred to the fight between the court beauties, *Mistress Middleton* and *Mistress Warmestre* (Marion Abbott and Helen Ware), which ended in *Warmestre's* grabbing a handful of false curls from the King-Charles-Spaniel wig of *Middleton,* and brandishing them before the adored *Chevalier de Grammont.*

In person and clothes Fitch was something of a dandy. He had an enormous love for beautiful things and his taste was impeccable. He was generous, loyal, a good friend. He never intentionally wounded a member of the cast of one of his plays, and to avoid this he preferred to pass upon the people before they were engaged. In my first production of his play he had to take what the gods provided since he was then in his beginnings, but in the revival he was most particular. One woman I engaged was without his approval, and he made up his mind that she could not play the part; that she would kill the play, etc. After the first performance in Boston, when he came home with me to supper, I tried to convince him that the lady had given a very satisfactory account of herself. But he was obdurate. "Why, Skinner," he insisted, "she is so damned dramatic that she couldn't even take a boiled potato off the dish without stabbing it." In his unreasonable obsession he inundated me for days with telegrams and notes imploring me to make the change in the cast. I couldn't do it. The play did not get to New York. There were difficulties in getting the right sort of theatre, and besides I found, after reviving it, the comedy a bit *demodée,* I think, in his heart of hearts, Fitch felt that too.

After the initial performance at Rockford, came a successful engagement at the Grand Opera House, Chicago. The critics were kindly. Miss Durbin, who had been the juvenile woman with Madame Modjeska, being especially praised for her sympathetic *Mistress Hamilton.*

Coupled with DE GRAMMONT for my tour was THE KING'S JESTER, my brother's translation of Victor Hugo's LE ROI S'AMUSE, a grim tragedy from which RIGOLETTO and Tom Taylor's FOOL'S REVENGE were taken. The JESTER was presented during the second week of the Chicago engagement. This served very well as a balance to the lightness of *De*

226

A BRIGHT SPOT IN ANY SEASON

Grammont; the bitter, lacrymose and revengeful jester *Triboulet,* and the flirting, foppish French gallant. Chicago was very good to us. I was my own boss now; I saw nothing but prosperity ahead. But from thence on through the season, it was a sadly different story. I could obtain bookings, but not audiences. In the larger towns our first-night houses had a good effect in advertising us for the balance of the week, but week stands were to be got only through the diplomacy and persistence of Buckley. No matter how loudly he and my advance agent, Goodfriend, trumpeted the virtues of their star, I learned that the public of Red Wing, Minnesota, and Montgomery, Alabama, merely took a chance on what the posters and lithographers promised in the entertainment at the "opry" that night. It was in a southern town that a member of my company, riding in a street-car, overheard an urchin who was gazing out the window at the pictorial printing on the bill-boards, ask his mother, "Ma, what is an ottis skinner?"

New Orleans was one of the bright spots of this first season—it would be a bright spot in any season, good or bad. We did a paying business at the Grand Opera House in Canal Street, formerly the Varieties Theatre, and now demolished. The owners of the establishment were the Varieties Club, a collection of choice old vatted spirits who had the hated privilege of entering the theatre free at any time. Two rows of arm-chairs were railed off directly back of the orchestra pit—the best places in

227

the house—and to this enclosure there was a private passage. These old nuisances, after dining and wining copiously, had a habit of clattering into their places during scenes of intensity and quiet, distracting the attention of the audience, and then going soundly to sleep.

But no small annoyance could dispell the charm of New Orleans. Some remembered features had vanished: the Louisiana Lottery tickets to be had at news-stands, barber shops and cigar stores; the big Keno hall on Royal Street, and the open cisterns and sewers which had fed the yellow fever epidemics had been covered. But there were still the French opera, the races, the marvelous cooking at Victor's, the Café Louisianne and Antoine's where one could eat buster crabs, oysters à la Creole and bouillabaise, and where the gouty-footed waiters never changed from year to year. Nor was the beer at the Cosmopolitan to be despised. Here, after the performance at night, we could be measurably sure to find the kindliest dramatic critic in the world— Major Nat Burbank of the PICAYUNE, in whose company there was always good talk about actors of other days in New Orleans. Madame Begué's Sunday morning breakfasts with the celebrated omelets and palatable red wine, down on the levee by the French Market, had not begun to deteriorate.

I went to Begué's one Sunday morning and finding the places in the favorite room opening off the kitchen all filled, our party was conducted to a room up-stairs where a number of young fellows—

very young—were already seated at the general table. Conversation eddied into pauses, and interest centered in our every mouthful of food. After the third course, a whispered conference took place; a youth was urged to his feet, his face one large blush. I presently discovered his embarrassment and faltering speech were directed at me. He was practically presenting me with the keys of the city and the welcome of its citizens. Reaching his climax, he stammered: "We are—we always like to —er—a— to greet people who—who give us as much pleasure as the visitor who honors this occasion, who has given us so much pleasure, and we— I should like" (here he got hold of himself for an effective finale) "to propose the health of our distinguished *hostess, Mr. Ottis Stringer!*"

As I was then looked to for reply I said that I had played every kind of part, except, perhaps, that of hostess; that though I presumed the compliment to be meant for me, the Ottis Stringer alias was unusual, and that I hoped they were enjoying our company as much as we were enjoying theirs. There was a terrible silence, and the tension wasn't broken until I reached over to take the orator's hand and tell him that I would forgive him if he would forgive me.

And one should not forget that bountiful dinner over at Maylie's near the Poydras Market, that started with an absinthe frappé in the barroom and finished in the dining-room with its sawdust floor, surrounded by casks of French wine, where

229

the proprietor, at the head of the big table, carved the meat for the guests. This was a stag dinner. Fat-bellied, thick-necked singers from the Opera were faithful to it; they sat in their shirt-sleeves, gorged and perspired like stokers.

Of blessed memory, too, is the shabby old Absinthe House with its marble counter and dripping taps, the Sazarac punch, the Ramos saloon where a corps of bartenders shook silver fizzes all day long; and the princely hospitality of the Pickwick and Boston Clubs.

A memory of the old Louisiana duelling days was given to me by Judge Clegg, a noted Crescent City jurist: a little pamphlet called, THE CODE OF HONOR, OR RULES FOR THE GOVERNMENT OF PRINCIPALS AND SECONDS IN DUELLING, published in New Orleans in 1873 by Clark and Hofeline. Its *raison d'être* is embodied in a foreword, the most significant part of which is the following:

"It is a digest of usages for gentlemen of the world in cases of personal difficulty, adopted by the best clubs in England and America as embodying the most discreet, moderate, and humane rules. . . . It is applicable to gentlemen who propose to settle personal difficulties according to the recognized proprieties of the most Southern communities. . . . The ruffianly rencounter, the blackguard street fight, sometimes vulgarly and absurdly confounded with the *duello,* are outside the pale of the code of honor and at war with its injunctions. It discountenances the bearing of arms, assumes that gentlemen do not wear them, and prohibits the combat in hot blood at the moment of injury."

230

ANTIQUES AND THE SOCIAL SCENE

One afternoon at a social gathering of men I felt myself almost within the rules of the CODE OF HONOR because I drank my wine before a belated guest had received his. He made a terrible fuss about it.

The fascination of the antique shops never failed. To drop in at Armand Hawkins' place, filled with dust and treasures, was a delight. This beguiling old prevaricator was never at a loss for documents proving the authenticity of his alleged Napoleonic and Bourbon *objets d'art*. I once bought from him a graceful brass bowl which he swore came from the home of a noted Creole family, and it later turned out to be a spittoon!

Matinées began at twelve o'clock. By half past two we were out of the theatre, joining the stream of promenaders on Canal Street, admiring the beauty of soft-eyed, smiling New Orleans matrons and maidens, and the dignity of calm aristocrats who might have been of the old noblesse.

I remember a tea at the home of the novelist, Molly E. Moore Davis on Royal Street—a house that had been the headquarters of General Jackson —when the curtains were drawn at four o'clock in the afternoon, candles lit and the prettiest girls in Louisiana wore their evening gowns and served refreshments.

It was my good fortune to make the acquaintance of Grace King, the author of NEW ORLEANS, THE PLACE AND THE PEOPLE, a work that, apart from its literary charm, is the best guide book to New

Orleans that I have ever found. One of its chapters is devoted to Jean Lafitte, known in the days of General Jackson as the Pirate of the Gulf. This fascinating rascal who alternated between respectability and piracy appealed to me as material for the theatre. I urged Miss King to outline the episodes in his life for a play, but she was over-timid of the idea, declaring that she had no sense of the theatre.

One morning when the sun was burnishing the oven-like tombs of Metarie Cemetery in which the dead of New Orleans are laid away because the moisture in the earth will not permit of interment, under the gray plumes of Spanish moss swaying from live-oaks, with the chameleons pausing on vines and epitaphs to cast curious glances at us, I asked my leading lady, Miss Durbin, to be my wife. As the lady said yes, it is possible that my fondness for New Orleans may be in part accounted for.

After our understanding had been complete, the lady of my choice found courage to tell me a secret. In the last act of THE KING'S JESTER there is a cruel situation wherein *Triboulet,* having bargained with the cutthroat, *Saltabadil,* to deliver the body of *King François* into his hands, receives instead the body of his own daughter *Blanche,* in a sack. Thinking it is the *King,* he kicks the body with demoniac glee before throwing it into the river. I thought I had been cautious in placing the sole of my shoe against Miss Durbin's arm before giving the necessary shove that indicated the savagery of my glee. I was sure that my foot action had been merely a theatrical gesture. Miss Durbin now confided to me that her left arm had been black and blue all the season.

From New Orleans we worked north again through Arkansas and played in Little Rock, Pine Bluff and Helena. At Pine Bluff we caught up with our advance agent, Si Goodfriend. He was at breakfast when I met him in a hotel where the food was a farce, making desperate attempts to cut into an orange. "I don't know," he said, addressing the orange, "whether you are a little rock or a pine bluff."

At Memphis I received a certainty for the opening of a new theatre, the Lyceum. As is common to such occasions, the building was not fully completed on the opening day—the temporary scaffolding on the stage had not been taken down, and during its removal a workman was thrown to the floor and killed. This disaster was not known to the beauty and fashion who, for the opening, made the auditorium like a scene from a play. Memphis belles wore their choicest gowns and with their escorts, occupied every available seat, each lady carrying a single American Beauty rose. The picture on the stage was surpassed by the picture in front of it. But the catastrophes of the day were not ended. At the finish of the first act, the iron curtain which was to descend slowly on the minuet of HIS GRACE DE GRAMMONT, fell with a crash, missing by not more than an inch or two Robert Peyton Carter who was just then on the front segment of the wheel. The man

233

on the curtain rope leaped up to check the fall, but the rope, which was of steel, tore through his grasp, skinning the flesh from the palms of his hands. This man was in the employ of the Lyceum Theatre for some years, and on my visits to Memphis never failed to show me his permanent scars.

The next afternoon at a reception a charming débutante who had been a member of an exceptionally conversational box-party the night before, found courage to say to me: "Mr. Skinner, why didn't you talk louder when you made your curtain speech. We couldn't hear a word you said?" "That's singular," I replied, "I heard every word *you* said." The satisfaction of my retort was rather dashed when the disillusioned miss exclaimed, "Oh, shucks! You've got gray hair!" This was a blow to one at thirty-six.

At Detroit, I made a revival of THE MERCHANT OF VENICE. I liked playing *Shylock* again. The play made a fair showing, though we hadn't much scenery for it. My leading woman graciously resigned the part of *Portia* to Sarah Truax, playing instead *Jessica,* in which she had been most charming in the Modjeska production.

The season wore on with scant returns. In spite of our auspicious beginnings, and though I never quite lost the belief that fortune's caprice would turn up aces, it wasn't always possible to blot out the memory of a procession of substantial salary envelopes, stretching back through years of Saturdays. It was sometimes difficult to keep a stiff upper lip—totally to ignore consequences. Paving the way to fame was a tedious process. The season's zero was met at Cincinnati where the week's receipts amounted to less than I later played to in a single night.

Already I was looking toward next year. Harry Hamlin, manager of the Grand Opera House, Chicago, introduced me to the Payne translations of François Villon's poems with the suggestion that there might be a play about Villon, and I fed the fires of my hopes by working out a scenario. I sent the result to my brother Charles, who took up the task of writing with enthusiasm.

April was bringing the tour to a close. Some bills were outstanding and could not be met—they were mostly for printing—but the company was paid. After that there was very, very little left in the treasury.

The closing date was on a Saturday at Corning, New York. The major part of the company left on an early Sunday morning train, leaving behind a little party, the principals of which were Miss Durbin and myself. It was our wedding day. The first wedding that had taken place in the new Christ Church at Corning. It was a beautiful day in April. Our assets were mainly rich hopes.

CHAPTER XV

THROUGHOUT the summer my brother and I worked on our play with the result that VILLON THE VAGABOND was given its premier in September, 1895, at the Grand Opera House, Chicago. This was the first of the Villon plays, and was presented in various cities for a year before Justin Huntley McCarthy's IF I WERE KING, written on almost identical lines, was produced by E. H. Sothern. It would be folly to pretend to say which was the better play, or intimate that any of the material of the McCarthy piece was taken from ours, but the similarity was striking. However, our consciences did not permit us to play ducks and drakes with chronology as did McCarthy's. His *Louis XI* was the conventional old character fellow that Irving had made known to us, while his *Villon* was a young man. Historically this was incorrect, but after all McCarthy took only a dramatist's license, while with us it served our purpose to keep historical verity intact.

Although my play was effectively staged and played, I couldn't get into New York. According to the estimate of the Powers that Were, I was a provincial star with a reputation to make. Perhaps

THE INEVITABLE HAMLET

I should have arrived quicker had financial backing given open sesame to Broadway theatres, but I was pounding away at the Herculean task of getting through on my own. I had looked for a significant improvement in my affairs during the second season, but results proved only slightly better. Hope and patience were obliged to go hand in hand led by determination. Once more I wandered over the map of the United States winning praise and encouragement, but discovering that on an income of this kind, you can't pay salaries. My favorite indc or sport became that of "sitting tight."

Two months from the date of the season's opening, I played *Hamlet*. Nearly every actor seems to be born either with *Hamlet* in his blood, or else he acquires *Hamlet* in his years of discretion. In some the virus so permeates that finally nothing short of an operation in the shape of an impersonation of the part can remove the disorder. William Gillette developed a particularly virulent case of *Hamlet*, and it progressed to the point of a complete scenic and costume equipment of the play which he later offered to dispose of to me. Eddie Foy for years was haunted by the spirit of the melancholy Dane. He was finally cured of his by MR. HAMLET OF BROADWAY, a musical farce.

The part has been acted by certain cranks and fake tragedians who have worn their inky cloaks to the delight of audiences that came to enjoy the delicious burlesque of the performances. One rather suspects that the "Count Johannes" (born plain

237

Jones and christened George), Doctor Landis and James Owen O'Connor had method in their madness and an eye on the box-office receipts when they exploited their freak *Hamlets*, although the going was rather rough in the face of the yawps of delight their efforts evoked. O'Connor, finding *his* inky cloak becoming spotted with vegetable stains, bags of flour and antediluvian eggs hurled from the front, was forced to portray his Dane behind a net stretched across the stage.

Nor has the part escaped attack from certain ambitious ladies. I recall the performances of a Mrs. Macready and of Anna Dickenson, a noted lecturer, who clothed their more or less shapely legs in black to their own evident satisfaction, if not to general admiration. Sarah Bernhardt played it.

Certain "boy tragedians" have been put forward in the part, from the celebrated Master Betty, who created a stir in London over a century ago and who later was discovered to be a very stupid youth, down to our own time. Indeed there have been few actors of serious parts who have not had their try at the character. Charles Fechter, vast of waist-line, with blond wig and tufted chin, certainly visualized two of the lines descriptive of the *Prince's* physique:

"O, that this too too solid flesh would melt!"

and

"Our son is fat and scant of breath!"

238

SHAKESPEARE'S INTENTION

The blond make-up was also adopted by Beer-bohm Tree whose *Hamlet* was enviously described by Irving as "funny without being vulgar." The truth is, no good actor ever failed in the part. It is the most completely human character in the whole range of the drama. You don't conceive it: it is you. Looked at through the opera-glasses of your temperament, *Hamlet* is endowed with your idio-syncrasies, while to me he may have entirely different attributes. He does not reason until he has to. He jumps at conclusions and when he finds his premises wrong, he tries another route. He has the feminine gift of intuition. I can not think him a philosopher. Shakespeare's own philosophy must have been as native to his thought as breath to his body, but it is past belief that in writing HAMLET he started with other intention than to make an *acting* play. Scarcely a device of the theatre has been left out in the dressing up of the piece. Whoever may have been the author of the plays, HAMLET was written by one who had as great a command of the tricks of dramatic construction as David Belasco. Small wonder that I desired to make my own experiment with *Hamlet, the Dane.*

Followed days on the train, nights in the theatre, walks afield, and hours in hotel rooms familiarizing myself with the lines and the many moods of the *Prince.* Only once did I become completely discouraged. It was in Bloomington—a link in the chain of profitless towns—where there seemed no light ahead. Why produce the play? No one will care. My wife was hearing me in the part with patience and sympathy. I turned to her and said: "It's no use; I am going to give up the fight. I haven't the courage to continue any longer."

It was a cruel thing to say to a bride of less than a year, but she bore it with philosophy. She knew my mood would change—and it did. But Bloomington has always remained a synonym for my darkest hour. The play was finally presented at the Duquesne Theatre in Pittsburgh, November, 1895. Later I played the part in Chicago where it happened that two other legitimate actors were appearing in the same play. Chicago was overrun with *Hamlets*—Creston Clarke, Walker Whiteside and myself. The public might have said, "A plague on *all* your houses," but I fared well, and I presume the others did, also.

In Toledo an astonishing innovation was introduced inadvertently in the graveyard scene. It was in an antiquated theatre whose name I have forgotten. The bier on which poor *Ophelia* lay was borne on by a group of white-robed maidens who formed a screen in front of the grave to conceal the lowering of the body. They parted and, going upstage, made room for the *Queen* to advance with a drapery filled with flowers. Miss Truax took a handful of the light paper petals, and with graceful Delsartian gesture held them for a moment over the grave as she spoke the line, "Sweets to the sweet; farewell." Then she dropped them. They fluttered down to within about a foot of the opening when they were seen suddenly to mount upward in a multi-colored spurt and sail off like so many butterflies. The bewildered *Queen* tried again with the line following: "I hop'd thou shouldst have been my Hamlet's wife"—but the perverse petals streamed up once more. Nervously concluding the speech with—"and not to have strew'd thy grave," she emptied the contents of her scarf over the hole only to have the flowers dashed back in her face. The grave had been placed over the heating plant of the theatre! I need hardly say that the gloom of tragedy was lifted from both audience and actors.

Brooklyn was a long way from New York in those stormy March days, but E. A. Dithmar of THE NEW YORK TIMES braved the elements and wrote in his Sunday review: "I found it well worth while to make the journey to Brooklyn," and he said encouraging things about my *Hamlet.* My tasseled handkerchief fretted him. I think to-day it would fret me too. Mrs. Skinner had found precedent somewhere for this "napkin," and I couldn't hurt her feelings. We hadn't been married long.

The tour took us to Boston where our engagement was played at the Park Theatre managed by the male *Mrs. Malaprop* of the theatrical world— John Stetson. This big, bass, blustering individual had sprung from street life in Boston to the position of prosperous manager. His usual manner was that of a war tank—he went through things if they stood in his way. One look at his aggressive face, square jaw and clouded *dead* eye was enough to cause timid ones to step aside. Perhaps many of the stories of his "malapropisms" were apochryphal, but he unquestionably had a penchant for big-sounding words. Once upon his return from Europe he expressed his satisfaction in being again on *terra cotta.*

A Biblical play was being presented at the Boston Globe Theatre under Stetson's management. Observing a tableau of THE LAST SUPPER, seen through a gauze drop, Stetson was disturbed because the scene looked scant, and demanded that more people be shown.

"But, Mr. Stetson," said the stage director, "there were only twelve apostles."

"I know what I want," said Stetson, "gimme twenty-four!"

For all his idiosyncrasies he was immensely popular, and he had a sympathetic side not difficult to approach. I discovered this in the dilemma which confronted us at the close of the engagement. Business had been quite terrible, and on the last Saturday night it was disclosed that not only were we indebted to the theatre for house charges but we hadn't the wherewithal to move to the next stand. My manager put the matter frankly before John Stetson. He accepted our I. O. U. for the indebtedness and advanced funds to enable us to move on. He wasn't altogether a bear.

Once more in the Middle West the going became easier. But the tour ended with my saddened eyes fixed on a woebegone bank balance. I spent the summer in writing a play of the cloak and dagger sort, modeled after a tale entitled THE HONOR OF SAVELLI, which I called A SOLDIER OF FORTUNE. This was produced in the autumn in Chicago. But before its production I took the company to St. Paul and Minneapolis and presented a list of legitimate plays: HAMLET, RICHARD III, THE MERCHANT OF VENICE, ROMEO AND JULIET, and Bulwer Lytton's THE LADY OF LYONS. Thus, with the new play, I was prepared for a season of repertory. *Richard* was the only new part in the classic list that I had not played before, and I thoroughly enjoyed the villainies, the subtleties and the intellectual adroitness of the crook-backed tyrant.

In a magazine article published long ago, Henry Cabot Lodge set forth the result of investigation into the character of the real Richard III. Records of undoubted authenticity show that the Duke of Gloucester was a much-maligned individual, given to deeds of generosity; that the murder of the two princes could not be laid at his door; that instead of tyrannizing over Lady Anne, it was the supposedly noble Duke of Clarence who persecuted her, forced her into the performance of menial tasks, and that it was Richard who, Lochinvar-like, rescued her from tyranny and bore her away. Later, as king, Richard proved himself a sagacious and beneficent monarch, governing England with justice and giving to the common people a civic and political freedom they had not before known. But Tudor history has written down Richard of Gloucester a schemer,

243

a tyrant and a murderer, and as such Shakespeare has stamped him for all time and given a terrible jolt to the old maxim that "truth is mighty and will prevail."

And, truly, I would much rather play the *Richard* of Shakespeare than that of Henry Cabot Lodge. I especially enjoyed the wooing scene with *Lady Anne*—one of the earliest incidents in the drama of hypnotic control. I do not know that the Elizabethans have said much about hypnotism, but Shakespeare certainly knew about it. How else can we account for *Lady Anne's* sudden acceptance of her husband's murderer as a suitor.

The delight of the ROMEO AND JULIET performance was the *Juliet* of Maud Durbin. Girlish, impulsive, imaginative and fair to look upon, she was easily *Capulet's* fourteen-year-old child, Verona's flower. Modjeska had coached her in the part, and she had caught much of the Polish artist's inspiration.

The pendulum of my travels swung east, then west—finally toward the Pacific Coast. We stopped at Lincoln, Nebraska, the early habitat of Colonel William F. Cody—"Buffalo Bill." It chanced that Bill's Wild West Show was in town that day. Under any condition I probably should not have had a full house, but what chance had *Hamlet* against Buffalo Bill?

The meager audience was listening to the early sorrows of the Prince of Denmark with apparent sympathy when the colonel came into the theatre a

244

little the worse for wear. All day long his friends and neighbors had been celebrating his advent with great conviviality. He looked at the little collection of people in the orchestra seats with a glazed eye that straightway kindled into indignation.

"Do you know what I'm going to do?" he exclaimed. "Look at that house! I'm going down that aisle and tell them that Otis Skinner is the best damned actor in America." Being thwarted in his threat, he came behind the scenes, deciding he preferred to issue his proclamation from the stage. Again he was dissuaded and I invited him to my dressing-room where he sat on a trunk swaying a bit unsteadily. The door flew open and my wife came in quite unaware that I had a visitor. The colonel rose, every inch a gentleman and a soldier, and stood erect, unswerving. He was in the presence of a lady: Off came the well-known sombrero. The colonel was a very prince. The introduction was formal. Scenting an air of restraint, if indeed no other atmospheric condition, my wife quickly withdrew and Buffalo Bill relaxed immediately to the trunk again.

Late one afternoon I stood on the platform of the Union Pacific Railway Station at Omaha with my face toward the setting sun. My company was aboard, our tickets—good for three months—from Omaha to California and back to the Missouri River were paid for. I felt I was on the threshold of adventure. Only a few days before I had received a letter from an acquaintance saying: "Dear Skinner: I hear you are about to go West. Don't! The plains are white with the bones of actors who have tried to get back."

My manager, reading a suggestion of doubt in my face, asked if I felt like weakening on the proposition.

"The first stop is Denver, and there's an awful lot of country west of that," he said.

"Well, that's where we're going," I answered, and we stepped aboard the train.

Denver, Salt Lake City and finally California!

We played from San Francisco to San Diego and back. The land of gold brought me nothing but the fairy-gold of legend. When I turned my face eastward at the end of June I was confronted by three thousand miles of railway and scant means of getting a company of twenty people, a carload of scenery, my wife and myself to our destination—Chicago.

I owed everybody—printers, transfer companies, scenic artists, property makers, my working force, and, above all, my actors. These last were patient and forbearing with me and took our reverses like true soldiers of fortune.

We had our railroad tickets back to the Missouri River—nothing more.

My manager camped in the office of the superintendent of the Southern Pacific Railroad at Sacramento for an entire day waiting a chance to plead with that potent person for authority to allow our scenery and baggage to go through as far as Omaha. Finally he got an audience with the hard-boiled official, and his pent-up eloquence as he pictured the desperation of our situation, won the day. We were off to pick up a few pence at Ogden and Salt Lake City. We traveled by day in the coach, and at night our women were given berths in the Pullman while we men took to the tourist sleeper. What cash there was in the treasury was held by Buckley against the necessities of meal stations where we breakfasted, lunched and dined *en famille* as frugally as possible. A frightful thing occurred on the way. At a cashier's desk of a meal station while the bell was ringing for the departure of the train, Buckley laid down a twenty-dollar gold piece among his silver, under the impression that it was a dollar, and didn't discover his mistake until we were fifty miles away. Then in our melancholy, befell the miracle—manna dropped from Heaven! At the supper station, nineteen dollars which we thought gone forever, returned to us by telegraph from the scene of the awful blunder.

Ogden and Salt Lake City helped us out a little —then a few Nebraska towns, and finally Omaha! There we played to enough cash to purchase our transportation to Chicago.

Our crusade was over.

CHAPTER XVI

THE kaleidoscopic memories of the next seven years have patterns brighter at times than others; a few shift into somber designs, but in each I find some glowing recollection that makes the pattern still beautiful.

In the summer of 1898, when America was at war with Spain, Jacob Litt defied tradition that a war play could not be successful when people were face to face with the actual situation. This had been the case when Bronson Howard wrote and tried unsuccessfully to present SHENANDOAH soon after the Civil War. Its success had come years later after the first wounds were healed. And now, after another generation, when for the first time the North and South were shoulder to shoulder in the cause of justice, Jacob Litt had been wise in reviving this effective melodrama.

It was the hottest summer I have ever known. We were wedged into McVicker's Theatre in Chicago, actors, supers, horses, cannon, powder-smoke, until it was an inferno. The audiences packed the theatre; patriotic feeling ran high, and yet the season was forced to end after twelve weeks from sheer exhaustion produced by the heat.

248

A CORPORAL ON HORSEBACK

One broiling afternoon during a matinée I, as *Colonel Kerchival West*, was in a scene with Frank Burbeck as *General Haverhill* when Augustus Cooke as *Sergeant Barket* was to enter on horseback with an important despatch. Cooke was a good actor but not a good horseman and it had taken some persuasion to get him to mount the docile old nag that had been lathered and dust powdered to look as if he had carried the breathless rider for many miles. This afternoon Burbeck and I had finished our scene and awaited the hurried arrival of the mounted corporal. In the wings we could see the weary beast being urged by the timid rider, but with no result. Finally the property man came to his assistance with a generous slap on the flank. The horse leaped forward, dashed across the scene, caught a glimpse of daylight through the open door to the alley, and when horse and rider were rescued they were tearing along State Street. Burbeck turned blandly to me saying, "That must have been the corporal riding by." The audience seized the situation and greeted Cooke with friendly applause when he finally brought on the despatch— but he was *not* (and was never again) on horseback.

That summer brought me the delightful acquaintance of George Ade. He was then editing a column in the HERALD, and he came often to the Virginia Hotel where, with Amy Leslie, Delancey Halbert and a genial group of Chicago writers, we talked of the war and our friends who had gone. George Ade's wit was brilliant, but he was shyly modest over his growing success. When my wife asked him to autograph her copy of ARTIE he said with genuine shyness, "No one ever asked for my autograph before." Several years later I went to a circus with him in Birmingham, Alabama. It was in every sense a real circus to go to a circus with George Ade. He had been a guest of the Ringling Brothers and long enough to learn the domestic history of every clown, bareback rider or freak connected with the great show. He was like a kid as he related to me the stories and secrets of these circus-folk. He chuckled with mirth as he led me to the platform where two sweltering creatures muffled in goat skins were being exhibited as Eskimos brought back from a farthest North expedition. The "barker" was holding forth how perilous had been the voyage, how these exiles yearned for their igloos, how difficult it was to provide blubber for their sustenance since they would die if they changed their Eskimo bill of fare. "Just listen to him," chuckled Ade, and then he whispered: "These two Eskimos are from Muncie, Indiana. I know 'em." It pleased him that they were natives of his own state. He gave them a friendly nod as we walked away, and one of them answered with a slow wink.

During these hot weeks we went always on Sunday to Grace Church because the Reverend Ernest Stires was the young clergyman there. He was chaplain of The Forty Club where his genial qualities had made him beloved. His sermon on the death of Gladstone was preached on the Sunday after the call to arms in the Spanish-American War had been answered by several men from Grace Church choir. The occasion made the service doubly impressive, and I felt in the force and appeal of the young clergymen his destined leadership.

The Forty Club was ever the most genuinely congenial group of men gathered together for the fellowship of dining and making welcome the visitor within their city. At that time the club was presided over by William T. Hall—"Biff" as he was known to his intimates. His death was a poignant loss to Chicago. I miss him yet after these twenty years. Bert Leston Taylor (B. L. T. of the TRIBUNE "Line o' Type" column) was another happy acquaintance. Roswell Field was often one of our coterie that summer. His brother, Eugene, I knew pleasantly but not so intimately. Among my rare and valued friends were Melville E. Stone and Herman H. Kohlsaat. These two did more kindly things, more thoughtfully helpful things than any men I have ever known. They have alike that unselfish quality in wishing to share their friends with others. Is there a truer kind of friendship?

Another rare person who came to us on one of those torrid days, and on more to follow, was Horace Fletcher,—he who is remembered for the new verb—to fletcherize. But in those days the problem of mastication was not the one in which he was interested. He had written two small books— MENTICULTURE OR THE A. B. C. OF TRUE LIVING, and HAPPINESS. Simple documents of metaphysics—

results of his own experience. We owed this new-
found friend to Joseph Jefferson who had given us
the books, saying that he knew their value because
he knew Horace Fletcher. I remember, in turn, the
praise the author had for Joseph Jefferson in his
generous appreciation of others. Mr. Jefferson, he
said had once told him, "I can recognize my superior in every one. I recognize my superior in a boot-
black, because he can black boots better than I. It
does not mean that in other things he is my superior, perhaps, but every human being has some re-
deeming, or some superior, quality for which I may
admire him."

Eight weeks' vacation came now, and I felt entitled to it after the three years' endurance test of
managing my own company with unceasing financial loss, and only saved from wreckage by the
SHENANDOAH engagement when the profits went to
pay patient creditors. Those eight weeks, with the
slow voyages to and from Europe, and the chance
to see again the plays in London and Paris, were
mental and physical salvation. The turn of the
memory-kaleidoscope of that holiday brings the
high gleam of Mounet Sully's *Œdipe Roi* at the
Comedie Française. It remains one of the greatest
events of the theatre I have ever known. That
actor—god-like in stature, magnificent in voice—
standing on the stage after the tragedy was finished and the audience had rushed to the front of
the orchestra with shouts and applause! It was one
of the most gratifying demonstrations an actor ever
witnessed.

252

A SHY THING IS COMEDY

JOSEPH JEFFERSON

There were a few weeks, altogether too few, with Joseph Jefferson—a man who made the acting of comedy a science. He was at all times ready to talk with his fellows about the detail and technique of the theatre. Although he was endowed with the temperament for the portrayal of humorous and pathetic emotion, had been bred from a long line of comedians, and found the manner of the theatre an easy matter, he was careful to the point of meticulousness in building up his effects. In this regard he was more like the French comedians than any American actor I have known. He nursed each line of his parts for its laughs or tears. "Never rush your comedy points," he once told me, "the quieter and more deliberate you are, the better your effect. I found that to be true when Billy Florence and I joined forces as a two-star team in THE RIVALS. I felt I mustn't take all the situations as *Bob Acres* but must give Billy a show as *Sir Lucius O'Trigger*. In the duel scene I had been used to work all the tricks of terror, shaking knees, trembling voice, ghastly face, etc., as *Bob* sneaks off the scene with his courage oozing out of the tips of his fingers. They used to laugh tremendously at it, so I piled it up. It rather took the attention from *Sir Lucius*. Of course I liked the laughter but I must be fair to Florence. So I didn't work at all. I gave *Sir Lucius* a look, turned and walked quietly into the wings and, by George! they shouted louder than ever. It's a shy thing—comedy. Chase it too hard and it runs away from you. When Mrs. Drew was playing *Mrs. Malaprop* she said one night, 'Mr. Jefferson, I'm not getting the laughs I used to get. What is the matter?' I replied, 'Mrs. Drew, it's because you read the lines as though *you* thought them funny. Try reading them seriously.' "

Commenting on his methods he said: "Work at your part like the dickens when you're studying your effects, but don't carry your tools into the theatre and let the audience see them. Leave them in the workshop. When I die I suppose people will say of me that I was one of the most mechanical actors in America and they will be perfectly right. I am. Most anybody can be funny; a clown in a circus is funny, but real comedy is the most difficult and serious business in the world."

He said that no two audiences were ever alike, and that was why he never tired of playing over and over again his old parts. One must not be caught napping in a performance for it is from the various and varying audiences that the tone and tempo of a performance are set. (How true I have found this to be!) "Besides," he added, "I always try to tell myself that I am playing the part for the first time."

He claimed that certain cities needed a little more force. " 'This is Pittsburg,' I always say to my company when we are there, 'and you must pull things open a little wider.' " (I don't think he would say that of Pittsburgh to-day—there is a new generation of theatre-goers, but I, alas! know other

cities where despite the new generation, or shall I
say *because* of the new generation, things have to be
"pulled a little wider.")

Our association was brought about by the tour
of a representative cast in THE RIVALS. Wilton
Lackaye was to be the *Sir Lucius O'Trigger,* Ver-
ner Clarges, the *Sir Antony,* Ffolliott Paget, the *Mrs.*
Malaprop, Elsie Leslie, coming back to the stage
after having been sent to school between the days
of her remarkable acting as a child, and the time
when she returned a beautiful young leading
woman, was to be *Lydia Languish,* I the *Captain*
Jack Absolute, and members of the Jefferson family filling in the other parts.

Although acting was the breath of life to Mr.
Jefferson, his fragile health did not permit him to
make long tours. This one was cut even shorter by
his sudden illness. During the brief tour, and I believe it was always his habit, he spent much time
with his painting. When the scenery was hauled
out of the baggage car, he would go down to the
railroad yards, set up his easel in the empty car,
paint landscapes and be happy. In my house hangs
a souvenir of my association with this gifted man—
a Rousseau-like forest and stream which he presented to me while the paint was still wet on the
canvas. This, with certain books and a few letters,
are the tangible mementos of my friendship with
Mr. Jefferson—a man who knew an infinite deal
about the art of acting.

He had a curious prejudice about mourning

worn in the theatre. The last evening we played at
Miner's Fifth Avenue Theatre in New York, he
said, "The play will go badly to-night. There is a
woman dressed in mourning sitting in a box."

1899—1900

The next turn of the kaleidoscope brings a tour
of ROSEMARY, by Louis N. Parker and Murray Car-
son, which filled the gap after the sudden ending of
THE RIVALS season. The South and Middle West
were new soil for this charming comedy—wholly
susceptible to its sentiment, and I thrived. If the
summer had been hot, that winter was cold. To be
snow-bound in Georgia was an unprecedented experience: the penetrating chill of half-warmed theatres, tedious railway journeys with delays from
frozen engines, waiting all day in a dreadful place
called Lulu Junction where an entire train-load of
passengers were half-fed at one eating house. It
was too hard on the dear Old Woman of the company. She struggled bravely through the performance at Augusta and we got her to Nashville, but
there she died. Somehow, until that sorrow occurred, I had never felt the loneliness of the road—
the isolation—the vagabondage.

The next year I again took an established New
York success through unbroken territory. This was
THE LIARS—one of the best of the Henry Arthur
Jones comedies.

Then came the happy result of my having made
a dramatization of Stevenson's PRINCE OTTO. At

MAUD DURBIN (Mrs. Skinner)
in Prince Otto

last a New York theatre was vouchsafed unto me!
In September, 1900, we came into Wallack's with a
success. I had not realized until after my version
was produced how many *Ottos* there were in the
field. I knew that Stevenson himself had said there
was a play in PRINCE OTTO, but he could not find it.
Others had. There were *Ottos* to the right and
Ottos to the left, but luckily I had been first to produce mine. Charles Warren Stoddard wrote to me
quoting a letter he had from Stevenson accompany-
ing a presentation copy of the novel. It said:

"If you like to touch on *Otto* any day in a by-
hour (Stoddard was then Professor of English in
the University of Notre Dame), you may tell them
(as the author's last dying confession) that it is a
strange example of the difficulty of being ideal in
an age of realism. That the unpleasant giddymind-
edness which spoils the book and often gives it an
air of wanton unreality as juggling with air-bells,
comes from unsteadiness of key; from the too great
realism of some chapters and passages (some of
which I have now spotted, others I dare say, I shall
never spot) which disrepairs its imagination for
the cost of the remainder. Every story can be made
true in its own key; any story can be made false by
the choice of a wrong key of detail or style. *Otto*
is made to reel like a drunken—I was going to say,
man, but let us substitute *cypher,* by the variations
of the key. Have you observed that the famous
problem of realism and idealism, is one purely of
detail?"

Curiously, I had felt that Stevenson had set up
his puppets only to throw stones at them later, but I

had worked out the play from the idealistic conception. To-day it would be the realistic which would be the natural procedure.

I was a little afraid to have the Stevenson family see the play, but Mrs. Strong and Lloyd Osbourne were kind enough to say they thought I had dealt faithfully with the book. It was an excellent company with Percy Haswell as *Seraphina*, Grace Filkins as the *Countess*, Mrs. Skinner as *Minna*, and George Nash starting on a long-continued career of villains, in the part of *Baron Gondremark*.

My friend Tom Nast's greeting after the opening night I have preserved with pride.

IN A BALCONY

To Sarah Cowell LeMoyne must be given the credit for the production of IN A BALCONY. Hers was the inspiration, and George Tyler had the perspicacity to realize that with careful advertising it could have a brief season. This it had—leaving a memory which endures as one of the genuinely artistic achievements of the American theatre. It was perhaps the most cohesive production with which I was ever associated. The one time when scene painter, musician, costume designer rose to the height of the poet, and I do not think we three actors of the short cast, Mrs. LeMoyne, Miss Robson and myself, ever approached a task with greater deference, or worked harder to make clear the difficult verse of Robert Browning.

Mrs. LeMoyne had been an actress but had re-

SEPTEMBER 4, 1900.

POST — MUSIC AND DRAMA.

"Prince Otto."

Mr. Otis Skinner's new romantic play, "Prince Otto," which met with a decidedly favorable reception in Wallack's Theatre

N. Y. HERALD.

"PRINCE OTTO" MADE A HIT

Th. Nast.
Sep. 4-1900

tired for a time to devote her talents to public readings. She had come back to the theatre with keen enthusiasm and it was her idea that we should produce this tabloid drama—a tragedy compressed into the space of one scene. She brought to the part of the *Queen* regal dignity and a deeply poignant sadness. I can still hear the vibrant ring of her voice as she cried out in the *Queen's* heart-hunger—

"There have been moments, if the sentinel,
Lowering his halberdt to salute the queen,
Had flung it brutally and clasped my knees,
I would have stooped and kissed him with my soul."

Eleanor Robson was lovely, young and on the threshold of a brilliant but brief career. She played the part of *Constance* with rare charm.

Browning was never kind to the theatre in the matter of ease of delivery. For over an hour this little tragedy moves on argumentatively—intensely, even volcanically. At the finish I found myself exhausted from the mere physical work of "putting over" *Norbert.* The result was well worth the effort. IN A BALCONY never failed to hold our audiences in breathless attention. I always felt that our real critics were in the gallery. Up there were people who knew more about Browning than I knew.

The tour had been carefully organized. Crowded houses greeted us. It was only for a month, but we swung from New York and Boston, south as far as Richmond, and west to the Mississippi, giving one or two performances in the principal cities. Sometimes we played a matinée in one town and a night

Otis Skinner

IN A BALCONY
Mrs. Le Moyne

Eleanor Robson

performance in another—as in Baltimore and
Washington. Browning Societies existed everywhere; audiences were well prepared. I doubt, now,
if In a Balcony will ever again be seen on a professional stage.

To make the programme of sufficient length
In a Balcony was preceded by William Butler
Yeats' poetic one act play, The Land of Hearts'
Desire. This was practically the introduction of a
new poet to the play-going public; his recent honor
of receiving the Nobel Prize has added still further
luster to that unique event.

A REVIVAL OF "FRANCESCA DA RIMINI"

I yielded to the persuasion that a revival of
Francesca da Rimini was timely. Both the Stephen
Phillips and the D'Annunzio tragedies had been produced but recently in their authors' countries—
England and Italy, and I believed then, as I believe
now, that in the matter of direct, culminating tragedy neither equaled the American poet's drama.

I find in comparing the two representations of
the Boker tragedy—the Lawrence Barrett production of 1882 and my own of 1901—that critics generally were kinder to the author at the later date. We
treat our poets better after they are dead. I am a
little amazed in turning through an old scrap-book
to find what almost universal praise the play received. Even in New York, where the first night
struggled against the outside din of a noisy New
Year, the critics were favorable. I hope I may be

pardoned for quoting from William Winter's review:

"It has great moments, and it is heavily freighted with terror and pity. With sincere and competent actors it could never fail. Mr. Skinner brings to the impersonation of this exacting character (*Launciotto*) ripe experience, stalwart vigor and superb energy, and while winning signal honor for himself, he arouses memory and inspires thought of many noble things, and he much refreshes hope for the future of the stage. There could not, in the dramatic world, be a brighter augury for the New Year."

Mr. Winter was not always so kind. Years later, when I built high hopes for THE DUEL, by Lavedan, he (as some wag said, "Now is the Winter of our discontent") showed his scorn of this new play from the French by coming solemnly down the aisle on the first night, wrapped and muffled in a heavy overcoat and scarf and never during the evening divesting himself of these garments although the theatre was cheerily warm. He was frozen to all interest in the night's work.

But whatever the praise and interest of the loyal supporters of poetic drama, FRANCESCA DA RIMINI lacked drawing power to reimburse me for all the funds that had gone into its production. At the end of the season I found myself again with a depleted treasury. I had lost what, at that time, was a hopeless amount—more than twenty thousand dollars. I should have fared no better had I taken the newer written version of Stephen Phillips

—superior and more modern though it was in verse. I saw the D'Annunzio FRANCESCA one bitterly cold night in Chicago when we were a mere handful of spectators to see that greatest of actresses—Eleanora Duse. She was a white flame as she entered the garden and stood by the flower-filled sarcophagus. She was Art visualized, personified, and yet intangible. She was not aware of her surroundings. She did not know whether we were a handful or a multitude sitting entranced before her. The play had a medieval atmosphere neither of the other two possessed, but it was brutal and yet, to-day, if the three versions were again presented D'Annunzio's FRANCESCA would be the one to have a possible success.

In my revival of the Boker tragedy, Marcia Van Dresser, beautiful and statuesque, played *Francesca,* Aubrey Boucicault was the *Paolo,* William Norris the *Pepe,* and I the *Launciotto.*

Boucicault had what might be called an ''actor's temperament,'' although I have known but few instances where the actor was not as normally balanced as any other human being. Aubrey undoubtedly inherited from his distinguished father much of his beguiling Irish wit, but he suffered from having been undisciplined in his youth and allowed to grow up pretty much as he pleased. In fact, he never seemed to have quite grown up. He was a curious contradiction. Likable in his deference and respect for his elders; ridiculously petty and vain in the theatre. A better dressing-room given to the leading lady than the one assigned to him, a mirror better placed than the one on his wall, threw him into a jealous rage. On two occasions he was unable to play—once because of a slight irritation in his eye, and again because his vaccinated arm pained him. Every mole-hill in life was to him a mountain. Not the least of my troubles in this season of general perturbation was keeping the peace between *Paolo* and *Francesca*.

My chief concern, however, was about the six choir boys we employed for the cathedral scene. These vigorous little chaps curled up like sleepy kittens on the long journeys and slept peacefully—not dreamlessly, however, for one lad sometimes talked in his sleep and it was always about home. They were the especial charge of the wardrobe woman—a motherly soul, but old Eugene Eberle delegated himself to keep them in check. (He had sons of his own.) He fussed over them far more than necessary, and insisted on buying heavy under "flannins" for one of them—much to the lad's discomfort. On one occasion one of the boys strolled off alone to an auction sale of farming materials. The bidding excited him and he joined in the competition until he became possessed of a farm wagon. The lad was terrified when he found what he had done, and poor old Eberle, grumbling and scolding, was dragged off to make explanations to the auctioneer.

We called Eberle, "Mr. Kill-Joy." If there was a catastrophe or disaster, Eberle was first to hear of it. He always knew when trains were late—when

1882

LAWRENCE BARRETT   OTIS SKINNER
LOUIS JAMES   BEN ROGERS

1901

AUBREY BOUCICAULT   MARCIA VAN DRESSER
OTIS SKINNER   WILLIAM NORRIS

FRANCESCA DA RIMINI

trouble was ahead. In the five years he stayed a member of my company we learned to laugh over his calamity-howling, for with it he had much kindliness and philosophy.

Apropos of the boys in the FRANCESCA DA RIMINI Company, I do not think the season was detrimental either to their health or mental progress, and yet, on general principals, I object to children on the stage. The few I have been obliged to use in my own companies, and those I remember with Augustin Daly's MIDSUMMER NIGHT'S DREAM, for example, had rather the advantage over other children of similar station in life, in that they were imbibing a culture their natural environment probably did not possess. I believe in legislation to protect the child, but not that he should be irrevocably barred from being in plays where his young mind may be benefitted rather than corrupted. I can think of several instances where, without the uplifting influence of the theatre, there might have been no development of a genuinely talented young actor.

Children, like dogs, horses or any trained animal, are usually more disturbing to a scene than a help. One is lifted from the mood of the play to admire the cleverness in training that has made it possible to teach the necessary words or tricks. I once relinquished my rights in a play after I had sought out the author and commissioned her to write it, because, when the finished manuscript was turned over to me, the problem of dealing with the child actor and the legal complications made it too difficult to undertake. This was Josephine Preston Peabody's THE PIPER, which later took the Stratford Prize in England, and was afterward produced in America at The New Theatre. I regretted giving up the play not only because of the author's disappointment, but for the sentimental reason that the inception of a play about THE PIED PIPER OF HAMLIN had come from my own child—just old enough to have the Browning poem read to her, and to have the tripping verse fascinate her little mind. "It would make a pretty theatre," she said, and she was right. I took the baby's idea to Josephine Preston Peabody because she wrote beautiful verse, because she loved children and because she had a sense of drama. I had no cause to regret my choice for, although circumstances conspired against my producing the play, it brought her high honors.

Alas! The plays one does not produce—that is another heart-breaking experience of an actor's life.

LAZARRE

No period in history has been more fertile for the dramatist than the French Revolution. It would take more than a five-foot shelf to hold the plays that have been written on various episodes in that tragic panorama.

I had felt there were splendid possibilities in a play based on the Lost Dauphin. There were several legends from which choice could be made, but the most picturesque seemed to be the one connected with America, and toward this end I had been collecting material for a play based on Eleazar Williams and the Oneida Indians, and had been in correspondence with the Missionary at the Indian reservation near Green Bay, Wisconsin, when in some anxiety Mary Hartwell Catherwood wrote to me that she was publishing a novel on this theme and would I consider dramatizing it before going on with my play. Here was a plot clearly developed, so the contract was made and a play written of this supposed Indian boy discovering himself to be Louis XVII, King of France. It made an effectively romantic play with the scene shifting from America to France and on to Russia and back again to the Indian Settlement in Green Bay. Curiously enough, I later played the Lost Dauphin of another legend—*Denis Roulette,* the French clock-maker in Henri Lavedan's SIRE, a better written and constructed piece, but at the time LAZARRE was picturesque and romantically satisfying.

My association with Mrs. Catherwood in the writing and production of LAZARRE gave me an insight into her deep love for the history and legends of America—especially of the Middle West where she had spent most of her life. She died shortly after the play was produced, and her going was a distinct loss, for she had still much to give in books she had planned dealing with the American pioneer. She had great patriotism, and a gifted pen.

One of the amusing high-lights of that season was our playing for one night in Sioux Falls, South

Dakota. Before the days of Reno, the divorce colony was Sioux Falls. The large hotel bore the aspect of a sanitarium, so filled was it with a fashionable clientele strangely different from the native inhabitants. When my wife and I were shown to our room, the facetious bell-boy swung open the door and exclaimed: "Mr. Skinner, you are going to occupy the room just vacated by the famous Mrs. M—." The room was adequately but cheerlessly furnished after the standard hotel pattern. The walls were quite bare except for a large calendar with only the month of December remaining, and up to that day of the month, the fifteenth, each was crossed off with a heavy blue crayon mark. This was the day of her liberation. We assumed that the previous months (one had to stay for eight) were tolled off with the same dreary blue-crayoned count.

About supper-time the electric lights went out. We groped through the meal, thinking it was merely a local disorder, but as we walked along the streets the town seemed unusually dark and on reaching the theatre we discovered the city lighting plant had ceased to function. Every available shop was sought for candles, of which only a meager lot of common or garden variety could be found. Candlesticks were not to be had, but a neighboring saloon donated empty bottles. These served (the candles fitted to stick into the bottle mouths) for the dressing-rooms and were then carried off to light the stage with feeble gleams. A railway locomotive head-light was fetched and placed on the upright

OTIS SKINNER IN FOUR FRENCH ROLES

ABBÉ DANIEL
in The Duel

DENIS ROULETTE
in Sire

THE HARVESTER
in The Harvester (*Le Chemineau*)

PHILIPPE BRIDAU
in The Honor of the Family
(*La Rabouilleuse*)

piano top in the orchestra pit. In front of this cruel glare we played important scenes, and then slunk back into shadowy gloom. Between acts each actor grabbed a beer-bottled candle and repaired down the steep stairway to the cellar dressing-rooms, while the head-light was turned round to light the orchestra (a piano and two fiddles) and to enable the nervous members of the audience to stare at one another—for the divorce colony was rather distinguished that year and the audience was quite as interesting as the play. We went through the entire evening with that ridiculous head-light and the bottle-filled candles. The audience seemed so hungry for entertainment that they accepted the play in all its hideous lights and shadows.

When we got back to the hotel, the clerk was quite indignant that the town's supply of candles had gone to lighting the stage. He handed me a half-burned wax taper (I strongly suspected a church had been robbed), requesting that when we were ready for bed it should be placed outside the door for some other guest. This I did, but I also forgot to turn off the electric switch. At five next morning the room was dazzling with the reestablished current. I looked out the window. All Sioux Falls was a-gleam. Everybody had apparently forgot to turn off the switch.

REHAN-SKINNER

Of the next season I can think only with poignant sadness. It had been arranged between George

269

Tyler and myself that I should star with Ada Rehan. We agreed upon a repertory of three plays: THE TAMING OF THE SHREW, THE SCHOOL FOR SCANDAL and THE MERCHANT OF VENICE. Miss Rehan had but to revive her old and favorite rôles, two of which seemed to be hers alone—*Katherine* and *Lady Teazle*. *Portia*, she had also played happily, if not so brilliantly. For my own part, *Shylock* had been a conspicuous rôle in my repertory for the first three years of my independent ventures. *Charles Surface* and *Petruchio* merely meant slipping into other shoes than the ones I had worn in the Daly Company.

From the opening rehearsal it was evident that the exquisite comedienne with whom I had the happiest memories of five years' association, was no more. One of the inevitable misfortunes that befall women of our profession had come to her: Miss Rehan was paying the penalty of years—acting was no longer a pleasure; it was an obligation. Augustin Daly was dead and without him she was helpless. She met the situation bravely, but she was tired; she was ill—often too ill to come to rehearsal. Sometimes, however, as *Katherine* the old fires would flash for a little and she would be almost her former self. *Lady Teazle* and *Portia*, though still sure in technique, were but echoes of the past.

The route had been planned in the belief that we could sweep through the East, South and Middle West with fine results; but it was a cruel thing to have expected of her. The way was long, and al-

ADA REHAN
as Katherine in The Taming of the Shrew

though we had the luxury of a private car for most of our journeys, there were hardships of travel she had never known in her heyday. It was rather the more tragic that the nearest and dearest thing to her should be a little black cocker spaniel that was her constant companion. Many times she was refused shelter in the more comfortable hotels because dogs were not allowed, and rather than lodge her little "Bobs" in the trunk room with the porter, or leave him in care of stage hands, she would drive off to a second-rate hotel. It was most exasperating to see the comfort she denied herself when it came to the question of the hotel or the dog. One night, in Kansas City, word came from the trained nurse, Miss Rehan's necessary traveling-companion, that Miss Rehan could not come to the theatre because Bobs was sick. With a very large audience to be dismissed, and much money to be refunded if the performance had to be abandoned, the business manager went to plead with her. At first she refused absolutely to consider leaving the sick puppy,—players or public meant naught to her, —but finally when a veterinary was called in and arrangements made for bulletins to be sent to her throughout the evening, she came to the theatre and the performance was saved. This seemed a little childish at the time, and I was provoked, but I am glad I said nothing, for when I contrasted this sad-faced, white-haired woman, always dressed, outside the theatre, as if clothes were merely garments for protecting the body from heat or cold, taking no interest in anything about her, with the radiant beauty of the Daly days, the comparison was more tragic than any rôle she had ever acted in the theatre.

One of the few amusing incidents of that season was during a rehearsal of THE TAMING OF THE SHREW. Walter Hale, genial, talented, lovable, had been cast for *Lucentio,* but was ill at first and went to the hospital for an operation. He returned to us amid much congratulation on his recovery, and we were putting him through a quick rehearsal when suddenly there was a roar of laughter. *Biondello* had spoken the line: "My master hath appointed me to go to St. Luke's, to bid the priest be ready to come against you come with your appendix." Walter Hale had been at St. Luke's hospital, and he had gone to have his appendix removed! Even Miss Rehan laughed that day.

THE HARVESTER

When, on a hot night in August, 1922, I saw, for the first time, a performance of LE CHEMINEAU at The P rte St. Martin Théâtre in Paris, and after I had, on the week previous in Dieppe, heard the opera arrangement of the drama, sung magnificently by a provincial company, I knew better than ever that it is one of the most poetically satisfying works in modern French dramatic literature. This was my old play, THE HARVESTER, produced eighteen years previously in America.

It had been a success in Paris some time before

OTIS SKINNER
as Charles Surface

there was thought of an English version, and then Beerbohm Tree produced one in London under the title of RAGGED ROBIN. The scene had been transferred from its French locale to Dorsetshire, and its language was so thick with *z's* and other dialectic hurdles, that it was baffling to London ears, and almost incomprehensible to read from the manuscript offered to me for production in this country. My brother Charles took the play as Monsieur Jean Richepin had written it, and turned it into poetic English prose quite worthy the French original. It breathed of fields and roads and sunshine and storm, for of these things no one had greater appreciation than my nature-loving brother. To bring the scene a little nearer home, we hit upon the idea of laying it in French Canada, and to this end I spent a summer in the picturesque parish of Les Eboulements where there was still a *Seigneur* to whom the habitants looked with respect and moderate awe. Domestic industries were still in their own hands. Homespun for the clothes to be worn in our play was bought from the women who had spun the yarn, dyed and woven the cloth. The characteristic *bottes sauvages* were made by the toothless old *cordonnier* at the bend of the road below the cottage in which we lived. Even the straw hats were plaited and shaped by a woman of the parish. Never have I produced a play with such pleasure. And in the playing of it I never had so sympathetic a company.

Night after night I have seen the members of

the cast standing in the wings listening to scenes in which they did not appear. Sometimes I used to feel that we were doing it for the enjoyment of ourselves, for audiences were not always understanding. On several occasions the beauty of the play brought forth an approving editorial from the press, but as often, the call of the road, the joys and sorrows of these simple God-fearing, home-loving *habitants* were lost to the casual spectator. It was like a butterfly seeking a flower garden in the Bowery.

Again a grim memory of the road. The train was drawing into Richmond, Indiana, after an ungodly early start from our last town, when I saw Ben Ringgold, of my company, looking terribly ill. He died in the cab with me as we were speeding to the hotel. That night, the dressing-rooms under the stage in the gloomy theatre were like a row of cells. As I passed along the corridor all the doors were open, and the actors sat there in silence as if afraid to shut themselves in with their grief, for Ben Ringgold was much beloved. He had served his profession for many years—his stories of a generation older than mine were rich in memories. We had not realized that his tired old heart could not stand the strain of hard travel.

"Gypsy, to the road again!" was the last line in THE HARVESTER. We started out on ours again next morning—the understudy taking Ben's place, while he had gone on The Higher Road.

Lizzie Hudson Collier, Marion Abbott, Mrs.

Skinner, Ben Ringgold and George Clark, he who had engaged me for one of my early appearances in New York when he produced HEARTS OF STEEL, and who later had been a member of the Augustin Daly Company during my time there, were the principal members of THE HARVESTER Company,—the most gratifying play of these seven years.

DE GRAMMONT REVIVED

The Harvester having finished his task, there came the question of the play to follow. I had seriously considered two Clyde Fitch plays: THE LAST OF THE DANDIES and MAJOR ANDRÉ. Both had qualities, but again they were both reminiscent of other and better plays of his—BEAU BRUMMELL and NATHAN HALE. I was sorry not to do ANDRÉ—it had a beautiful last act. Later, when it was produced, a a couple left the theatre one evening evidently much disgruntled. Said the man, "This is a nice kind of play you picked out. The hero getting shot in the last act."

"Well, I'm sorry, dear," pleaded the wife, "but it isn't my fault. That is what happened to Major André."

"How the devil was I to know that!" growled the man as they disappeared into the crowd.

That is the chance an author takes in writing a play of historical characters. He flatters his audience that they know quite as much of the subject, and have remembered their history quite as well as he, when, in truth, the average audience cares very

275

little about the subject-matter of a play. We talk about cultivating public taste, and I believe an audience is, generally speaking, moderately intelligent, but the average person, like the gentleman who did not know about Major André, hates to have history taught him in the theatre.

And so I did produce a Clyde Fitch play, but not a new one. It was the revised HIS GRACE DE GRAMMONT, freshened in lines and trappings after these seven years.

CHAPTER XVII

BEFORE my fortunes passed under the management of Charles Frohman I had met the little Napoleon of the Theatre but twice; once in a poker game at the old Lambs' Club on Twenty-Sixth Street in my Daly's Theatre days at the time he had made his first ten-strike by his production of Bronson Howard's SHENANDOAH, and then, much later, when I made an arrangement with him to take out ROSE-MARY for a tour. One does not develop an unwonted warmth of friendliness in a game of poker, and as for the business meeting, it was strictly a formal occasion wherein terms were agreed on; that was all.

Charles' brother Daniel, in his LIFE OF CHARLES FROHMAN, has told of the humble beginnings of this man whose name became a synonym for theatrical supremacy in two continents. Little schooling had C. F., but his was a temperament born for success in whatever enterprise he might have chosen. His early struggles and the uncertainties attending his first managerial efforts stiffened his resolutions and enlarged his capacities. Through it all he had preserved his vision. His ideas were so great that their very presence seemed to overwhelm his utter-

277

ance. The mental pictures he saw, he lacked power to describe. At rehearsal he would run into a verbal hiatus now and then—but always by gesture or an expression of his face managed to make his meaning known. He seemed to have a timidity in the presence of language. But if his tongue faltered his eyes conveyed his message. They were eloquent eyes. He would begin—"Er—a—Otis—you know—a—you know—er—"

"Yes, Charlie," I would reply, "I know. I've got it." It was a kind of telepathy. One caught his meaning before he spoke.

Not that he was a silent man. With two or three of his friends he could be most eloquent, and it was said, with his foes as well. In his office in The Empire Theatre I have listened by the hour to his descriptions of plays he had seen or read. On these occasions, he would leave his chair and pace to and fro, stopping now and then to act certain scenes, and his tongue never faltered for a word.

His friendships were warm and his hatreds bitter. One of the oddest and yet firmest of his friendships was that for James M. Barrie. I am told that when he was a guest of Sir James in England, the pair would sit through long silences—quite content, Barrie puffing away on a big pipe, and Frohman negotiating a cigar. Quaintly opposite—the sensitive, fragile creator of *Peter* and *Wendy* and *Dear Brutus,* and the little rotund commercial manager. But they met on common ground in the land of their dreams.

278

CHARLES FROHMAN

HIS FAMOUS LAST WORDS

I recall his pride when, one morning at The Empire, he stopped my rehearsal to bring Sir James down the aisle of the empty theatre and introduce us. It was this friendship for Barrie that sent him to his death. Barrie had written that he would like to have Frohman pay him a visit, and nothing would stop his going. He embarked on the *Lusitania*. When the ship was sinking, after the assault of the German submarine, it was a quotation from Barrie that was preserved to us by a fellow passenger, as his last words: "Why fear death? It is the greatest adventure of life."

The unknown had great fascination for him. He once said to me, "If I knew that every play I produce was going to be a success, I'd quit the business." Every play he produced was a new adventure for him.

He had his weaknesses—amiable ones; the wonder is that they were so few. He was singularly clean; as Augustus Thomas said of him in a masterly funeral oration, to be with him was to come into the presence of decency. He was vain of the eminence he had gained, and loved all references to his power. He always wished to see Charles spelled in full, and was inclined to be peevish over letters addressed to Chas. Frohman. He liked to think of himself as the creator of his theatrical stars—the Pygmalion of many Galateas. This was probably the reason why there was a shade of constraint at the beginning of our acquaintance; I was a ready-made star delivered into his hands. But

this suggestion of formality was of short life. And
I learned, too, that any assistance in direction from
his stars annoyed him somewhat. He wanted to be
sole authority in production. He hated to acknowledge himself in the wrong. Once we had a little
argument about a piece of business in A CELE-
BRATED CASE. I yielded, though unconvinced. At
the next day's rehearsal he said, "You were right
about that scene." Then seeing my look of satisfaction, he added, "Now don't rub it in!"

C. F. was inordinately fond of pastry, particularly pies. They beckoned to him from pastry-shop
windows. An especially alluring pie would pursue
him to his very office desk, where he would ring for
an office boy to go in haste to purchase the delect-
able thing that he might devour it to the last flaky
crumb. An odor from a pie bakery was always his
undoing. His weakness for rich foods undoubtedly
contributed to a digestive disarrangement that became an all too constant companion, and because he
never took physical exercise, presently wrought
havoc with his system.

A point on which he was particularly jealous
was that all vital suggestions should come from him.
I discovered this when we produced Henri Lavedan's SIRE. The theme, the worship of royalty by
an aristocratic Frenchwoman of the old régime, did
not strike a sympathetic note with the first-night
audience at The Criterion Theatre in New York. It
did not exactly fail, but I did not scent a special success for the piece. I was feeling rather downcast

over the result, for our engagement was booked for a number of weeks, when a brilliant idea occurred to me—the revival of a play which had scored heavily three years before. I felt we could turn our indifferent engagement into a popular run. I hastened to the Frohman offices with my bright idea and sprang it with great emphasis and enthusiasm. He was rather swept along with my fervor at first; said 'twas a happy thought and might work out. At the theatre that night, however, he came into my dressing-room and said no, he had decided to keep SIRE on for the full engagement.

Speaking about it later to his brother, Dan said to me, "Ah! you should have let Charlie think the idea had come from him, and he probably would have accepted the suggestion. You were too sudden with him."

From the members of my profession, big and little, I can not recall hearing a word of dislike or hatred for Charles Frohman. He had a way of making an actor think he was doing him an honor by accepting an engagement from him. I recall his saying, "Why shouldn't I like actors? Actors and authors have made me."

His ambitions were boundless, his personal wants few. Money had no meaning to him for itself; for its mere possession he cared not a straw. So long as it gave him the call on the works of nearly all the English and French dramatists through offers of such terms as they had never been accustomed to, and so made his life one grand procession of first nights; so long as "Charles Frohman Presents" stood at the head of the announcements of many plays, and many stars; so long as he managed many theatres in New York, the larger American cities and in London—he was happy.

He was not a great stage director, but he had an instinctive and unusual knowledge of stage effect. He studied his audiences and watched their reactions.

Much of his later life was spent in the seclusion of his apartment in the Knickerbocker Hotel—imprisoned by a painful malady of the leg which at times caused him the utmost torture. Through all his suffering his eye never lost its look of courage, nor did his philosophy desert him.

He gently bemoaned the fate that kept him from my first night in New York as *Hajj* in KISMET. "I can't be there," he said, "but I shall know everything that you are doing. They are going to call me up on the telephone after every act. I shall see your whole performance." Half an hour before the rise of the curtain a messenger brought a note scrawled in blue pencil to my dressing-room. It said: "This is your night and that makes it mine also. Good Luck! Charles Frohman."

The play was a triumph. The next day Mrs. Skinner and I called on him. He was propped up on his couch, the morning newspapers strewn about him, beaming with satisfaction.

"Weren't you nervous?" he asked my wife.

"No, Mr. Frohman," she answered. "I had

seen the performance in Washington, and I felt confident."

"Mrs. Skinner, you can never be confident. Otis might have sneezed in the wrong place. That sort of thing has happened."

The immediate cause of my enlisting under the Frohman banner was my need of a play, and a particular one. That play was Henri Lavedan's LE DUEL. I was looking for a vehicle to follow the revival of HIS GRACE DE GRAMMONT when I received news of the success of this piece at The Théâtre Français in Paris. It was the work of a distinguished academician dealing with the strife between Church and State, religion and materialism (always a poignant issue in France), and it had stirred the emotions of the Parisian public. Its chief protagonist, the *Abbé Daniel,* an impressionable and fanatical young priest, seemed to me an excellent part for my clientele. I knew Frohman held the American rights, and I wrote to him. His reply was brief and characteristic. "If you want THE DUEL, come under my management and I will produce it for you."

Another interchange of letters, arranging terms, and the business was finished. That was the way that C. F. always directed his affairs if it were possible, and this was our contract throughout his lifetime—a tacit understanding, a letter agreeing to the production of a certain play—nothing more. We each had confidence in the fidelity of the other: our mutual interests prospered: our friendship

283

grew. From thence onward it was, "Charles Frohman presents Otis Skinner."

THE DUEL was given at The Hudson Theatre with a cast that included Fay Davis as the *Duchess*, "the woman in the case," Guy Standing, who later won his knighthood in England by his valor in the World War, playing the contending, agnostic brother of *Abbé Daniel*, and Eben Plympton, a talented, forceful but extremely temperamental and egotistical actor in the colorful part of the *Bishop*, originally played in Paris by Paul Mounet.

This Lavedan masterpiece ran to the season's end at The Hudson, and the following year went on tour from Boston to the Pacific Coast, reaching San Francisco twelve months after the Great Fire. The most important member of the new cast was that able artist, E. M. Holland, who gave a tender and beautiful performance of the *Bishop*.

My second production under Frohman management was a play with a curious history. It had been under advisement for several seasons. This was a translation from the French of Émile Fabre's dramatization of Balzac's LA RABOUILLEUSE. It had made a sensation at The Odéon in Paris where Firmin Gémier had died in gore and glory nightly through a long run. C. F. had purchased the rights of the play for America, and commissioned Paul Potter to make the translation, an almost literal one, which was subsequently subjected to much overhauling by Frohman, William Gillette and Clyde Fitch. Later, I, myself, had a go at the manuscript.

284

I LIVE IN SPITE OF MYSELF

Fortunately all these cooks did not succeed in spoiling the broth of this vital and admirable play—a French *Katherine* and *Petruchio,* in a sinister and melodramatic setting.

One of the idosyncrasies of C. F. was his horror of death scenes. Had he produced KING LEAR, I believe he would have wished it to end happily. (SIRE would have met a better fate had Lavedan's scoundrel hero, *Denis Roulette,* been killed by revolutionary bullets as the author intended.) *Colonel Philippe Bridau* must not be killed, "But that was a big point in the Paris performance," I said, "people came to see Gémier die." "Well, they won't come to see Skinner die. Why should you die? Nobody will want you to. You've been a good fellow all through—all comedy and gaiety. Do you think they will like it if, after all these fine scenes, you come in covered with blood and fall over a chair?" The play was his property. He was stubborn. I couldn't convince him, so *I lived.*

I had not seen the French performance, and though I appreciated much of the humor and picturesque quality of the shabby, bantering, dominant Napoleonic *Colonel,* I was not prepared for his irresistible comedy. The play was christened THE HONOR OF THE FAMILY. We opened the season by a trial performance at New Rochelle. Everything was unpropitious for the event. Hardly any press announcement had been made—the company wore that aspect of ghastly cheerfulness that actors always assume in face of anticipated disaster. A

mere handful of people composed the audience—
and to crown all, it rained pitchforks. The storm
beat upon the metal roof of the sparsely-filled theatre, making as much racket as the actors on the
stage. It was an awful night. The play began
apathetically and proceeded on leaden feet. At the
very end of the first act, while the precious lady and
her lover are preparing to make away with old *Rou-
get's* money, *Philippe* bursts unexpectedly on the
scene—bangs his stick on the table, tells the plotting
pair that they've got to get out—then strolls out to
smoke a cigar. It is the falling of a thunderbolt,
and the scene lasts less than a minute. I know no
more effective entrance in the whole range of the
drama. The audience screamed with delight. When
I came on again in the next act, they chortled once
more, and somewhat to my own amazement, I discovered the *Colonel* to be a comic figure. The audience had taught me the exact mood of the part, and
proved what I have often found, that the right audience is the greatest stage director in the world. The
play was a success from that moment. It ran for
two years, with half a season at The Hudson Theatre, New York. Ten years afterward I made a
profitable revival in a forty-week tour of the entire
country.

When the sun of Charles Frohman rose on Man-
hattan, managers of individual stock companies
were prospering in their theatres. Daly was at his
zenith, Daniel Frohman's little theatre, The Lyceum on Fourth Avenue, was popular, A. M. Palmer

had had a string of successes, and although Wallack's was living largely on its past reputation, it was still in the running.

Ill-fortune befell these managers within a few years. Whether or no Frohman had anything to do with it, I can not say—probably the public's whims were changing—but it is an undoubted fact that he put the theatre into a new position in New York. He was the first to produce plays wholesale. I lament the tragedy of his taking off, but I believe that Charles Frohman died at the psychological moment. He had been much lauded by the critics of the theatre, also much blamed for his commercial methods. His general importation of material, instead of an encouragement of the works of American writers, aroused bitterness in some quarters; but when all is said, his record stands for ideals and high achievement.

But now Fortune's wheel was once more at the turn; other producers were contesting his supremacy. He no longer had the field to himself. His affairs were becoming involved. The fires of ambition and activity which he had stoked so ardently were burning him out physically. He was growing tired.

But even shipwreck and drowning could not annihilate C. F. The pain-wracked body, which had been washed ashore, came home for a leave-taking from his old business comrades who with some of us that had been under his management, Gillette, Faversham, Sothern, Miller, Wilson and myself, formed the cortége of his pall-bearers. Forgotten was the picture of that ghastly last hour aboard the *Lusitania.* The real man who did not fear death because it was life's great adventure had gone on. "Nothing in his life became him like the leaving it." As the synagogue organ rumbled forth the Chopin funeral march we, who were bidding him God speed, walked with firmer tread. It was so supremely a great achievement which "Charles Frohman Presents."

CHAPTER XVIII

I have decided that the pleasantest experience a man may have is to live through a critical illness, and then enjoy the comfort of a successful convalescence. To read complimentary notices, quite of an obituary character, dug from the morgue of the newspaper office, and to find after all his work has counted for enough to warrant his being spread even on the editorial page; to receive telegrams from friends whose paths had not crossed his in years, and from strangers as well; to have as many flowers as a débutante; to be, for the moment, the Danaë of a golden shower of solicitude; these things are a tremendous stimulant to one's vanity, and make it almost worth while to go down into the Valley of the Shadow to be snatched back by a great surgeon.

And even the *going down* is not all of the adventure. You behold yourself in a mirror after the barber's visit, and wonder of what tribe of aborigines you are a member. Half your hair has been shaved off—the right half. Presently you are wheeled down a corridor in a tumbril, and you think of *Sidney Carton* and the guillotine.

Who is this white-sheeted person?—Mormon

289

prophet—Ku-Klux—Trappist monk? He is the anesthetizer! While you are wondering about him he puts your face inside something and says, "Now take a *deep breath.*" You see it all rather dreamily because of the two shots of morphia in your arm. A deep breath? Easy enough. Crack! Something snapped—everything is pink and—

You are doing a muscle dance on the bed—a woman's voice says "We must stop that." You hear something about "surgical shock"—"oxygen," but you don't know, and it is blank again.

Such was my privilege in May, 1913, after some slaughter-house of a theatre in the list of cities comprising my second season's Kismet tour had supplied me with a lusty and ambitious germ of mastoiditis. I had just strength enough to pull through the concluding three weeks, and then take a train from Boston to Indianapolis and be rescued by Doctor Lafayette Page.

No poet that I know has sung the joys of hospital life—there are few joys to sing about—and the particular one chosen for my retreat reduced pleasure to a minimum. A water-stain in the wall directly over my bed became by turns a landscape, a map of Europe, and a huge grotesque face so unstable that I could never depend on its keeping its individuality for two minutes. Its nose had a habit of creeping into its chin, or of becoming a whole flock of noses. I derived vast cheer from my nurse. By way of encouragement, and to show me I was not in desperate straights, she sat by my bedside and told

290

me tales of operations, and of special maladies which she herself had suffered. She was a confiding soul and stirred my sympathies deeply when she confessed that her hair, which had made me quite her slave until one night when I saw most of it hanging on the back of a chair near her trundle bed, was "dipped."

On the fourth morning after my operation, when the May sunshine was creeping through the foliage outside my open window, imprisonment grew loathsome. The creature on the wall had been scowling at me from among his myriad noses ever since the first daylight. Every nerve in me was in rebellion; I determined to escape. On the roof was a walled promenade. I shammed sleep, and my nurse stole out for a flirtation with the internes down the corridor. My bath-gown beckoned to me from its hook; after repeated and weak-legged efforts, I wabbled into it, swaying and dizzy, and peered down the passageway. No one. The self-operating elevator carried me to the roof and to freedom. In the pocket of my bath-gown I found cigarettes and matches. I was having a glorious time when a rescuing squad burst upon me and carried me back in disgrace.

From what far-away lumber camps they procure hospital cooks, I have not discovered. Fortunately, my investigations were unnecessary. Food in hot dishes flowed from the kitchens of many homes, particularly from the William Bobbs' and the Tarkingtons'. My thrice-a-day tray from the hospital

291

kitchen with its inevitable mashed potatoes, alternating canned peaches and pears, unfriendly biscuits, and a particularly virulent brand of tea, I bestowed upon my golden-haired nurse who, in gratitude, read to me the laudatory obituary notices kindly people had clipped from the papers and mailed to me.

Some day I want to write a hospital comedy.

After about ten days of coddling, James Whitcomb Riley came regularly and bore me, bandaged and turbaned like an Arab, away for rides in his limousine; brief, at first, then longer as my strength came back. He had twice suffered paralytic strokes and required much assistance in moving about. His right hand was quite helpless. His left, however, was still workable and generally held a long cigar which he smoked on these excursions. Whether our route took us through the town or afield, the car was sure to be followed by fond glances. One day, quite away from the city's smoke, we halted at a prosperous farm-house. In response to the chauffeur's knock a lank tall man in working clothes appeared. Seeing his caller, he turned and shouted, "Come on out, ma! It's Riley." And the old couple brought their gentle worship to the poet, who fairly bathed in it.

He spoke seldom on our drives, seeming content to have me tell stories of my experiences in the theatre. Occasionally he would think of something quaint and interesting, and would relieve me of the burden of conversation. Once I roused his indignation: I spoke of Whitman. It was as a red rag to a bull. He loathed Whitman's verse. I was describing Whitman's appearance when, as a youngster, I had seen the picturesque old poet on the Camden ferry—gay in attire, his collar open at the throat. "Yes," snarled Riley, "showin' his *brisket*."

He was much interested in having me read aloud to him THE SILENT VOICE, the new play I was to produce. And he insisted that we should be photographed together in his little sanctum on the third floor of the publishing house of the Bobbs-Merrill Company.

In earlier years Riley had been fond of convivial parties. It was from one of these, the story is told, that he returned early in the morning to his rooms at the Denison Hotel, and gave orders that he should not be disturbed. About noon Senator Albert Beveridge called. The clerk tried to explain that Mr. Riley was not feeling well and wished to see no one. The senator insisted, and writing the single word, "Beveridge" on a card asked that it should be sent up. It was some time before the bellboy could get an answer to his knock at Mr. Riley's door. Finally a sleepy voice:

"What is it?"

"A card."

"What does it say?"

"Beveridge," replied the boy.

"Beverage! Take it back. That's what was the matter with me last night."

Before my calamity gave me the boon of the

Hoosier Poet's friendship I had known him slightly. We met at a supper party in the early days of my Indianapolis engagements. I found him moody and uncommunicative. He was often that way; never dependable at a dinner party. If his neighbors attracted him he would talk; if not, he was dumb. His sympathies in matters of friendship were bottled up; he had to be quite sure before he let them out. He did not look the conventional poet—though why a poet should look conventional, I do not know. But for his occasional far-away manner and the humorous pucker of his mouth when a fantastic thought would strike him, he might have been taken for a very commercial sort of gentleman.

Only once during this supper did he become really animated. It was when Doctor Page's wife was relating the unromantic circumstances of going to her fiancé just before their marriage to have her tonsils removed. Riley's eye twinkled. "What a charming wedding present," he remarked. "A pair of tonsils."

The personnel of this party was notable. Besides Riley, it included Meredith Nicholson, General Lew Wallace, May Wright Sewall and Booth Tarkington. General Wallace sat, massive and dignified, his old military authority clinging to him in spite of the change that successful literature had made, in the piping times of peace. He seemed to realize that he was one of Indiana's great men. I feel it an honor to have known him.

Of Nicholson, a reserved and quiet man whose

JAMES WHITCOMB RILEY—OTIS SKINNER

fame had been more that of a poet than novelist and essayist, I saw but little that night. Later, I was to know him better.

Booth Tarkington had not been long out of college but already his literary genius was fore-shadowed. He was presented to me this night as the author of a play, THE PRODIGALS, which the Dramatic Club had given with success. There was in his manner a sort of old-school gallantry and deportment—rare in these, and even in those, days. Instinctively courteous and sympathetic, with a cultural understanding and a fondness for the fine things in art and literature. To know Booth Tarkington is to love him.

In spite of a peculiar hesitancy of speech, he is an admirable raconteur whenever he is in the mood, and has always an eager audience. His intensity in narration is sometimes apt to make him forget his surroundings. This evening he was seated next my wife at the end of a long table. I was at the right of the hostess at the other end. The occasion was cordial but formal.

The oysters had received due consideration from all except "Tark." Just as he was about to dispose of his last one, he launched a long story into the willing ear of Mrs. Skinner—one of the best listeners I know. In the general talk, no one noticed any delay except the hostess, who, anxious that things should move like clock-work, was disturbed; she could not give the butler the signal. Our remarks grew fewer and more constrained, until we both realized that we were becoming hypnotized by Tark's behavior. His oyster, suspended like the coffin of Mahomet, regularly rose and fell between his mouth and the table. I could see hope glow in my hostess' eye whenever the oyster seemed about to disappear, but each time Booth would strike a new angle in his story and the fork would halt on its journey and start slowly downward. We began to make little *sotto voce* bets on it. I was a sad loser before the hostess signaled the waiters to remove the course.

I look back on pleasant evenings in the homes of friends where I have had stimulating talks with Governor (later Vice-President) Marshall, Albert Beveridge, Maurice Thompson, the author of ALICE OF OLD VINCENNES, and with Charles Major, who wrote WHEN KNIGHTHOOD WAS IN FLOWER. Major was a Shelbyville lawyer; a big, breezy, overgrown boy who went at his story-making with the ardor of a college athlete. The characters in his novels were the most real people in the world to him. It is related of Dumas *fils* that he wept copiously over his DAME AUX CAMELIAS. I am positive that Charles Major not only wept, but laughed and swore as well, over the children of his brain.

One of the centers of hospitality was the house of Mrs. May Wright Sewall—a woman of rare culture, highly intellectual and vitally interested in the higher education of women. Her private school for girls set a standard of thoroughness. She had always a welcome for people of the theatre. I knew her first back in the Modjeska days. She was a vigorous anti-liquor advocate, and in the days free from prohibition, Mrs. Sewall's table was a spot where alcohol found no place. Her feasts were simple and bountiful, but no wine welcomed the guest within her walls. At the head of the table stood a chair which had been the seat of her late lamented husband—empty now save for a pot of ivy. If she referred to Mr. Sewall she would turn to the chair with an affectionate gesture as if he were present. A ghost at the feast could hardly have been less grewsome than the pot of trellised ivy. It was not easy to drown one's edged nerves in draughts of iced water.

As a recompense for having to play one night in Lafayette, Indiana, I made the acquaintance of the young editor of a local newspaper, George Barr McCutcheon, who then had ambitions as a playwright—an acquaintance that has ripened into an abiding friendship.

Not many miles from Indianapolis lies Dayton, Ohio. On an afternoon of an engagement there, I was preparing for a siesta in my hotel room, when the colored head-waiter rapped at the door and handed me an engraved visiting card reading, "Paul Laurence Dunbar."

"He asks if you will see him for a few minutes," asked the waiter. The negro poet who had written some of the tenderest verse of his race! Certainly I would.

Presently he came, the undiluted African, young,

good-looking, very black, neatly dressed, and modestly apologetic.

"Mr. Skinner," he said when I had made him welcome, "you were very kind to me a year ago in Chicago. You read a play of mine."

I remembered a play with the seventeenth century poet, Herrick, as its hero that had been handed in at the box office of the Grand Opera House. It had been left without explanation, and I only knew the identity of the writer by the name on the title page.

It was rather a scant play in volume, hardly producible, but of literary quality, full of appreciation of that poet of Arcadian romance. Altogether it was a remarkable work, when one realized the background of its author. I returned it by post to the address given, writing him of my regret that I could not produce his play. I had forgotten the episode until this day in Dayton.

"I called to thank you for your courtesy," he said.

He went on to tell me of his ambition to write a real play, and the inevitable difficulty he had in obtaining a hearing because of his color. "What has my color to do with the merit of my work?" he asked with a note of protest. "I've written plays, quite a number of them; some have been produced by Williams and Walker, but they were musical farces and written for my own people. I can make a living at it, but it isn't worth while. I want to do something real and fine."

FRIENDLY ENEMIES

What could I say when he lifted this curtain on the tragedy of race prejudice? Nothing, but extend my sympathy and advise persistence in keeping at the game. The soul of a true poet was imprisoned under that black skin. He never realized his great ambition; shortly after he died of tuberculosis.

While THE HONOR OF THE FAMILY was still on tour, I made a contract with Booth Tarkington and Harry Leon Wilson to collaborate on a play for me. Because of the recent hit of THE MAN FROM HOME they were besieged for plays by managers, but they agreed to my plan with enthusiasm. It concerned a desire of mine, long cherished, to portray an actor of the old bad school—one of those simple fellows given overmuch to "sound and fury," whose mental horizon was bounded by back-drops, wings and footlights. I had known so many of them!

The two men, singularly opposite in disposition, had a bond in common in their enthusiasm for the theatre. Wilson had been for some years the editor of PUCK—a rather sensitive man, warm in his friendships, and impatient in contradiction.

The joint authors sailed for France, leaving me their promise to have a rough draft of the piece ready in July when I should go over to Paris. They kept their word, and one evening at Tark's handsome apartment near the Luxembourg Gardens, the comedy was read. Never shall I forget that evening. Booth read the manuscript while Harry Wilson, pacing up and down like a caged panther, made comments which began with mild suggestions here and there, progressed to acid criticism and finally, when an *impasse* was reached from which appeared no orderly retreat, into fierce protest. Then Tarkington's spirit was roused and he came back at H. L. In the wrangle, I attempted to inject an idea or two. It seemed to me we were becoming inextricably mixed. I began to have a strange impression of the method of collaboration of the two authors. I saw my ship in a fair way to go on the rocks. The reading over, I went to my hotel and spent a restless night.

Bright and early next morning came the two partners—buoyant, hopeful, smiling, declaring that last night's session had been one of harmony and understanding. And I am sure it was. I wasn't used to their method of collaboration—that's all. What I had taken for cross-purposes and temper, was merely the adjustment of two eager, artistic conceptions. Friendship between these two had existed too long, too staunchly to admit of any real misunderstanding.

The rock on which they had split the evening before was a piece of stage business intended for comedy effect. H. L. declared it wasn't funny. Booth insisted it was. Wilson, having been the editor of a humorous journal, claimed to know a funny thing when he encountered it—a statement that no one who has delighted in his incomparable MA PETTINGILL stories, and his Hollywood classic, MERTON OF THE MOVIES, would wish to deny. But Tark was adamant. The business stayed in, and proved in the acting, to be effective.

The episode is illustrative of the trials and heartbreaks of play-making—an emotional business which can come nearer to sundering friendships and destroying good feeling than anything I know.

From the turmoil emerged an amusing comedy, replete with touches of human nature, which Booth christened YOUR HUMBLE SERVANT. It had a prosperous career of a year and a half, its New York presentment being at the Garrick Theatre. Of Booth Tarkington's little idyll of Western Pennsylvania, MISTER ANTONIO, which I later produced, I shall have something to say further on.

During this season, in a week's engagement at Macauley's Theatre in Louisville, I saw much of Henry Watterson at the Pendennis Club, and at the little "Chile Club" room near the theatre, redolent with the memory of many midnight feasts and the odor of *chile con carne,* where he joined John Macauley now and then in a welcome to the visiting players.

Once there came to the club to join our group a youngster with a slight stammer. I had known him for several years as one of Marse Henry's boys. He used to come to my hotel and talk books. He had little to say, but he was an excellent listener. When he did talk it was of his love of books and his admiration of their authors. He had a flattering attitude of deep respect for the opinions of others—the earmark of the perfect interviewer. He has proved himself preeminently so— He was Isaac Marcosson.

Wherever Henry Watterson was, there was the

center of the stage—like the renowned McGregor whose seat, no matter where, was always the head of the table. In talk he was much like his editorials, eloquent and convincing when he was warmed to his subject. His eyesight was not the keenest. His one serviceable eye was strained to the utmost in scrutiny, giving him an almost savage appearance which belied the genial nature it hid.

On one occasion he walked into my dressing-room at Macauley's Theatre after a performance and said, "You're going out to supper with me." It wasn't an invitation; it was a command. "Marse Henry" could rarely see why his wishes should not be obeyed, and when they promised such hospitality as his, who would wish to gainsay them?

I accepted with eagerness. He included in his invitation my business manager, Walter Collier, and my leading lady, Miss Comstock. We proceeded to a German restaurant Mr. Watterson favored, where his particular beer was kept on tap. There was much food and much beer, and over the dishes swirled the talk of "Marse Henry." It was of old days in the theatre, old plays and old players. It grew late; other guests finished their suppers and departed; still we sat and still the Watterson barytone rumbled on.

It was in the small hours when we left the restaurant. I knew that he lived at some distance, and it was before the days of taxicabs, so I suggested that he take a room at the Louisville Hotel as my guest. We found a staid-looking horse-cab for Miss

302

A DREAM OF GREATNESS

Comstock, and we three men walked. The night was heavy with fog rising from the Ohio River, making halos about the street-lamps, and a drizzle of rain was falling. Just before we reached the hotel Mr. Watterson stopped us and putting one arm over Walter Collier's shoulder and the other over mine, said, "Boys, it's coming; it is in the air! Watch the developments. As sure as we stand here I am to be the next governor of Kentucky. From the governor's chair there is just one more step— the president of the United States! It has been written."

"Marse Henry" may have been dreaming that dream for years. But the powerful editor of the LOUISVILLE COURIER JOURNAL became neither governor nor president.

CHAPTER XIX

ABOUT the time that Edward Knoblock wrote KISMET, there was a flood of Oriental plays, but Knoblock was early in the field. The scheme of the play had been a dream of his since his graduation from Harvard University. After his story had taken definite shape he went to Tunis to write it, among the sounds of street criers, muezzin calls-to-prayer, the whining of beggars and the stenches of an Arab city. Completed, he brought his piece to English and American markets and for a long time the manuscript went the rounds of managerial offices to be declined by readers who saw nothing in it. Charles Frohman sent a copy to me, asking my opinion, several months before Oscar Ashe produced it in London. When I told Frohman that it seemed to me a play of unusual interest and picturesque quality that would require a small fortune to produce, he said, "Well, we will think no more about it."

When KISMET scored its great triumph in London, American managers fell over one another in their eagerness to secure the rights.

It was produced lavishly by Klaw & Erlanger and Harrison Grey Fiske at Washington in Decem-

304

ber, 1911, and then brought to New York to crowd the Knickerbocker Theatre until the ensuing summer.

An arrangement was made by which I was temporarily released from my contract with Frohman, to play the part of *Hajj, the Beggar,* for three years.

During rehearsals the manager of the Knickerbocker said to me. "I hear you commit a murder in this play." "Yes," I replied, "two, and both of them quite sanguinary." He shook his head gloomily and said that sort of thing would never do for Broadway, which only proves that managerial prejudgments are things not to be relied on.

Knoblock made a fortune from the royalties of KISMET, and *Hajj* brought me more wide-spread success than any part I ever played.

In the previous October I sailed for London to see about my costumes, designed by Percy Anderson, and to learn some conjuring tricks necessary to the play from Devant, of the firm of illusionists, Maskelyne & Devant, who were masters in their line. As a result I returned with enough apparatus to set up as a rival of Thurston, but it was found too elaborate and the many tricks of sleight of hand that *Hajj* was to perform before the *Caliph* were reduced to the simple feat of producing fire from an empty brass bowl.

The run of the play in New York settled down to an easy triumph, and the elaborate machinery of the production ran on well-oiled wheels.

When we took to the road the following season the going became more difficult. Carrying a troupe of fifty people who were augmented in each town by a regiment of supernumeraries and an enormous quantity of scenery and properties was something like running a circus. Carpenters and electricians were sent a week in advance to arrange the line rigging in the theatres and cut the stage for the big water tank in the harem scene.

Also in advance was the drill master for the local mobs of supers. This task was performed by Gregory Kelly, whose talents have since brought him into prominence. The bathing pool of the harem in which I had to drown the wicked *Mansur* was always a source of anxiety. Bathing girls had to dash about in it and to keep them from perishing on cold winter nights and to preserve the life of our *Mansur*, Hamilton Ravelle, steam had to be turned into it during the day and its temperature carefully watched.

Once in Chicago, while setting this scene, the temporary flooring above the tank was removed and the stage hands were well-nigh suffocated by a geyser that arose from below. The flow of live steam had been on for twenty-four hours. Somebody had forgotten to turn it off.

Here was an awful situation. The scene was vital to the play; the girls had to go in—I had to drown *Mansur*. The curtain was kept down for half an hour. Blocks of ice were requisitioned from the neighboring hotels, restaurants and saloons. They

OTIS SKINNER
as Hajj in Kismet

melted in the bubbling water. An attempt was made
to drain the pool by the escape taps and refill it
from the hydrant. Finally the pool ceased to resemble Old Faithful Geyser and the curtain went
up, but the water was very far from cool; the bathing girls gave wild shrieks when they plunged in
and they came out like boiled lobsters. When I
flung Ravelle in his eyes nearly started from his
head. His dying cries were strangely out of keeping with the text: "O, my God! Get me out of this.
I'm scalding!" Before I had a chance to complete
the illusion of thrusting his head beneath the water
he was saying things that closely resembled blas-
phemy, and after an interval of complete incoher-
ence when the scene was over he dragged himself to
his dressing-room, vowing he would never play the
part again. But he did; he lived to go through a
still more terrible experience.

One bitter night in Baltimore it was discovered
that not an ounce of steam had been turned into the
tank and the water was at freezing point. It would
have taken several hours to make an impression on
its temperature. There was no help for it, and
poor Ravelle wasn't even warned. No words can
describe his amazement when he struck the icy
water, but the realism of his drowning was never
equaled by him or anybody else. At the end of the
act his blue body was wrapped in hot towels, hot
drinks were poured down his throat, his feet im-
mersed in a steaming tub until finally his teeth
ceased to rattle like castanets. Strangely enough

when I did the play for the films several years afterward, it was Ravelle who was selected for the part of *Mansur*. He had much trouble and discomfort in his drownings before the camera but it was in sunny California and he neither boiled nor froze.

I can not but regard the three seasons as *Hajj, the Beggar,* as a species of chastening and castigation. Draughty stages, uncomfortable dressing-rooms in unsavory country theatres, swathed in a few scraps of thin rags, my feet, legs, arms and chest with no covering but a wash of brown paint, rolling about on unswept, unsanitary stages that were trodden upon by supers and muddy-footed stage hands and the *Caliph's horse,* who was never over particular—it is almost a wonder that I survived. I did nearly succumb. It was after my second season that I went to the hospital with my case of mastoiditis.

Toward the end of the run the part began to get on my nerves. The work became so mechanical through repetition that the words would sometimes seem almost meaningless to me. I began to have a sense of separation from my performance. I seemed sometimes to be three people—myself—*Hajj*—and a dim something that was watching us both.

Terror lest I forget my lines would visit me. Had I allowed myself to drift I might have reached a nervous collapse, but reason brought me away from such peril. Placing myself before myself and telling myself that I was physically and mentally sound and that nothing could happen to me, I soon put the little demons in my nerves to rout.

308

FORGOTTEN LINES

But one does forget one's lines sometimes in the long run of plays. It is impossible to keep impulse and freshness away from the atrophy of reiteration.

I once had a terrible quarter of an hour in THE HONOR OF THE FAMILY, in Pittsburgh. At a matinée on Saturday, during the third act my mind was wandering in what by-paths I don't know but they certainly led neither to nor from the play, when suddenly all became blank; I hadn't the least notion of who I was or what I had to say. After a deal of sputtering and extemporizing I brought myself back and got on the track again. But the episode left me almost physically sore, as if some one had given me a Jack Dempsey punch.

That night when this scene approached, I felt myself becoming panicky, and when the speech arrived wherein I had struck my snag at the matinée, I dried up completely and all intelligence vanished. Percy Haswell who, as *Flora Brazier,* was playing the scene with me caught the infection and was stricken dumb. We looked over to the prompter and he grew rigid with panic. We sat like statues, It seemed hours before a word was spoken. There wasn't a soul in my company who could have told the speech on the instant.

The prompter hadn't even his manuscript—for several months he had ceased to refer to it. And he had actually to rush to his dressing-room, open his trunk, get his prompt book and return to his post before he could throw us the life line. Meanwhile we had sat staring at each other until the audience must have thought we were giving an exhibition of double hypnotism. The next day I studied *Colonel Philippe Bridau* all over again.

When the moving picture, THE BIRTH OF A NATION, was produced the enthusiasts saw something more than a mere novelty. They saw in this new form of dramatic or theatrical expression the downfall of the spoken stage. They argued that the motion picture would at some future day bring together a combination of the arts—drama, music, painting, literature, plus the best of stage lighting and decoration, and so successful would this mingling be that no one would want to see a mere play.

THE BIRTH OF A NATION, with the rides and gatherings of the Klan, demonstrated that the movie as a story-teller is superior to the stage in certain respects. The gatherings of a great crowd, the bringing together of conflicting forces and the facility for telling parallel stories were at once things which the stage could not do. One of the hardest tasks of a dramatist is to get his people on the stage; in other words, to bring people all into one room.

But aside from the movie's advantages in story-telling and for staging great scenic effects, such as fires, waving trees and storms, the motion picture has not demonstrated that it is the bringing together of the arts; in fact, it is a process or a medium and not an art itself. This seems to me particularly clear in the case of the actor. Granted that he were a great pantomimist, his work must still be subject to the camera; it is an accepted belief in the movies that the camera man can make or break the actor. He can.

This was my dominant thought when I found myself journeying out to California in the early summer of 1920 to break into the movies and film KISMET. I knew nothing of moving-picture work; I must win the camera man. I found him waiting for me at Hollywood, an employee of the Robertson-Cole Company, with which organization my contract for two months' services had been made.

Tony was an Italian, an expert in his work, and had been looking forward to the pictorial and photographic possibilities of this Oriental play eagerly—even excitedly. Before twenty-four hours had passed I invited Tony to lunch at a little restaurant opposite our studio.

Tony had been expecting from me the usual condescending attitude toward my task that is often exhibited by those whom the film world rather slightingly refer to as the *"speakies."* I soon disillusioned him. "Tony," I said, "I'm here to learn. The director can tell me much. You can tell me more. Watch me, and when I go wrong let me know." Tony, the prince of camera men, promised—and I profited by his vigilance.

For my first day in the pictures it was decided to do the prison scene. *Hajj* had been arrested for thieving at the bazaar. When I saw the set I was tremendously pleased. The greatest care had been taken, and the whole was really impressive. As the floor was supposed to be earth, dirt had been brought in and an uneven surface produced with the utmost fidelity. In the theatre the actor enters with the knowledge that the walls are painted canvas, that they could not easily be anything else, and often he sees the brush strokes.

In this prison scene, in the theatre, I always had to be careful when I was chained to the pillar that I did not shake the canvas scenery and give the audience a glimpse of shivering masonry. But here, I thought, this substantial set should conspire to produce very real acting, but when I acted *Hajj* before the camera I was always conscious of a director sitting with a megaphone, and two camera men—there were always two—each with the visor of his cap turned over the neck. When a scene was long enough, and I lost myself in working up for a second to what seemed like definite impersonation, I would hear the disillusioning word "cut" from the director. Sometimes I wished that we might, when we were lashed up to the playing of a scene, go on with it to its natural conclusion.

The captors of *Hajj, the Beggar,* led him into the set and threw him down a flight of very real steps. I slid for some feet over the uneven floor and my right leg, bare and stained to the hue of the Oriental beggar, was skinned from thigh to ankle. There was a rush of distressed assistants. I was helped to my feet and I gazed ruefully at my bleeding leg. "I am going to like this business," I said.

"Are you game for another shot?" asked the director.

"Yes," I replied.

When antiseptics had been applied and the raw places repainted we did the same incident twice more.

On the second and third falls I was able to protect myself a little. That was my first work before the camera, and that was how the filming of KISMET began.

My first day in the pictures I saw one very great difference between the movie and the theatre. Not only is the human element or personal appeal entirely lacking when the picture is projected, but in the acting, that collaboration between the audience and the players so necessary to make a finished performance on the stage, is entirely missing.

Directors quite early saw this lack and have attempted to supply the nervous thrill of real acting in the theatre by having music played during the action of filming—soulful ballads during "sob scenes" and lively strains in the comic and strenuous ones.

Orchestras range from a band of half a dozen down to a concertina. Ours was the largest accordion I ever saw and was played for hours on end by an ever obliging and smiling musician named Mac-Niel. One day we were having a bit of difficulty in lashing our little *ingénue* into agonies of despair over her hapless plight. It was a "close-up" of her single figure. The little lady sat with her face in her hands trying to feel abandoned, forlorn and hopeless, but her sensitive system refused to func-

313

tion. The assistant director was patting her on the back telling her in whispers that she was a forsaken and abused girl, the cameras were trained on her electrically-lit face, the operators, crank in hand, ready to "shoot"; the director slumped in his chair, his megaphone tapping the ground directly under the machine and looking vastly disgusted. MacNiel's accordion was at its soulfullest.

After a minute of two of patient waiting the unhappy maiden looked up and said, "Play, KISS ME AGAIN," then buried her face once more.

MacNiel promptly obliged her; presently her pretty face rose from her covering fingers, streaming with tears, and the camera men ground furiously.

A stage play is not a play until it is before an audience. Prior to the first night of a play I have worked for four weeks, and my performance is as good as I can make it on that night, but I do not feel until I have worked in a part four weeks more, and those additional weeks before an audience, that I am thoroughly familiar with the part or at home in it.

In the movies things are rarely gone over more than three times, and thus a great deal is lost.

My daughter Cornelia, for whom a part was devised, a sort of general messenger in the harem, was sent to find out from the eunuch, a huge negro, who the man was in the next room. Being given no instructions she invented a flowery speech which she thought was in keeping with the play of KISMET and with which she addressed the black.

AN IMPROMPTU ORIENTAL

Her speech was something as follows: "Who is yonder fair stranger I saw within the palace gates? Thou knowest all the secrets of *Mansur's* palace. Speak, or your life shall be the forfeit."

"You can search me, lady," responded the black.

At another point we were having difficulty with a man who played a small part, a captain of the guards. Two people had been tried and neither found satisfactory. Finally the director espied a man working in another part of the studio on a scene in a wild West picture.

He was called over and given the Oriental costume for the part. He knew nothing of our play KISMET; he had perhaps never heard of it.

He was supposed to say a line from the play: "Seize him. Thou must go before the *Wazir Mansur.*"

All he heard was—at least what he said was— "We-ah! Oo! Sewer!"

This man showed up very well on the screen, photographed effectively, and at the right moment the line he should have said was printed boldly as a caption.

The extravagance and waste in the making of pictures have been largely due to the producer. The producer of KISMET, for instance, talked in millions, thought in millions and perhaps he thought that he spent millions. If a show on the stage cost fifty thousand dollars to put on, then at least five hundred thousand dollars should be spent on it in the "movies," and the verdict of Hollywood must be that the film is at least ten times as good as the play.

315

FOOTLIGHTS AND SPOTLIGHTS

KISMET seemed to me a very beautiful production, and every effort was made to make it correct and elaborate. At the first of the private showings in New York, Edward Knoblock, the author, pronounced the filming beautiful and exact. In one scene in which some girls danced, they danced upon glass beneath which black velvet had been placed. I mention this to give some idea of the extravagance of production. I am not prepared to record whether this was worth while or not.

But there were other wastes besides that of money. On my own contract there was a great deal of waste. I was engaged to work from nine o'clock to six, and I was prepared to do so. Actually we worked from eleven to four and spent eight weeks taking the picture instead of five.

In one scene in which I was supposed to go to the palace to meet the "wife of wives," it was decided that I should go by water, so a façade of a palace was constructed in a depression of the hills at Glendale, which was outside of the "movie" lot. City water was pumped into the depression for forty-eight hours until we had a lake. In the meantime an Oriental boat such as is still used on the Ganges was constructed. It is shaped something like a gourd and is called a gofar; a name, by the way, interesting in the light of what happened. First we found that the boat leaked, and it was necessary for me to bail it out with a tin can. I could not do this and scull. Then it was found that I could not scull the boat at all. It moved, but not forward.

EXAMPLES OF WASTE

During all this experimentation the surface of our lake became covered with plaster, chips of wood and a thousand other things. First a man in a row-boat with a rake would go out and brush up our lake and then I would make an attempt with my gofar. Meanwhile my daughter, in the part of the general messenger of the harem,—a part not in the original play at all,—was standing on the palace platform waiting to let me in. She had just about a four-hour 'wait.

At last it was decided that it would be necessary for some one to pull the gofar across the lake. Fence wire was attached and a man concealed on the other side who pulled while I sculled proudly. Then it was discovered that the fence wire showed, and piano wire was substituted. This proved a success, but when the picture came to the showing the whole incident of *Hajj* and his trip across the lake was cut out.

In the original play the black sword-bearer *Kafur* was played by a white man who covered his entire body with lamp-black and then used oil over this so that he was a shiny, gleaming mass. Effective but troublesome this proved, especially on the road; for the man who played the part always had to be taken in a cab to a Turkish bath after the performance. In the "movies" a similar make-up proved disastrous because of the reflection or "halation" of the oiled skin, and a real negro was necessary. An ideal man was found. He was used in the early work. Unexpectedly at the very end it was necessary to do a retake of an early scene. The black had disappeared and we waited for some days till he was found in Salt Lake City. Lack of planning is often responsible for delay and for waste of this sort.

One great fault of the pictures, it has always seemed to me, is the fact that they are so much alike in little things. Almost every picture has a dog or a cat. The temptation of course to use animals and babies in the picture is very great, because they are perfect "movie" actors. They never get self-conscious. A goose walking down a country road has all the lordly manner of his race. In a picture I saw recently, a dog closes a door for no reason that I could guess except that the director had at his disposal a dog that could close a door.

Dogs do not need to be well trained to be effective in the movies. In KISMET, at the very opening of the picture, *Hajj* is seated on his stone in front of the Mosque. A dog comes down the deserted street, sniffs at *Hajj* and then runs away. This was accomplished in the following manner: Under my rags I had a bit of meat which I gave the dog. Every time we rehearsed he got the bit of meat. Naturally, he ran toward me. When he had the meat his master called and our dog ran toward his owner and out of range of the camera. Many people have spoken to me about this very clever dog.

I am not decrying the films, they are a great source of amusement, fine entertainment, even educational, but when it comes to acting in front of the camera—that is another matter. The motion picture might be called the child of pantomime and photography. A week before the camera, should give any one who has had theatre experience a knowledge of what to do. There are certain tricks of course. The actor will soon learn that he can make violent quick motions toward the camera but not across, as from left to right. This, for a few days, may hamper the man who has been in the theatre. Also he may find it difficult, as did Sir Herbert Beerbolm Tree, who was engaged to make a series of pictures in Hollywood, to keep within the camera lines—lines of chalk or tape which converge at the camera and spread out V shape to mark the range of action. Sometimes out-of-doors the line is drawn with a stick in the sand, or a post with a white flag is set in the ground. Really staying within the mark is not difficult to manage, but the confined space is not always conducive to the best acting, judged by standards of the theatre. At long distance violent action is permissible, but close to the camera only the slightest facial expression may be used. A deliberate raising of the eyebrow, which in the theatre would scarcely show, may convey much in the greatly magnified picture.

CHAPTER XX

In the spring of 1910 I had an argument with an eminent clergyman concerning the PASSION PLAY at Oberammergau. He held that the Bavarian peasant players, in their religious zeal, touched heights that the professional actor could never reach. My contention was that an actor, trained to emotional portrayal of all kinds, could best express the emotion of any drama. Neither of us had seen the performance; we were backing our stubborn personal opinions. I learned my lesson in humility in July of that year when I saw ardent, unselfish and temperamental acting with every mark of careful stage direction. These Bavarian peasants were not inspired amateurs; they were disciplined actors. The clergyman and I were both wrong, and both right.

What first stirred my admiration was the handling of the mob. The big stage, with its six hundred and eighty-five people surging with frenzied dynamic force, was a shifting of color and grouping, the like of which we had never seen in any theatre. To the smallest tot in the mobs and tableaux, each had his part and his pride in the perfect whole.

A HAUNTING FIGURE

My mind flashed back to recollections of mobs in Shakespearean productions when the *Velveteen Knights* stood in the background, but the *Brocade Lords* marched in attendance. Not much intelligence or enthusiasm were exacted from sandwichmen and park benchers engaged at two dollars a performance, alas! But in Oberammergau, when for two hundred years all the village——

In the vast impression the drama left with me, I found myself confused as to its details. To "see the wheels go round" I stayed on for a second performance.

In a Catholic country where the people are accustomed to worship their sacred characters in symbolic service, it is remarkable that the Passion Play should be most human. This human note was struck by nearly every one of the players, and only notably departed from in the case of the *Christus*.

The outstanding figure, not only by reason of its somber passion, but by the artistry of the player, was the *Judas* of Johann Zwink. From his first entrance, apart from the other disciples, this furtive, isolated man presented a haunting figure, and in his final scene when he unwound the girdle from his orange-colored robe by which to hang himself, he roused not execration but pity.

I had a little talk with Zwink and found him a sad man, weary of the load of remorse he had borne for twenty years. He was the *Judas* for three revivals of the Passion Play. When I told him of my delight in his performance, his tired eyes kindled, and with spread fingers across his chest he said: *"Ja, ich kenne Judas; ich verstehe Judas. Aber, ach! Ich kann Judas nicht spielen."* It was the modesty of the true artist.

Another fine performance was Hans Mayr's *Herod.* Splendid in stature and wearing his trappings with regal grace, he presented a picture of a cynical man of the world, wearied of this irritating disturber. Christ, to him, was but of the *canaille.* One could not imagine a better portrayal of degenerate royalty.

The value of personality was striking in the disciple group. Except for *Peter* and *John* they have but little to say and almost nothing to do, and yet the memory of their patriarchal figures is so vivid that it is something of a surprise to realize they had been silent figures. After years, the sturdy figure of *Peter,* and the boyish, exalted *John,* the beloved —and *Andrew* and *Thaddeus,* sweet in their old age —come before me as if the play were yesterday.

There was immeasurable sadness in the Duse-like moments of the *Mary* of Otillie Zwink, and much tenderness in Marie Mayr's sensuous *Magdalen.*

My single disappointment was in the *Christus* of Anton Lang. It is probable I should have felt this in any performance. The impersonation of any great historical character is always difficult, and in the case of *Christus* the difficulty is well-nigh insuperable. Lang looked the traditional Christ of stained-glass windows and the effeminate Italian paintings—always the Man of Sorrows; never the

Man of Action. He would never have raised a storm in Judea as would, for example, the inspired ascetic of Munkacsy's painting.

There was one place in the Oberammergau performance where realistic treatment was, in a way, destructive to the value of the play. It was in the detail of the Crucifixion when a little bag of "property blood" burst and oozed as the Roman soldier pierced the side of *Christus*. But this was succeeded by a rarely beautiful piece of work when the body was lowered from the Cross. Not an awkward or hurried movement, not a false gesture, not a commonplace suggestion, but a precision that made an impression of awe and reverence. Lang's body was of considerable weight—no easy task to remove it inert from the great height. It was a supreme achievement.

I had entered the village in a frame of mind to appreciate the PASSION PLAY, but hardly anticipating that it would remain one of the abiding memories of a lifetime. My family and I had driven by landau northward over the Austrian border into Bavaria. After leaving Ettal the men we passed along the road looked different. The costume was familiar, but their long hair gave them a strange appearance. *John*, "the beloved disciple," rode past on his bicycle. A fair-haired lad working with some hay-makers, said he was "Adam's child." It was a day on which no performance was held which accounted for the highways and fields being the scene of much domestic activity. As we drove into the village some unusual interest seemed attached to our landau. A little crowd followed after us, and as we dismounted before the house in which the ubiquitous Thomas Cook and Sons had domiciled us, there was a real stir. The way was cleared; a photographer, mounted on an improvised stand, snapped excitedly until an individual waved him to desist with shouts of *"Nein! nein!"* It all seemed very flattering but incomprehensible until our host explained that they were awaiting the arrival of royalty. I had been mistaken for the King of Saxony! An hour later His Majesty arrived by train and walked from the station quite incognito. That evening we saw him brush through the corridor of our little hotel, bareheaded (and I must admit, baldheaded) and, with his two young sons, mingle with the throng outside quite unrecognized by the tourists who had, by this time, filled the village to overflowing. His democracy did not extend so far as the common dining-room, for during our meals we waited long for service and could hear a commotion up-stairs. Doctor Charles Francis Murphy, of Chicago, glanced up at the low ceiling creaking beneath the tread of hurried feet and said: "Heavy! Heavy, hangs over our heads."

It was an interesting group at the dinner table that day when we came back for the two hours' respite from the play. Ambassador David Jayne Hill and Mrs. Hill were there from Berlin. William H. Crane had motored from Munich, Doctor Murphy,—he of the famous "Murphy button,"—a Russian princess who had been thoroughly objectionable by rising at intervals throughout the play to take snap-shots, a prominent merchant from Philadelphia. In that small dining-room five languages were being spoken; it was then the feeling of pilgrimage was borne in upon us.

Our host was, in daily life, the Posthalter; and in the play, his was the rôle to stand before the house of *Pilate* and read the death warrants—important positions both.

To remain in Oberammergau for a second performance we were obliged, through pressure of previous reservations, to remove to humbler lodgings. The Posthalter's wife with regal dignity (and why not since she had been hostess to royalty?) lifted her cumbersome train skirt from the rain-soaked street, and guided us courteously to the small *gast haus* where our host was, in the play, care-taker of the sheep in the Temple Scene. We were delighted to find his *beer stube* was a favored resort of the players. The beer was excellent. Here, after the performance, *Christus* and *Pilate, Judas* and *John* and *Herod,* freed from their antagonism in the Sacred Drama, sipped their foaming seidels and smoked their porcelain pipes in amity.

The second performance I watched with calmer feelings, and yet the impression was even more intensified. I left the village knowing I had been for a week among artists of rare quality—men and women not only deeply reverent in their religion, but deeply religious in their dramatic reverence.

FOOTLIGHTS AND SPOTLIGHTS

Among all my emotional reactions of the theatre, none has exceeded in intensity the experience of participating in the Easter Sunrise Service on the summit of Mount Rubidoux in California in 1918.

Two years previous, while resting before an engagement at Riverside, I had yielded to the spell of this ceremony in joining the line of pilgrims who journeyed up to greet the Resurrection Dawn from the mountain top. An automobile was placed at my disposal, but I preferred to go afoot up the zigzag path. I didn't want to talk to any one.

It was three o'clock when I started under the stars and a clear half-moon; the world bathed in night. The spirit of the moment on the climbers; there was even an occasional ripple of laughter, but it was low and not strident. Below us lay the city—a gridiron of street lights with one electrically lit church tower brighter than the rest. We were aware of the encircling ring of distant mountains only by the deeper gloom of the somber band that cut off the stars.

Finally my section of the procession reached a rocky shoulder that gave out to the summit and lo! shining in the radiance of a soft search light, the Cross—Golgotha glorified!

I passed the barrier to the space privileged me by my special ticket, and as I clambered up the rocks some one greeted me; it was John Mc-Groarty, the author of the California MISSION PLAY who had been up there since midnight with his sen-

326

timental soul in a riot. He was reporting the occasion for the LOS ANGELES TIMES. Together, with our backs to the rock at the foot of the cross, erected in memory of Fra Junipero Serra, we watched the stream of automobile lights on the road coming down from Los Angeles along the valley of the Santa Ana and winding up our mountain. We could now make out the moving mass of people swarming over the three peaked ridge of Rubidoux and picking out perches of vantage on every rock shelf. It grows lighter over eastward—the Sierra Madras are a silhouetted sheet of black cardboard —the west lying water-course of the Santa Ana catches the dawn, its mists turning to Whistler-like vague purples and violets, and all the while the blinding flashes of lights from arriving automobiles, the whirr of motor engines, and the subdued hum of voices. The city street-lamps are out; the illuminated church tower stands alone; we see Riverside in the morning twilight.

The participants of the programme are here. George Osbourne, the veteran actor, who is to recite GOD OF THE OPEN AIR, climbs up beside us, his white head bared, and asks do we think it sacrilege if he smokes his pipe. McGroarty, doubly sympathetic from draughts of something that has sustained his night's vigil, declares it most fitting and Osbourne lights his cut plug for the soothing of his nerves before the ordeal of the Van Dyke poem.

The east is becoming dazzling. Packed about us are eighteen thousand souls. Behind me, in a crevice of the rock, a pale girl is stretched on a rug; the climb has been too much for her, but she is not unhappy. It is as if she were offering a glad sacrifice of her strength.

An official looks at his watch; it is ten minutes after five; he signals the cornetist. The first notes of THE HOLY CITY ring out to the morning. The men take off their hats. The choir sings an anthem in subdued tones, and we repeat the Lord's Prayer. Marcella Craft is standing on a platform ready to sing HEAR YE ISRAEL. Her white dress shimmers in the morning light; her head is lifted; her body erect in exaltation. As she begins, the rim of the sun comes over the crest of the Mother Mountains; the little singer is bathed in splendor.

Christ is Risen!

George Osbourne recites GOD OF THE OPEN AIR, his old soul shaken, but his voice triumphant. Marcella Craft sings again and then thousands of voices join in the Doxology. The multitude streams quietly down the foot-paths; the motors chug again.

McGroarty says, "My God! I haven't tasted meat all Holy Week. Order me all the beefsteak and bacon there is at the Mission Inn."

Still tremulous with feeling from the rites of the mountain top, I sought Frank Miller, host of the Mission Inn at Riverside, who might almost be said to have put the town on the map, and who certainly is responsible for the glorifying of Rubidoux, and told him I should not die content until I had made myself a part of the programme and recited GOD OF THE OPEN AIR, even though I came across the continent for the ceremony.

"You will find us waiting for you when you come," he said.

Fate decreed that in two years I should again find my tour lying through California, and leading me to Riverside to fulfill my promise.

As in 1916, I again journeyed through the darkness on foot to the summit. It was even more profound this year—terribly profound—for the hand of war was on the world and our own men were being killed in France. A Boy Scout standing at the foot of the memorial cross, holding the American Flag, symbolized the sacrifice of the country's finest youth and the liberty for which they offered their lives.

Some one placed a telegram in my hands; it was an Easter message to the people on the mountain from Doctor Henry van Dyke, then overseas. I was to read it to them: it was a cry for salvation,

"Right is stronger than might. Light conquers darkness. The final victory over Prussian paganism is sure. If we want to share in it we must do our part in winning it. We must be fearless of death and suffering, willing to follow the pathway of the Captain of Salvation through Gethsemane and Calvary and Hades to the dawn of an immortal day."

The programme of hymn, prayer and anthem proceeded. Madame Mariska Aldrich was the soloist. For myself, I was in a distinct trance—my

whole body was numb. To this day I have no remembrance of how I recited the Ode. As I commenced the opening lines:

"Thou who hast made Thy dwelling fair
With flowers below, above the starry lights,
And set Thine altars everywhere
    On Mountain heights,
In woodlands dim with many a dream"

the sun rose over the Sierra Madras and blinded
me. I was aware of a fiery sea of color, and of an
awful force pulling at my vitality. The recitation
ended, I sat back dazed. Madame Aldrich's magnificent voice in FEAR YE NOT, OH ISRAEL! roused
me.

Before the Benediction the people sang AMER-
ICA. For a moment it seemed the stereotyped thing
to do, until suddenly when the third verse came—

"God bless our noble men
    Bring them safe home again!
God bless our men.
    Chivalrous, glorious,
From work laborious,
Send them victorious,
    God bless our men!"

Then we heard the guns over in France.

The crowd disappeared down the mountain, subdued and hushed. At the Mission Inn I went to
bed exhausted and slept for hours.

THE CALIFORNIA MISSION PLAY

IT was not a good play, technically speaking.
And yet, why was it not a good play? Because it

seemed a bit old-fashioned in construction? Because it was episodic? Because it was sentimental? Because the actors preached a little? These all could make the judicious grieve, and the author might have taken his manuscript home to rewrite it, one ear to the ground for "what the public wants." But, heaven be praised! this play had no such history.

Its inception came from deep reverence for the history and legend of those brave Spanish fathers who endured the hardships of adventure that we might to-day have the King's Highway dotted at intervals with some of the most picturesque ruins to be found in America—The Spanish Missions.

It sounds rather a foolish confession that a man should feel a clutch in his throat at the idea that a bay had been discovered which should be known as San Francisco, but that was the effect it had upon me. The lady sitting beside me, frankly wept. A bay was a fine thing to discover, but why choke and weep over it? Because the dramatist had not been afraid of his own emotion. He had dealt so simply, so sincerely with his material that the audience fell at once into the romantic spell of the play. John Steven McGroarty is an Irishman, a Californian and a poet—fortuitous combination for romance.

Adventures of explorers, hardships of pioneers, the courage of our ancestors in the struggle for life and liberty would furnish dramatic material for a pageant in any one of our forty-eight states, but nowhere could the setting be so picturesque, the characters more sympathetic than in this story of Fra Junipero Serra and his missionary work with the Indians of California.

So strongly has the MISSION PLAY impressed me that even now—nine years later, I can not pass a Mission bell along *El Camino Real* without visualizing the little Franciscan barefoot padre pushing along through sand and cactus. And the Bay of San Francisco, that most beautiful harbor, now filled with ships that reach the furthermost ports, has always for me a tiny sailing vessel, *San Antonio,* bound back to waiting Spaniards, starving and disheartened in the South.

This is the test of a play. Not whether it is written according to accepted standards, not whether it defies an old tradition to create a new one. But whether it can produce upon an audience the effect that is enduring. THE MISSION PLAY has this quality. Lofty in ideals, noble in sentiment, it should have an annual, or at least a triennial representation in its own environment with San Gabriel Mission as neighbor, that the people of this country may have always with them the legend of the dauntless Junipero Serra.

THE PILGRIM PLAY

WHEN I think of the Easter service on the summit of Mount Rubidoux, and the MISSION PLAY at San Gabriel, I make of them a trio in inspired achievement with the PILGRIM PLAY at Hollywood, in the writing and production of which Christine

A LASTING INFLUENCE

Wetherill Stevenson accomplished the almost impossible. Twenty years before, an actor, James O'-Neill, had been arrested in this same California for daring to act the part of The Christ, and now in this pageant-drama, (a transcription, scene after scene from the New Testament), not one murmur of impiety has been raised, and the reverent impersonation of Jesus, as portrayed by Henry Herbert, has been received with appreciation.

The PILGRIM PLAY has been compared to the PASSION PLAY, but they are not comparable. One is a great tradition brought to perfection with years until its breadth and scope are heroic. The PILGRIM PLAY is a poetic, dramatic narrative wherein even the painful climax of the crucifixion is softened into a tableau in diffused light.

The coming together of many people on any occasion where lofty ideals are aroused can not fail to have lasting influence. The Rubidoux service, the MISSION PLAY and the PILGRIM PLAY should be permanently endowed and safeguarded from commercialism. Only in their own setting do they belong. The mountain can not be moved for the Easter service, the MISSION PLAY belongs where the bells on the King's Highway remind the traveler of the patience and fortitude of the Franciscan fathers, the PILGRIM PLAY belongs in the Cañon where Christine Wetherill Stevenson visualized it, and where she gave her life in its development.

CHAPTER XXI

THE BULL FIGHT AND CHRISTIAN SCIENCE

THE June of 1921 took me to Spain. I found myself dreaming away valuable days in the provinces of the Basques, San Sebastian and Burgos, among fishermen, muleteers, peasants and priests, when it dawned on me that I had no right to be idling—business was calling me southward to Castille. With vast reluctance I tore myself away from northern Spain and embarked on a train which with exasperatingly slow progress at last delivered me at Madrid. My journey was for the purpose of purchasing mantillas, high combs, Andalusian costumes, bull-fighters' clothes and the paraphernalia of the bull-ring, and also to meet the novelist, Señor Vicente Blasco Ibañez. I had contracted to produce a dramatized version of BLOOD AND SAND. The contract was made in this country by the Charles Frohman Company and the Señor's American representative, Paul Kennaday, from whom I bore my note of introduction. He received me literally with open arms, such was his anxiety to get the business over with that he might return to southern France, his present home. But he was cordial and gracious. He did not at all measure up to my preconceived notion of a Spaniard. He was built like a gladiator;

in manner he was high-strung, temperamental and at times irritable, not in any way typical of his fellow countrymen. I arrived on the edge of the enthusiastic reception given him by his loyal admirers after a prolonged absence from his native land.

He assumed to have no longer any interest in the great national sport.

"Ah, I do not go to the *corridas*," he said in French—our language of communication. "They bore me. For the first ten minutes of a bull-fight, if I am forced to go, I watch and then I read a newspaper." However, when I with some timidity suggested that it was a gruesome sight to see the bull disembowel the scrawny nags ridden by the picadors, he turned on me like lightning.

"And how do you defend the sport of your own country—Le Boxe? Two human beings standing up hammering and gouging! So! So!" And he indicated the action with forceful gesture.

The moral question we did not argue. Bullfighting was, nevertheless, our common interest whether it bored him or horrified me. By a stroke of luck the bull-fight this day was a gala occasion arranged for the benefit of the Spanish Red Cross. Royalty would attend, and the arena would present a gorgeous spectacle.

Blasco Ibañez took me to the Plaza de Toros in the morning where we saw the magnificent horned beasts, arrived by train from the Andalusian plains, goaded by drovers and beguiled by tame bulls into dark stalls, there to remain for four hours until they should be released for torture in the dazzling light of the arena. Already the encircling galleries were gay in decorations of national colors—red and yellow; banners and pennants with royal devices hung from the king's box and that of the tribune of the judges. After the bulls were safely stalled we went to the stables where sorry-looking horses were waiting their ghastly doom. The bleak little chapel with white-washed walls and simple altar where the Virgin of the Dove listened with compassion to the prayers of the fighters, was to me no less foreboding than the adjoining surgery with its five spotless cots ready against accident.

Two hours before the *corrida* we drove to a house in the Street of Good Success to see Grañero, the most brilliant young *torero* in Spain, make his toilet. The details were exactly as Ibañez has described them in BLOOD AND SAND. Grañero looked such a boy—he was really not twenty. Where was the burly *torero* of my imaginings—the swaggering *Escamillo* of CARMEN or the stalwart bull-killers of the Goya pictures in the Prado? I could not rid myself of the feeling that presently, in full regalia, he would be transformed into something bigger—as an actor in his make-up—but he looked more delicate than ever when his valet finally squeezed him into his new thousand *duro* costume. His breeches were drawn on with much difficulty only after the valet and a friend had lifted him bodily and shaken him down as one shakes a tightly packed bag of sugar. He submitted to the various proceedings with an air of gentle melancholy. He might have been a young priest preparing for holy orders. Nothing about his manner was hectic or nervous. Here was an artist preparing for his work with a reverent spirit. I was not surprised to learn that he played the violin. His white hands, with their delicate fingers, suggested that he might play well. Blasco Ibañez had known him from childhood. They were both native of Valencia.

We waited outside to see him start off amid the cheers and good wishes of the crowd before his door, and then Blasco Ibañez left me at the arena where by now eighteen thousand people were gathered. The band was playing. The queen arrived; a little later came the queen mother. The boxes were filled with fashionably dressed men, but the women wore over their Parisian-designed gowns, the Spanish shawl and mantilla. The day being blazing-hot, the shawls were taken off and thrown over the balustrade of the boxes, making a riot of color indescribably gay—even Zuloaga could not have painted it.

A fanfare of trumpets. The heavy gates are opened, and the parade of the *toreros* begins. The time-honored amusement is dated in the costumes worn by the two *Alguacils*—mounted on splendid horses and looking as if they had dashed out of a Valesquez picture. Matadors, banderilleros, picadors, lance at rest on their gaunt, partly-blinded nags, scarlet-bloused mozos, (they who sweep up the shambles) and the mules, bedizened in jingling and tasseled harness who will later drag out the carcasses.

The foremost fighters of the day march together —Belmonte, El Gallo, Varelito, and the youngest of all, Grañero. From having spent an hour in watching him make ready, my interest in his safety had grown until it now seemed as if I had known him always. He is very white; very serious. He might be offering himself for some hazardous quest in which all our safety depends. Knights of a crusade could not have set forth with greater solemnity.

A bugle sounds—the arena is cleared—the gates are opened——

The story of the bull ring has been told graphically many times; told in the revolt and bitterness of shocked sensibilities or told with admiration and enthusiasm.

Two bulls were in turn so quickly despatched by Belmonte and El Gallo that I had not recovered from the horrifying details sufficiently to realize that the third bull, meant for Grañero, was not "playing fair." He was a coward. He refused to fight. The crowd hissed; the judges ordered the beast removed and a fresh one let in. Was it fate that this should happen to my *espada?* This hero of a hundred successive *corridas* could not be disturbed by a cowardly bull. The amulets I saw him slip round his neck would surely protect him! But

338

—there he lay—stretched out on the sand, and presently he was borne away to the surgery leaving the bull to be given the death stroke by El Gallo.

I had a feeling of terror. I felt responsible. It was I who had watched him dress; I who had asked him questions about his costume; I who had been last to touch his hand as he left his apartment. Perhaps I, the foreigner, had brought him ill luck. But here was I again getting the bull-fighter and the actor mixed in my imaginings.

There were four more bulls to be killed. But I would not see them. I left at once. News of the accident spread over the city, and even before I reached the hotel Blasco Ibañez had learned that the accident was not fatal. The next afternoon I went again to the apartment in The Street of Good Success, for Grañero had been carried there from the surgery. He was able to see me, and somehow his cordiality gave me an intense relief. I had not been his evil genius of the day before! Accidents happen—one gets a little careless. He gave me his photograph, and although the accident had made walking a pain, he limped over to his desk and wrote on the picture

"Al eminente actor
Norte Americano,
Otis Skinner.
Manuel Grañero.

This was on the twenty-first of June, 1921.

A despatch in a New York newspaper of May 7, 1922, bore this news:

FOOTLIGHTS AND SPOTLIGHTS

"Madrid: The matador, Manuel Grañero, was killed in the arena this afternoon, his body being crushed against the barrier by a savage bull and horribly mutilated."

The gentle lad was the victim of the blood-lust of an insensate people.

When the play, BLOOD AND SAND, dramatized by Tom Cushing, was presented in America, a curious thing happened. In the third act the hero, *Juan Gallardo*, is brought in on a stretcher, his leg, broken a month before in the bull-ring, is still in a splint. At a juncture in the scene, *Juan* disobeys the doctor's orders and cuts the bandages from the wounded leg. Mistrusting his superstitious faith in the cards that have told him his wound has healed, and doubting whether he should have gone against the doctor's command, he gingerly lifts his leg from the cot, holds it out while he bends his knee—his brow in a cold sweat of terror lest the leg should prove to be permanently stiff. The foot finally resting on the floor, he rises slowly until his entire weight is on the broken leg. Every night somebody in the audience fainted. At first we laid it to the close theatre, for the season had opened while the weather was still hot. But when night after night and week after week these faintings continued, until one night the distracted ushers had twenty people on their hands, we knew we had a serious problem. Each usher carried a bottle of smelling-salts; and aromatic spirits and ice water were always on hand for the third act. It seemed almost too serious a

340

matter to go on with. I reduced the pantomimic action to a minimum, even then the power of suggestion had its effect on certain sensitive people. More men fainted than women, and always more young men than old men. The war and hospitals may have had something to do with it. One young man said he would not have fainted had it not been for the wound he saw when the bandage was removed. There was no wound. Purposely I had made the situation as free from realistic details as possible.

In the last act when *Juan* is carried in covered with blood, not a soul minded.

It was a harrowing experience. I should never want to go through it again.

And yet this power of suggestion lies at the very core of the appeal of the theatre. It worked in quite an opposite way in a play I had produced several years earlier—THE SILENT VOICE, made by Jules Eckert Goodman from the material of a short story by Gouverneur Morris entitled THE MAN WHO PLAYED GOD. The hero was a highly strung musician who had been stricken with deafness, and had learned to understand the speech of others through lip-reading. By the means of powerful marine glasses he was enabled to bring distant groups in the park across the way into close observation, learn their many secrets and little tragedies and aid them through the assistance of his valet.

This part entailed upon me the assumption of

341

various characteristics of the deaf—the rigid attitude, the intent stare at the lips of others, the closed dead vocal tones of the deaf, and indeed all the mannerisms I could discover.

One night at the Hermitage Club in Nashville, where a friend had given me a visitor's card, I had difficulty in getting from the waiter the exact status of the club rules. My wife and I had had an exacting day in the theatre, and we wanted some beer with our supper. A sympathetic group of club members, having supper at an adjoining table, was watching us. A man arose, and coming close to me yelled into my ear that unfortunately visitors had not the privilege of ordering anything to drink, but would I accept the courtesy of his locker. For a moment I was amazed at the man's shouting—then I realized that he and his friends had been to see THE SILENT VOICE.

Once an entire class of deaf children from a Buffalo institution came to the play, and we altered the stage business as much as possible for their benefit, playing so that they might see our faces. What they actually got of the play was perhaps not so important as the incentive to persist in their study of lip-reading.

The play carried a note of optimism. Although not expressed as such, the piece had a Christian Science theme sufficiently accented to impress many people very deeply. That was one reason why a party of perhaps a hundred Christian Scientists attended the opening performance in Boston. I had been rehearsing long and arduously

all day for the all star production of A CELEBRATED
CASE that was to follow in New York immediately
after the close of my season. I was very tired. On
my first entrance I discovered, to my dismay, that I
had overworked at rehearsal and my voice had fled.
I was living up to the title of the play! I got
through the first act with much difficulty, and in
the state of dire panic that always assails me when
my voice goes. During the second act I was re-
lieved to find myself able to make almost under-
standable sounds. In act three my voice had a
familiar timbre, and in the concluding act it was
nearly normal.

I had noticed after I had been on the stage for
a few minutes that there was a slight commotion in
the audience—people were whispering—a general
message seemed in despatch throughout the house.
Explanation of the occurrence was vouchsafed me
the next evening when I had fully recovered. The
manager of the Hollis Street Theatre came to my
dressing-room to tell me that when the Scientists
in the audience became aware of my plight word
was passed from one to another, and from their
entire number I was given C. S. treatment. He was
amazed at the result: I was no less so.

I am not a Christian Scientist, and yet——?

CHAPTER XXII

A space back I made mention of another play by Booth Tarkington. This proved to be my vehicle for three seasons, affording pleasure to audiences, and profit and actual recreation to me.

Never was a more engaging, lovable Dago than *Tony Camaradonio;* he is the expression of all that is tender and imaginative in Tarkington. This piece was written after Booth had for two years or so been avoiding any sort of play-writing, and had devoted his time to novels and stories.

One day I received a letter from him which read: "I am beginning to have a feeling that I'd like to write another play, and that I'd like to write it for you." That was the way Mister Antonio began. At first the central figure was not an Italian at all. He rose mistily in Booth's mind. "I want," he said, "to write a *beautiful* man. I haven't got him yet." So I commenced as one thing and was repeatedly transmuted into another. I was re-nationalized again and again. Banker, farmer, electrician, policeman, I was continuously torn up and thrown in the waste-basket.

Finally Tark found his *beautiful man* in the hurdy-gurdy man, and gave him for companions an idiot and a jackass.

344

LIBERTY BONDS IN DIALECT

There is scarcely a city of importance in the country where this son of Sorrento has not appeared. Several of our little jackasses grew weary of the burden of dragging the cart during these three seasons, and one had his leg broken, but still *Tony* went on his way grinding out THE TOREADOR and ONWARD, CHRISTIAN SOLDIERS from New York to California, showing hard-hearted mayors and ministers that assertive Godliness is not goodness, and that bigotry can be the friend of no man.

MISTER ANTONIO was first produced early in war-time. All actors were called on to exert their influence and eloquence for war relief, speech-making, bond-selling from stage, hall and street stand. Many of us shouted ourselves speechless in the open.

My duty was to make a nightly appeal in front of the drop curtain for the buying of various issues of Liberty Bonds. Ultimately I dramatized this little appeal and caused *Tony Camaradonio* to narrate his reaction to the call of patriotism—the story of relatives in his own Italy who were fighting in the Trentino, etc. This *entr'acte* made a sort of extension of the play, and being given in *Tony's* dialect generally met with a liberal bond-buying response.

Something occurred after a matinée in Washington that must have been the result of patriotic enthusiasm. The principal air of *Tony's* hurdy-gurdy was ONWARD, CHRISTIAN SOLDIERS. That afternoon the audience had been especially responsive both to the play and to my bond-selling appeal.

When the final curtain fell and the orchestra continued the hurdy-gurdy's anthem, which it always played as the audience filed out of the theatre, a tall woman, handsomely dressed and heavily veiled, advanced to the orchestra rail and lifting a marvelous mezzo-soprano voice, sang as one inspired. The outgoing spectators checked their exit—the musicians catching the infection of the moment, played on—repeating the refrain again and again while the inspired songstress sang on, seemingly lost to her surroundings.

War-fervor—patriotism? Undoubtedly. Still a play must have some good in it to produce such an effect as that.

War work in the theatre extended beyond the régime of MISTER ANTONIO. The women of the stage were tireless in their activities, organizing, making, giving and doing, while the men beyond the age limit for service could only give and plead for funds to help carry on.

While the Victory Loan campaign was on I was filling an engagement at The Lyceum Theatre, in New York with an English comedy that failed completely—HUMPTY DUMPTY. The recollection of the piece even at this date gives me something of a chill. It was the only play I ever produced that had no success whatever. My business manager said he always felt like going out to the box office and saying to prospective ticket purchasers, "Don't go in; you won't like it." The comedy was all right, but it was a case of mistaken judgment on my part.

346

Eleanor Woodruff   Otis Skinner   Capitano   Robert Harrison

MISTER ANTONIO

THE BEST LAID PLANS

It was too English for America and too English for me. It didn't last long, but while it existed and while things were going ill with the unsympathetic HUMPTY DUMPTY, I was nightly selling bonds during the *entr' acte* at The Lyceum.

On the last night of the play, and also of the Victory bond drive, I conceived a scheme. Like many others I had invested myself poor in these pieces of war paper. I figured out how much ready cash was available. By dusting all the financial nooks and corners I found I could collect fifteen hundred dollars with which to purchase a final installment of bonds. I unfolded my plan to my wife; she thought it an excellent scheme. The proceedings were to be progressive. In my Bond appeal after the third act, I would offer to take a fifty dollar bond for every one in the audience that would do the same. After ten of these should be sold, then I'd offer to buy a hundred-dollar bond with each further purchaser for five more sales. That would make a thousand dollars. Then I could reach the climax with a five-hundred bond which would bring me to my limit.

The game of matched sales proved to be of interest. People began buying at once. Offers came rapidly when an officer in uniform, his armless sleeve pinned to his breast under his decorations, rose and said: "Mr. Skinner, I'll buy a fifty-dollar bond. I haven't the money to buy more." This brought an outburst of enthusiasm, and Mrs. Skinner, unable to control her pent up feelings, sprang

347

to her feet in the box where she had been sitting and cried: "I'll take a fifty-dollar bond for every man in uniform in the house!" It was beautiful patriotism but it was disaster to my plans. My nicely arranged progressive sale tumbled like a house of cards. I accepted the inevitable. "Will all the uniformed men in the theatre stand up?" I asked. "Turn up all the lights, Mr. Electrician." When the audience was revealed in the full illumination it showed a liberal sprinkling of khaki and blue in orchestra and gallery, while the balcony was one solid mass of dough boys. My startled wife gave one look and turned ghastly. "I made the bid," she said faintly, "but my husband has to pay for it."

My manager, seeing the balcony advance sale quite negligible, had packed it full of soldiers!

CHAPTER XXIII

REVIEWING my forty-six years on the stage I am confronted with the striking changes that have accompanied their progress. When I began, stock companies existed in most of the principal theatres of America. The comparatively few regular dramatic stars filled their season by taking the cities each in turn, and being supported by these stock companies in their repertory of plays—Traveling or Visiting Stars was the technical title they bore in the announcements. A few stars were beginning to make season tours supported by their own traveling organizations.

Theatres generally were in the hands of old experienced managers, many of whom had formerly been actors, and even at that date made an occasional appearance in a favorite rôle. Each manager carried the business of his theatre unconnected with any booking agency. Vaudeville was unknown outside a few discredited places that gave what was then known as "Variety Shows." To be sure there was Tony Pastor who used annually to take to the road with a troupe of specialists from New York. Negro Minstrelsy, however, flourished, and went gaily through the land with posters, bands and parades, Occasionally one would encounter a touring

349

burlesque troupe whose entertainment was of very low order indeed. Theatrical Syndicates were unknown; the work of organizing of the various theatrical interests throughout the country would have been looked on as an impossibility.

The advance agent of the period was not the well-educated individual he is to-day. The few traveling companies were preceded by a hard-boiled hustler whose chief accomplishments were the securing of the best bill-boards for his "paper," making the best deals with railroads and transfer companies, the placing of stereotyped advance notices and advertisements in the newspapers, and the capacity for making a general large noise; a sort of ballahoo side-showman.

Play-writing was for the most part a poorly paid profession. Scarcely any one could make a living by it. If, now and then, an original play saw the light, it was commonly the work of one who made his living by other literary or newspaper work. Often the actor ventured into the play-writing field and produced plays that were pretty sure to be effective in situation and character. A few names on the long list of American actor-playwrights are John Brougham, Dion Boucicault, Anna Cora Mowatt, Lester Wallack, Steele Mackaye, Edwin Milton Royle, Edward Harrigan and Augustus Thomas. The author of HOME, SWEET HOME, John Howard Payne, was an actor and had seventeen produced plays to his credit. But the dramatists of to-day can make more money by writing failures, than

those of forty-six years ago made by their successes. Nearly all the newer or modern plays were either translations, or of English origin. Shakespeare, the classics, standard printed pieces—these were generally the fare the managers put forth.

Later on, a new class of theatre sprang up—the theatre of melodrama. These places held undeniable attraction—both the quality of the plays and the prices of admission were cheap. But they bred a class of writers of fertile invention and untiring industry—the forerunners of the American dramatists of to-day. These places held their popularity until they were thrust into limbo by the advent of the moving picture whose first development was along the lines of sheerest sensationalism.

Romanticism has retired—realism has taken its place. The highest respectability was a themic necessity—virtue was rewarded; right was might; love conquered; retribution was inevitable. But now the play with an unhappy ending is not doomed. The final curtain may fall on general death and damnation. Realism stalks triumphant. The panorama will shift again—just how I can not say; there are many predictions as to the future of the theatre; whatever the change it will come so gradually that it will not seem radical until it is in turn placed in perspective along with changes that have gone before. The scene to-day, lighted in chiaroscuro worthy a Rembrandt, would have seemed an incredible attainment in my beginnings when gas footlights and borders, together with the illumination

351

of the blended calcium gas from iron cylinders placed in the wings, changed scenes from daylight to sunset and to moonlight. But now the soft mellow beauty of stage lighting has evolved so gradually from those hot wiggly little wires of the first incandescent lights that it is not a matter of wonder to an audience how these things have come about.

Acting has changed. Versatility, once the choicest possession of the player, is being bred out of the stock. Actors are no longer chosen for their ability to express every and any character, but for their physical and temperamental approximation to one particular character.

Stage direction has changed. In the old stock companies there was little or no constructive direction or any working out of the niceties of acting. Then came a period of intensive instruction—the exaltation of the meticulous, with the actors made into automatons—parrots of the director. This, in turn, is passing away. I find many directors silent at rehearsal to-day, seemingly content to allow actors to find their own salvation. Perhaps they are waiting for an inspired moment, or maybe they are Svengalis hypnotizing their people.

But in all this mutability one vital, ineffaceable thing remains—The Spirit of the Drama. The patronage and love of the public for the theatre grows. More thoughtful people than ever before are writing about and exploiting the drama. More imagination and originality are going into the work of play-

OTIS SKINNER
as Sancho Panza, 1924

writing. Dramatic workshops are being introduced into colleges. Little Theatres are springing up over the land, and in some of the young actors recruited from their limited fields to the professional stage, I see a great and glorious hope.

When I ask myself what my forty-six years in the theatre have brought me, my mind goes to Robert Louis Stevenson who, in a "letter to a young gentleman" said:

"But even with devotion, even with unfaltering and delighted industry, many thousand artists spend their lives, if the result be regarded, utterly in vain: a thousand artists, and never one work of art. But the vast mass of mankind are incapable of doing anything reasonably well, art among the rest. The worthless artist would not improbably have been a quite incomplete baker. And the artist, even if he does not amuse the public, amuses himself; so that there will always be one man the happier for his vigils. This is the practical side of art: its inexpugnable fortress for the true practitioner. The direct returns—the wages of the trade—are small, but the indirect—the wages of life—are incalculably great. No other business offers a man his daily bread upon such joyful terms.

". . . But to those more exquisite refinements of proficiency and finish, which the artist so ardently desires and so keenly feels, for which (in the vigorous words of Balzac) he must toil like a miner buried in a landslip, for which, day after day, he recasts and revises and rejects—the gross mass of the public must be blind."

In taking an inventory of my professional experience, I find that I have played in all, three hundred and twenty-five parts; have appeared in sixteen plays of Shakespeare, acting therein, at various times, thirty-eight parts, and I have produced under my own direction thirty-three plays.

This list of experiences has brought me to Cervantes and *Sancho Panza*—the most joyous, sympathetic and philosophic of clowns—transferred to the stage from DON QUIXOTE, by the Hungarian dramatist Lengyel, and done into English by Sydney Howard. And in the homely theory of this simple Squire of the Knight of the Rueful Countenance that "One must work and love—and pray sometimes," I bid my patient reader adios!

THE END

INDEX

INDEX

INDEX

358

INDEX

INDEX

INDEX

361

INDEX

INDEX

INDEX

INDEX

INDEX

INDEX